CW00621691

COMPTON INTERNATIONAL FUNDRAISING LTD
Compton House, High Street, Harbury,
Warwickshire, CV33 9HW, United Kingdom

Pinpointing Affluence
in the 21st Century

Increasing Your Share
of Major Donor Dollars

Judith E. Nichols, Ph.D., CFRE

05   04   03   02   01   5   4   3   2   1

Library of Congress Cataloging-in-Publication Data

Nichols, Judith E.
    Pinpointing affluence in the twenty-first century : increasing your share of major donor dollars / Judith E. Nichols.
        p.   cm.
Includes index.
    ISBN 1-56625-165-6
    1. Fund raising.   2. Rich people—Charitable contributions.   I. Title.

    HV41.2 .N5296 2001
    658.15'224—dc21   00-012255

Bonus Books, Inc.
160 East Illinois Street
Chicago, Illinois 60611

Second Edition

Typesetting by Point West, Inc., Carol Stream, IL

Printed in the United States of America

Contents

Introduction

MANY FUND RAISERS MIS-TAKENLY THINK that the desire to be philanthropic drives the giving process. They assume that our donors are philanthropists first, driven by an overwhelming desire to make a difference, rather than propelled by the world they inhabit towards that conclusion.

> Unfortunately, most of us waste precious time and effort dreaming of catching the attention of the wealthiest individuals. Although the number of gifts of one million dollars or greater from individuals has doubled in the last decade, there are still few philanthropic millionaires available—each year, there are less than 1,000 gifts of over one million dollars reported by *Giving USA*. In seeking gifts of wealth, we focus too often on a rarely-attainable ideal donor.

In a very real sense, philanthropy is the end result of a logical chain of events that shapes an individual's thinking and concerns. If fund raisers don't understand the environment that individual inhabits, we miss the clues that enable us to facilitate that person towards meaningful giving.

What are these clues? They're available all around us in the demographic and psychographic information savvy marketers have been using for years to reach consumers. They can open the door to a much wider audience of prospects, able and willing to provide our not-for-profits with support.

In truth, we structure our development programs without taking into account the realities of who has the money and is willing to give.

> It makes much more sense to try to identify, cultivate, and form charitable partnerships with the much larger group of nearly 19 million persons capable of giving gifts of $1,000 to $100,000 than the very few able of high six-figure and over gifts!

The revised and greatly expanded edition of *Pinpointing Affluence: Increasing Your Share of Major Donor Dollars in the Twenty-First Century* continues to explore the development strategy I have been researching and refining in my own fund raising since the early 1980s.

In *Changing Demographics: Fund Raising in the '90s,* my first book published by Precept Press, I suggested a then-radical concept: that our donors and prospects were not all alike. The book has become a classic. I am gratified that so many of my colleagues agree that demographic differences—age, sex, race, and ethnic backgrounds—along with psychographics keys—attitudes, values, and lifestyles—need to be understood by fund raisers.

In *Targeted Fund Raising: Defining and Refining Your Development Strategy,* I proposed that once you know who your current donors are and your future prospects will be, a more logical fund raising program evolves. Again, many of you applauded my approach. My colleagues agreed that knowing who to ask, how to ask, and how much to ask for are basic building blocks of a strong development program.

One of my most popularly received books, *Growing from Good to Great: Positioning Your Fund-Raising Efforts for BIG Gifts,* encouraged fund raisers to switch paradigms, suggesting the time had come to move away from fund raising strategies focused solely on acquisition and put greater efforts into after-marketing. Using case examples, I was able to demonstrate that increasing renewal rates provides not-for-profits with the financial stability they need and sets the stage for a dialog on upgraded giving.

When the first edition of *Pinpointing Affluence: Increasing Your Share of Major Donor* was published in 1994, readers were invited to stretch their thinking yet again. I asked you to consider how you could strengthen your fund raising if you rethought who the **best** donors really are and put more of your time and energy into capturing those prospects with the capability and willingness to give.

Like the earlier edition, the revised edition of *Pinpointing Affluence* moves back and forth between demographics and psychographics and fund raising—weaving a logic between background and strategy.

- In the first section, *Understanding Why We Need a New Approach,* I've outlined the strategies that make sense for today: concentrating on how to redirect your fund-raising strategies to access larger contributions.

- In Part Two, *Meet Today's and Tomorrow's Donors,* we review the broader demographics and psychographics of the American population, seeking an understanding of who the players are now and in the near future.

- Then, in Part Three, *Finding Affluent Prospects Demographically and Psychographically,* we look at a variety of ways we can locate this upscale group and discuss ways of marketing to the affluent. This section has been heavily updated with additional chapters added, dividing out affluence in the workplace. You'll find information on self-employed professionals, small business owners, and on entrepreneurs.

■ Parts Four and Five focus on fund raising strategies.

● In Part Four, *Fund Raising Strategies that Make Sense,* the underlying philosophy for fund raising in the twenty-first century is outlined.

● In Part Five, *Creating Donor and Prospect Involvement,* specific recommendations for more effectively reaching affluents through each methodology are given.

I hope the new edition of *Pinpointing Affluence* encourages you to rethink your development program again and again. **Fund raising cannot be static: our society does not stand still.** The world changes, our donors and prospects change, and we must change too.

Judith E. Nichols, Ph.D., CFRE
March 1, 2001

PART I

UNDERSTANDING WHY WE NEED A NEW APPROACH TO FUND RAISING

Few fund raisers set out to deliberately create stress for themselves. Yet, in striving to reach ever-increasing goals, many development officers actually use the least effective strategies for choosing donors and methodologies!

Part One of *Pinpointing Affluence in the 21st Century* makes sure you're positioned properly. These chapters provide the information you need to convince yourself—and your gate-keepers—that a development strategy emphasizing major giving makes sense and that, to succeed in this, you will need to focus on affluent individuals.

■ **Chapter 1** explains why you should focus on major gifts and challenges you to review your current development program to see if, in fact, you are doing so.

■ **Chapter 2** refines the focus further. Current trends in giving advise you to make nine out of every 10 major donor prospects individuals rather than companies or foundations.

■ **Chapter 3** suggests a reality check. With less than one thousand donors who give one million dollars or more annually, is it wealth or affluence you want to target?

■ **Chapter 4** introduces you to affluent Americans: over 19 million strong and growing.

1

Why You Should Focus on Major Gift Giving

I'M GOING TO MAKE AN AS-SUMPTION that in choosing to read this book, you are admitting to a bias: given a choice, you would rather bring in a large gift for your organization than a small one.

Put bluntly, your not-for-profit's goals and objectives require donors who can and will give

- five hundred dollars, not five dollars.

- ten thousand dollars, not ten dollars.

But, too often, we treat all donors and prospects as if they are equally able and willing to help. In truth, fund raising should **not** be done democratically. We should be spending more of our time, energy, and resources with those at the top of the donor pyramid than with those at the bottom.

The numbers bear this out:

Eighty percent of gifts come from 20 percent of donors.

OR

Ninety percent of gifts come from 10 percent of donors.

AND EVEN MORE FREQUENTLY

Ninety-five percent of gifts come from just 5 percent of donors!

● **A minority of your donors give a majority of your funds.** Try this experiment: Run a list of your last full fiscal year's donors, prioritizing from the largest donor to the smallest. Chances are that before you are one-quarter to one-third down your list, you will have more dollars represented at the top than at the middle and bottom.

● **This wisdom holds true for all organizations.** Even in religious organizations—the last holdout to this rule—a minority of church members now give a majority of funds. Although typical in other charities, the move away from tithing and stewardship is a new situation for religious organizations.

WHY AREN'T FUND RAISERS FOCUSING WHERE THE DOLLARS ARE?

Several reasons come to mind:

- Organizations are applying a "buckshot" approach to staffing

- Organizations have not defined the organizational needs

- Organizations don't know who to ask

- Organizations don't know how to ask

Let's look at each of these concerns in turn:

● **Is your organization applying a "buckshot" approach to staffing?** You can't do everything equally well. The typical development shop—whether one person or a staff of 20—ignores this reality. Fund raisers automatically work every strategy area from major gifts, the annual fund, corporate and foundation relations to special events, and even product sales. The result is that each area is too thinly staffed to reach a critical mass of success.

The director of development needs to decide what makes sense for his/her shop and develop a plan that supports those decisions.

The hardest part is often getting your gatekeepers—the CEO and board—to understand why you're not doing everything.

Questions to answer:

■ **One-Person Shop:** What percentage of my time is spent in each fund raising activity? What percentage of dollars is this bringing to my organization?

■ **Multi-Person Shop:** How is our staff distributed among the various fund raising activities? How does this expense relate to income?

● **Has your organization defined its needs?** Many not-for-profits spend a disproportionate amount of time raising gifts of $10, $25, and $50 because they assume that donors won't make large gifts for operational needs. As a result, volunteers and staff restrict their major dollar requests to specific equipment, facilities renovations, and scholarships.

The problem here is communication. Often donors and prospects simply don't know what it takes to deliver the programs and services you do so well. You need to work with the administrative and program delivery staff to show how the copy machine, vans, and—yes, even light and heat—make a difference to your clients.

Questions to answer:

● Do your communication and solicitation approaches take donors and prospects "behind the scenes"? Do you use case examples that help caring people understand your day-to-day activities and the costs involved in continuing them?

● **Does your organization know who to ask?** Many not-for-profits looking for larger gifts zero in on the same list of persons and organizations without doing the basic research. *Wealth alone gives you a suspect.* It is only when you add interest and accessibility that you have a prospect. You have to identify the connections that would justify asking for a commitment.

And, you're probably focusing on a small proportion of the many prospects who can make major gifts. You need to know where to look to identify a broader base of wealth and affluence.

Questions to answer:

● Why is each of my major donor prospects on my list? Is my organization a strong match? What type of project would interest each? Who could get me in the door?

● **Does your organization know how to ask?** Everyone hates to ask for money—fund raisers, CEOs, and board members alike. That's why it doesn't get done. To raise money, you must ask.

Most of the problem lies in our understanding—or rather lack of understanding—of why people make gifts. We still tend to think of fund raising as adversarial in nature, that somehow the development officer or volunteer is forcing or tricking the prospect into doing something s/he doesn't want to do. Training on the role of the cultivator/solicitor is essential.

Questions to answer:

● Do your staff and volunteers understand their role in the cultivation and solicitation process? Do you provide regular, ongoing training sessions with role-playing opportunities?

Understanding why you are not focusing on major gift giving is the first step in reordering your priorities. The next step is understanding *who* makes the larger gifts. We'll discuss that in Chapter 2.

CHAPTER TWO

Why Nine Out of Every Ten Major Donor Prospects Should Be Individuals

THE NUMBERS SUPPORT IT. You should be focusing the vast majority of your fund raising efforts on raising your major donor dollars from individuals.

Charitable gifts by Americans reached $190.16 billion in 1999 according to *Giving USA*—which is compiled yearly by the American Association of Fund Raising Counsel. This impressive amount is equivalent to one-third of the federal budget, or 2 percent of our national income—a significant increase of more than $15 billion over 1998's $174.52 billion.

Giving by individuals always leads the way. Personal giving accounted for nearly three-quarters of the overall increase in charitable giving for 1999 with a gain of $12 billion.

Of the $190.16 billion received in 1999:

> - Individual gifts totaled $143.71 billion, 75.6 percent of total philanthropic giving.
>
> - Bequests totaled $15.61 billion, 8.2 percent of total philanthropic giving.
>
> - Foundations gave $19.81 billion, 10.4 percent of total philanthropic giving.
>
> - Corporations donated $11.02 billion, 5.8 percent of total philanthropic giving.

Looking at each sector in depth reveals that individuals are the major source of donations for most not-for-profits:

● **Arts Giving:** Many corporations continue to reduce the share of their contributions that goes to art groups. Most private foundations expect little change in their spending patterns of approximately 14 percent of grants going to arts, cultural, or humanities projects.

● **Education Giving:** Half of all corporate gifts to education go to just 40 institutions. Alumni provide nearly 40 percent of contributions at both colleges and secondary schools. Corporate support to the lower grades represents just 4 percent, while it supplies about 22 percent of total voluntary support to higher education. Education and library grants receive a large percent of foundation gifts—26 percent.

● **Health And Hospital Giving:** Two-thirds of all gifts to hospitals come from individuals; corporations and foundations give approximately 13 percent each.

● **Human Services Giving:** While foundation giving has increased slightly to human services organizations, it's been for demonstration projects rather than for the operating costs such organizations crave. And, corporate dollars have not grown at all. In areas of potential controversy—AIDS, domestic violence, child abuse, reproductive rights—it has, instead, diminished.

● **Religious Organizations:** Almost 100 percent of support to religious organizations comes from individuals. The Ecumenical Center for Stewardship Studies states that, although a trace comes through foundations, corporate support of religion is virtually non-existent.

● **Women's Programs Giving:** Less than 5 percent of all foundation grants made yearly go specially for programs to help women and girls. Foundation grants for arts and culture programs represent one of the areas in which women receive the smallest share.

The real story on corporate and foundation funding isn't pretty: If you are focusing your fund raising efforts on corporations and foundations, rather than on individuals, you are competing for significantly fewer dollars:

● **In real dollars, corporate contributions have declined and there is no reason to expect future contributions will show any real gains.** Acquisitions and mergers, slow corporate growth, and downsizing have taken a toll on corporate giving.

- Much of corporate giving today is *NOT* philanthropic. Rather it is tied to marketing goals with clearly defined expectations and a return-on-investment orientation. Corporations are quantifying ROI (rate of investment) in terms of increased customer sales, and/or recruitment and retention of employees.

● **Fewer than 11,000 foundations exist that give away $50,000 or more per year.** The best estimate is that there were approximately 20,000 foundations in existence in the United States in 1980. By 1999 this number had doubled to more than 40,000. Of these foundations, 10,445 had at least $2 million in assets or $200,000 in annual giving. Their combined assets of

about $304 billion accounted for 92.3 percent of all founda-
tion assets, and their combined grants of about $14.3 billion
accounted for 90 percent of all foundation giving. The 14
largest foundations each held assets of $2 billion or more and
the next 86, in size of assets held, each had $419 billion or
more.

● Start-up costs are often the easiest kind of support to secure as many foundation people consider themselves the "venture capitalists" of the nonprofit world. By providing start-up
support they can legitimately take credit for enabling a new
enterprise to begin operation.

● For most funders, location is the single most important
criterion in awarding grants as they prefer to spend their
money close to home. Among the 8,700 largest foundations—
those with assets of $1-million or more—only 23 percent, or
2,000, give on a national or international basis. Foundations
in 10 states gave away the majority—about 71 percent—of all
foundation grants.

● Foundation giving is rarely unrestricted. According to The
Foundation Center, under twelve percent is given for general
operating costs. Approximately

  • 40 percent of foundation grants go to specific pro-
    grams.

  • 25 percent of foundation grants go to capital projects.

Individual giving is nowhere near its potential.

Even though individuals give far and away the vast majority of philanthropic dollars in this country, their potential for
increasing the money they give is mind boggling. Let's return to
the $190.16 billion that living individuals gave to charities in
1999. How generous was it?

● *Using the AAFRC economic model to estimate annual
charitable contributions, donations equaled 2.1 percent of gross*

domestic product, the highest level by that barometer in 28 years. However, Daniel Feenberg at the National Bureau of Economic Research suggests another yardstick of measurement, related to personal consumption. He calculates that 1999 donations equaled 3 percent of personal consumption expenditures up slightly from 1998 and a significant jump from the 2.5 percent in 1995 but still below the 3.3 percent of the late 1960s.

● According to Independent Sector and AAFRC, the average contributing household gave $1,075, or 2.1 percent, of household income. In 1995, contributing households reported an average contribution of $1,017, or 2.2 percent, of household income. From 1995 to 1998, after inflation, the average household contribution decreased by 1.2 percent.

● To put philanthropy in perspective, let's compare it to other discretionary purchases. That's the "pocket" from which most charitable gifts are made. Few people put giving before their needs for food, clothing, and shelter. Today, Americans have a lot of money left over after taking care of essentials. According to the Bureau of Labor, the share of income spent on food, clothing and shelter has decreased from 76.2 percent in 1901 to 37.7 percent as of 1995.

According to John and Sylvia Ronsvalle in *The Poor Have Faces,* we spend the following yearly:

- more than $3.5 billion on cut flowers

- $5.5 billion in quarters on pinball and video machines

- $12 billion on candy and $29 billion on diets

- $44 billion on soft drinks

Conclusion: There's plenty of potential for increasing individual giving. Obviously, what we need to do is to identify those that have the ability to give the most—and motivate these individuals to give more. In the next chapters we'll look at the wealthiest Americans and explore their charitable giving records.

CHAPTER THREE

America's Rich: A Reality Check

*H*aving examined the alternatives, a development strategy that focuses on individuals clearly is the logical choice. Where do you start?

Yes, those at the very top should be your very best prospects. Many more people are wealthy today than in the past. In 1999, the world added 1 million new millionaires, bringing the total to seven million. Fifty-five thousand of them are worth $30 million or more. The combined wealth of the seven million is $25.5 trillion; they control $44.9 trillion.

A very large percentage of the wealthy are American. There are 514 billionaires in the world. America at the last count had 170 billionaires, compared with just 13 in 1982. In addition to the 170 billionaires, the United States boasts 250,000 decamillionaires and 4.8 million millionaires—with more on the way.

Year	Millionaire households	% of all USA households
1989	3.0 million	3.2%
1992	3.1 million	3.2%
1995	3.4 million	3.4%
1998	4.1 million	4.0%
2001	5.0 million	4.7%

SOURCE: *USA Today,* January 25, 2000

The wealthy are growing wealthier. Between 1990 and 1995, the most recent years for which the Internal Revenue Service figures are available, the wealthiest segment of our nation has increased by 14 percent.

● The number of taxpayers who reported an adjusted gross income of $200,000 or more reached nearly 1.3 million in 1995.

● Nationwide, earnings for the poorest fifth of the population rose less than 1 percent between 1988 and 1998, but jumped 15 percent for the wealthiest. Whereas the poorest fifth's income grew only by $110—from $12,880 to $12,990—the wealthiest fifth grew by $17,860—from $199,620 to $217,480.

● Households with investable assets of $1 million or more have doubled in the last four years.

If these trends continue, the wealthy will increase to 7.4 million in 2010.

WHO ARE THE WEALTHIEST AMERICANS?

The top 1 percent, about 1 million American households, report an average wealth in 1995 of $7.9 million and average annual income of $625,000. Half inherited wealth with an average inheritance of $782,000. The typical rich person is 55 to 74, a college graduate, perhaps with a post-graduate degree. He is white, married, self-employed and working full time, and healthy.

As assets and income drop, the demographics change slightly. Americans with $2.5 million in assets, as of 1997 or who had at least a $250,000 income were 52 years of age. In addition, they are/have:

• Homeowners	96%
• Caucasian	92%
• Married	88%
• Executive or professionals	66%
• Republican	52%
• With children under 18	52%
• Post-graduate education	47%

Sixty percent of millionaires live in just eight states:

- New York (home to 17%)

- California (10%)

- Massachusetts (7%)

- Connecticut and New Jersey (6% each)

- Ohio, Pennsylvania, and Texas (5% each)

Almost 20 percent attended Ivy League schools. Yale University alone produced about 4,300 millionaires and Harvard follows with 3,100.

The wealthiest of Americans also share core values. Often, they:

- Have a middle-class sensibility

- Are savvy, value-driven consumers

- Are redefining the meaning of success

- Seek financial stability

- Actively maintain and preserve their youth

- Use new technology to realize goals

But the demographics and psychographics of the wealthy are rapidly changing. About 100 new millionaires are being created each month through the multimillion-dollar lotteries taking place across the country each week. Women are just starting to enter the ranks of the rich on their own, the rich are getting younger, and Blacks, Asians, and Hispanics are appearing in the very rich community.

Today, we recognize that there are three kinds of wealth:

1. Old wealth—from families that made money several generations ago and whose members are active in a variety of civic endeavors. The Social Register tracks approximately 32,500 individuals known for having "old money"—inherited fortunes, typically created around the turn of the century. Over three-quarters of surnames are English (not Irish or Scottish or Welsh).

2. The Millionaire Next Door—modestly living professional or small business owners who invest wisely and give frugally. According to Thomas Stanley who coined the phrase

in his book of the same name, your average millionaire next door:

- is a 57-year-old married man with three children.

- is self-employed in a practical business such as farming, pest control, or paving contracting.

- works between 45 and 55 hours a week.

- has a median household annual income of $131,000.

- has an average household net worth of $3.7 million.

- owns a home valued at about $320,000.

- is first-generation affluent.

- drives an older model automobile and buys rather than leases.

- attended public schools but is likely to send his children to private school.

3. New wealth—extremely wealthy entrepreneurs who earned their money in technology, real estate, corporate mergers, athletics, or entertainment. They are often younger and new to philanthropy. Whether or not you have gone to college is becoming more significant in determining status in America than what your parents did for a living. A rising number of wealthy in their own right are younger than those coming from the traditional inherited wealth or "millionaire next door" backgrounds; increasing numbers of wealthy women and minorities are found here.

The sources and sites of America's big fortunes have changed dramatically: in 1982, 85 percent of the wealthy inherited their fortunes with 40 percent of their monies coming from mining, oil, or gas and the locations were Texas and New York. Today, success is less likely to be inherited than it was in earlier years: it's communications or media (45%) and software or computers (26%) and California is the state.

Finding the wealthiest Americans is fairly easy. Each year, it becomes easier to find out who's got what:

● *Forbes* and *Fortune* magazines are eager to tell us who's dropped off and on to their lists of billionaires and millionaires. According to *Forbes,* the world's billionaires club expanded in the year 2000 to 482 from 465, pushing the combined wealth of the richest 200 working people in the world upward of $1.1 trillion—a $100 billion increase from 1999.

The USA—represented by Bill Gates, Lawrence Ellison, Paul Allen, and Warren Buffet—holds the top four spots. Spots 5, 6, and 7 went to German retailers Theo and Karl Albrecht; Prince Alwaleed Bin Talal Alsaud of Saudi Arabia, a global investor; and S. Robosn Walton, whose family started Wal-Mart. Japanese software magnate Masayoshi Son ranked eighth followed by Michael Dell, founder of Dell Computers at 9 and Canadian media magnate Kenneth Thomson at number 10. Heavily representing the trend towards the new wealth being the wealthiest of the wealthy, five of the top 10 among the working rich are 47 years old or younger.

● *Business Week* reveals the salaries of top CEOs. *Inc.* shares the names of top entrepreneurs.

● *Working Women* points out the top females while *Hispanic Business* and *Black Entrepreneur* acknowledge leaders in the minority communities.

> The problem is that you're not alone in knowing who are the wealthiest of the wealthy: your fund raising colleagues—at more than 1.5 million not-for-profits—are researching these same names!

What happens when we take a closer look at wealth and philanthropy. How eager are those at the top to give it away? *A relatively few give a lot and the vast majority give little.*

● **Major gift giving has decreased proportionally, not increased.** While there were over 60,000 millionaires by 1989 compared to just 4,281 in 1980, there were only 888 gifts of over $1 million compared to 418. In fact, by the end of the 1980s, in terms of average annual giving, the wealthy were giving 60 percent less than at the beginning of the decade.

● **The wealthiest Americans—those who earn more than one million dollars annually—appear to be decreasing the share of their income that goes to charity.** Contributions from the rich have declined from an average of more than 7 percent of their reported after-tax income in 1979 to less than 4 percent in 1990. While changes in tax laws may explain why the wealthy are giving less, this decline, according to leading observers quoted in *Business Week,* is "downright stingy" and the lack of generosity is "our shame and disgrace."

The truth is that it is the poorest who give the largest percentage of their income—5.2 percent in 1998. This compares with just 2.2 percent for those earning $100,000 according to Independent Sector. Although total dollars given are greater from the wealthy, the proportion of giving is actually much greater for the poor. Sadly, the most generous donors are not the wealthy, but rather the poor and the widowed.

But don't lose hope.

● **Among households with a net worth of more than $50 million, the amount and percentage of income contributed to charity increases with the respondents' level of wealth.** Among families with a net worth of $100 million or more, for example, the average contribution was $5.5 million, or 57 percent of income. Among families with a net income of $5 million to $10 million, the average contribution was $65,780, or 10.6 percent of income. Families with a net worth of $1 million to $5 million contributed an average of $13,113, or 3.5 percent of income.

● **The new philanthropist is as likely to be a 30-something Internet millionaire setting up his or her own foundation,**

retiring early to help build schools in Chile or running for political office. Personal involvement is a key part of the new giving. According to Larry Ellision, cofounder and former CEO, Oracle Corporation: "The goal is not to be the richest guy in the graveyard. I don't care how much I'm worth when I'm dead. How do I make myself feel good? The only way I know to make myself feel better is to make the world better. Don't mistake that for altruism. It's egotism. Call it enlightened egotism."

● **It's taken a while, but many multimillionaires of the technology boom are now giving something back.** High-stakes giving is no longer dominated by the society matron writing checks to a well-heeled foundation. For many years, the multimillionaires of the booming technology industries didn't feel very secure in their newfound wealth and weren't at a point in their lives where they thought much about their legacies. Now that's changing. Silicon Valley CEOs, along with other newly rich Americans, are finally stepping up to the collection plate. And just as they've transformed American business, members of this new generation are changing the way philanthropy is done.

● **Our newest "lucky" millionaires appear less reluctant to share.** Preliminary studies show that lottery millionaires have a greater tendency than do other tycoons to redistribute their wealth among family members and charities. "What's interesting about lotteries," explains University of Southern California marketing professor Jagdish Sheth, "is that they redistribute resources, not from the rich to the poor, but from the poor to the poor. The poor are the largest players and the largest recipients of lottery funds."

To what charities do the wealthiest make their gifts? According to the U.S. Trust, which does an annual survey on affluent Americans, the wealthiest 1 percent of Americans (those with an adjusted gross income of more than $225,000 or a net worth of more than $3 million) most frequently contribute to: human services (88%), education (84%), children and youth services (76%), and religious organizations (69%). They make their largest contributions to religious organizations (30%), education (22%), and human services (16%).

And, according to *The Chronicle of Philanthropy*, most of those contributions go to a small number of non-profits. In fact, about one in six dollars is given to one of the 400 largest U.S. charities. The money goes to one of:

138   Colleges and Universities
 42   United Ways
 32   International Groups
 24   Religious Organizations
 23   Community Foundations
 22   Health Charities
 22   Hospitals and Medical Centers
 20   Human Services Groups
 14   Jewish Federations
 11   Environmental & Animal Related Groups
  9   Museums and Libraries
  9   Youth Groups
  8   Arts Groups
  8   Miscellaneous Educational Organizations
  8   Public Television Groups
  4   Public Affairs Groups
  6   Other Non-Profit Groups

Unless you are one of that small minority of organizations who can find a logical link to that even smaller number of donors at the very top who are willing and able to make the very largest gifts, the truly wealthy may not be the best individuals on which to focus your prospecting efforts.

Is there a better prospect pool for many charitable organizations? Yes! It is the growing number of affluent Americans. We'll discuss this exciting prospect pool in Chapter 4.

CHAPTER FOUR

Turning to Affluence

*T*HINK AFFLUENCE RATHER
THAN WEALTH. Don't automatically focus all your major gift
fund raising efforts on the very small pool of easily-identified
persons at the pinnacle of wealth in your community. Instead,
concentrate on the more logical, broader base of ***affluent
donors***—individuals with a household income of $75,000 or
greater.

**Stop thinking of major donors only in terms of gifts of
assets.** The average millionaire only has a yearly income
of $120,000. Remarks Dr. Thomas Stanley, author of *Market-
ing to the Affluent* and *The Millionaire Next Door,* "That's four
or five times what the average family brings in, but it's not
megabucks."

In fact, the richest 5 percent of Americans had a 1995 average income of just $188,962—a growth of just one percent
since 1975. The top twenty percent averaged just $108,411 in
income. It's here that the growth is—35.4 percent since 1975.
And 80 percent of the wealthy are first-generation millionaires, understandably cautious in making sacrificial gifts. Neither they nor the majority of our affluent prospects are
able—are willing—to strip themselves of assets to make gifts of
five figures.

**Instead of "ultimate" gifts, think more boldly about an-
nual gifts.** Look for prospects who can—and will—make yearly gifts from $1,000 to $100,000 regularly. While only 1 percent

of individuals number themselves among the upper class, 14 percent are upscale households—more than 19 million householders. Half of these upscalers have incomes higher than $66,000 and 15 percent (about four million householders) have incomes greater than $100,000. In addition, there are about 1.5 million households with a net worth of over $1 million.

■ **A dramatically increasing number of households now qualify as affluent.** *America's middle class is rising fast.* The real median income of households rose by 1.2 percent from $35,082 to $35,492. Real median earnings for women rose 2.4 percent to $23,710, about 74 percent of the median for men of $32,144. That's the highest percentage for women on record. The biggest gain, 2.2 percent, was posted by the 20 percent of families with the highest income.

● **According to the 1997 U.S. Census, released in 1998, the median family income is $40,611,** but the amount varies widely among ethnic and racial groups. It's $42,646 for white, non-Hispanic families, $25,970 for black families and $24,570 for families of Hispanic ancestry. The median net worth of families is $56,400. But among those with college degrees, the median net worth totals $104,100.

● **The proportion of American households with incomes of $100,000 or more has tripled during the past 30 years** from 2.8 percent in 1967 to 9.4 percent in 1997—a total of nearly 10 million, five times the number in 1967. The number of households with incomes of $50,000 or more grew from 13 million to 36 million during those years. Behind today's record level of affluence is the aging of the dual-income couples of the Baby-Boom generation into their peak-earning years. We can expect household incomes to rise for another 10 years.

● **During the past six years, 4.4 percent of American households have transitioned up and out of middle-class status and into the top stratas of income in the United States.** Today, more than 20 percent of households earn more than $75,000 versus 16 percent in 1992. By 2003, households with incomes over

$100,000 will grow by 15 percent, including a 17.1 percent leap among households that take in more than $150,000 a year. (At the same time, the number of under-$50,000 households will grow 3.2 percent; more than 12 million of them will claim incomes of less than $10,000—5 percent more than in 1998.)

■ **It's not what you earn; it's what you have to spend that counts.** After taking care of the necessities of life, two-thirds of all households had at least some discretionary income in 1994, with an average of $13,476. All households with income of $80,000 or more have such spending money. And discretionary income is growing: 80 percent of today's American households have discretionary income. And, as incomes increase, the amount of discretionary income—money used for purposes other than the necessities of life—increases significantly.

● **Householders aged 45–54—those in their peak earning years—are the most likely to have discretionary income, with an average of $16,222 in 1994.** The top 10 percent of households (those reporting annual incomes greater than $100,000) control more than 70 percent of the country's discretionary income. On average, their discretionary income surpasses $68,000—nearly four times the national norm.

● **More than 55 percent of persons aging from 35 to 50 have discretionary income and account for 40 percent of all discretionary income in America, by age, with an average of $19,900 per household.**

● **Education pays, too.** Households with a college degree are most likely to have money: they account for 58 percent of discretionary income, by educational attainment.

● **And size matters:** two-person households make up one-third of all households with discretionary income, and have roughly $18,000 at their disposal.

■ **Affluence is spreading throughout our nation, regardless of ethnicity, race, and gender.**

● **African-Americans:** There are currently more than 259,000 households with an annual income over $100,000. The share of affluent African-American households has tripled since 1994.

● **Asian-Americans:** There are currently more than 111,000 households with annual incomes over $100,000.

● **Latino Americans:** There are more than 193,000 households with annual incomes over $100,000.

● **Women:** There are 220,000 households with annual incomes over $100,000.

The Affluent Market is one of the fastest growing markets in America. Higher productivity, two income households, lower taxes, more college-educated adults, and lower inflation, among other dramatic developments, have combined to produce new levels of affluence. In the past decade, affluence in the United States has increased at a phenomenal rate, enlarging an already under-tapped market of potential donors.

● From 1972 to 1990, the proportion of households earning $50,000 to $74,999 a year rose about a sixth to 15 percent; the share making $75,000 to $99,999 climbed by a quarter to 5 percent; and the percentage above $100,000 doubled to 4 percent, or 4 million households. Since 1984 the number of affluents has doubled—and these are low-inflation years, so the increase in numbers is genuine. All indications are that their ranks will continue to grow.

● As of 1996,

   • 979,626 households declared incomes of over $200,000.

   • 65,646 declared an annual income of more than $1 million, with an average of $2,473,442.

   • there are 45,000 couples who both earn over $100,000.

The Spectrem Group, a financial services consulting firm, defines an affluent household as one with an income of $100,000 or more, or with a net worth—not including principal residence—of at least $500,000. That covers 16.7 million American households today. Those at the top of the affluent market ($100,000 annual income and/or $500,000 net worth) are growing at an annual rate of 5 percent a year (not adjusted for inflation).

If these trends continue, the number of the most affluent households will increase to 19.6 million in 2010.

ARE THERE SOME GENERAL CHARACTERISTICS I SHOULD KNOW ABOUT AFFLUENT INDIVIDUALS?

It used to be that the affluent and generous givers had a number of socio-economic and demographic characteristics in common. Both were white, male, between the ages of 55 and 64, Protestant, highly educated, married (or widowed), and professionals. At the start of the twenty-first century, however, we find a diversity in our society that goes well beyond anything we once imagined. As a result, the affluent have diversified as well, and so should your major gift prospects.

Today, education is the common thread. According to Judith Waldrop and Linda Jocobsen, in *American Demographics,* "education and income go together like wine and cheese."

● **The most affluent counties in America are also among the best-educated.** In Fairfax County, Virginia with an affluence level nearly six times that of the rest of the United States, 42 percent of adults aged 25 and older are college graduates compared with only 20 percent of all Americans that age. Seventy-four percent of all adults have gone to college, the median household income is $59,000, and more than half of workers are managers, professionals, or technicians.

● **The Baby Boom generation is the most highly educated generation in American history.** With 48 percent of Baby Boomers (those born from 1946–1964) having either attended or graduated from college, we can look forward to a continuing groundswell of affluence as they move into the prime earning years of their careers.

● **Increasing access to higher education is increasing affluence as well.** The percentage of adults who are college graduates increased from 8 percent in 1960 to 23 percent in 1995. Educational attainment and monthly income is highly linked: in 1993, those without a high school diploma earned $906 monthly compared to the mean of all persons earning $1,687, those with a Bachelor's degree earning $2,265, and Professionals earning $5,534.

DEMOGRAPHIC FACTS ABOUT AFFLUENT AMERICANS

Affluent Americans can be found throughout our country. Of course some locations are more blessed than others: only one of the richest area codes is for a central city. There are 13 area codes where the median household income is higher than $50,000 and only one—San Francisco's 415—is a central city. Arlington and Fairfax, Virginia (703) is the richest code. Seventeen of the top 20 richest codes are big, wealthy suburbs. The exceptions are Hawaii (808), Alaska (907), and Minneapolis (612).

The Affluent Index provides a fascinating profile of who today's affluent Americans are. Using an index of 100 as average, an index of 175 reflects a 75 percent above average incidence:

By Household Incomes

● Households with incomes above $100,000 comprise 5 percent of the U.S. population. They are strongly college graduates (282) and post graduates (366) and age 45–54 (174). Overwhelmingly, they are top managers (789).

● Households with incomes above $75,000 comprise 10 percent of the U.S. population. Like the wealthiest households, they show strongly as college graduates (263) and post graduates (315) and tend to be age 45–54 (174). They make a strong showing in top management (581).

● Households with incomes above $50,000 comprise 27 percent of the U.S. population. Like the $75,000 and $100,000 households, they show strongly as college graduates (206) and post graduates (223). Almost as many are aged 35–44 as tend to be aged 45–54 (174). They make a fairly strong showing in top management (320).

By Individual Employment Income

● Individuals with employment above $75,000 comprise 2 percent of the U.S. population. Much more likely to be male (186) than female (21), they are strongly college graduates (373) and overwhelmingly post graduates (556). They cluster in ages 35–44 (175), 45–54 (215), and 55–64 (167). They put top management off the chart at 1,891.

● Individuals with employment above $50,000 comprise 6 percent of the U.S. population. Still much more likely to be male (183) than female (25), they are strongly college graduates (334) and overwhelmingly post graduates (434). They cluster in ages 35–44 (180) and 45–54 (205), but drop off in ages 55–64 (130). They are overwhelmingly in top management (1,178).

By Affluence within demographic subgroups

● College graduates—19 percent of the U.S. population—have an index of 334 for having an individual employment income of $50,000+ and an index of 206 for a household income of $50,000+. They are heavily professionals and managers (334) and top management (327). They are most likely to be Baby Boomers, with the largest grouping age 35–44.

● Post graduates—8 percent of the U.S. population—have an index of 434 for having an individual employment income of $50,000+ and an index of 223 for a household income of $50,000+. They are heavily professionals and managers (441) and top management (447). They are most likely to be Baby Boomers, with equally up above groupings in ages 35–44 and 45–54.

● Professionals and Managers—17 percent of the U.S. population—have an index of 387 for having an individual employment income of $50,000+ and an index of 220 for a household income of $50,000+. They are heavily college graduates (334) and post graduates (411). They are most likely to be Baby Boomers, with equally above groupings in ages 35–44 and 45–54.

● Top Managers—2 percent of the U.S. population—have an index of 320 for a household income of $50,000+. They are heavily college graduates (327) and post graduates (447). They are most likely to be Baby Boomers, with the strongest grouping in age 45–54.

● Working Women with household incomes of $50,000 are 1 percent of the U.S. population. They are overwhelmingly college graduates (338) and post graduates (507), professionals and managers (424), and ages 35–44.

The bottom line: large numbers of Americans could be more major donors to your charity. By fund raising to "those in the middle" rather than at the top—affluent, rather than wealthy— your organization will gain two valuable pluses:

● **More of your fund raising income will be less restricted.** The higher the gift, the more control donors want to exert. It is easier to encourage donors who give from $1,000 to $25,000 to designate rather than restrict their gift-giving or to leave its use fully to the judgment of the organization.

● **You will be less dependent on the whims of one or two donors.** We've all been there—for two or three years, Mr. and Mrs. Jones have given the top gift to your not-for-profit. You've become accustomed to counting on their continuing generosity.

Suddenly, for whatever reason, this year's gift doesn't come and you're scrambling to make up 30, 40, or 50 percent of your gift income.

> Redefining "who is a major donor" is an important first step in shifting to a major gifts development strategy that expands to include a broader base of gifts from the affluent as opposed to one that focuses only on the wealthy.

By redirecting its focus from the small, over-solicited base of the wealthy to the broader, often-ignored base of affluent prospects, your organization will increase its success in fund raising.

But, before we can move ahead to the specifics of where you will find affluent prospects, it's important to understand what is changing in today's and tomorrow's donors. Because affluence reflects our society's increasing diversity, your donors and prospects will be found in all ages and in all shades. It's important to have an overall understanding of the individuals we will come in contact with during the next ten to fifteen years. Who are they, demographically and psychographically? Moving on to Part Two of *Pinpointing Affluence in the 21st Century* we'll explore this vital information.

PART II

MEET TODAY'S AND TOMORROW'S DONORS

America has changed dramatically during the past 100 years. With the twenty-first century just beginning, the U.S. Census Bureau has chronicled just how much has shifted demographically. The changing picture of the U.S. since the early 1900s includes a near doubling of life expectancy and a dramatically decreasing proportion of white, non-Hispanic Americans.

To begin, there are a lot more of us—in 1900 we were just 76 million. The Commerce Department's Census Bureau projected the resident population of the United States as of January 1, 2000, at 274,024,000 and foresees U.S. population doubling by 2100 to 571 million people. Continued immigration and an increasing number of potential parents could add nearly 300 million people.

Thanks to improvements in medical care, life expectancy of Americans has shot up. In 1900, a typical man could expect to die at age 46; a typical woman, 48. By 1997, life expectancy had reached 74 years for men and 79 for women. The number of Americans aged 65 and up grew from 3 million to 34 million. Death rates were cut in half, from 17.2 deaths per 1,000 people in 1900 to 8.6 in 1997. Influenza and pneumonia, for example, killed 202 out of every 100,000 people in 1900. By 1997, the rate had fallen to 33 out of 100,000.

Other demographic ups and downs:

● *Immigration is up:* Between 1901 and 1910, 2 million immigrants came from Italy and 50,000 from Mexico. Between 1991 and 1997, 1.8 million came from Mexico and 54,000 from Italy.

● *Household size is down:* The average American household in 1900 included 4.8 people; in 1998 it was 2.6 people.

● *Education is up:* In 1900, 11 percent of all 14- to 17-year-olds were enrolled in high school; in 1997, more than 93 percent were in grades 9–12.

● *Divorces have skyrocketed more dramatically than the population,* up almost hundredfold, from 200,000 to 19.4 million.

● *And the women who stay married aren't staying home.* In 1900 there were 800,000 wives in the work force. Now it's around 34 million.

Two important definitions:

- Demographics are sets of characteristics about people that relate to their behavior as consumers. Age, sex, race, marital status, education, and income are used most frequently. Because marketers rarely focus on a single person, we look for such similarities so we can mass market to groups of individuals.

- Psychographics are the measure of attitudes, values, or lifestyles. Taken from surveys and observations, they can be integrated with demographic measure to put "flesh" on an individual or group of persons.

Within the general American population, do you know who your current donors are and who your best prospects would be? What are their backgrounds? How do they spend their time? What do they do to earn a living? To *Pinpoint Affluence in the Twenty-First Century,* let's start by defining who our donors are, today and in the future:

● **Loyal and Predictable**

- Civic Elders (Depression and Swing Babies)

- Emerging (Minority) Populations

● **Idealistic and Affluent**

- Boomer Mid-Lifers

- Today's Working Women

● **Influential and Emerging**

- Pragmatic Busters (Generation X)

- Protected Boomlets (Generation Y)

Chapter 5 reviews the five generations born in the twentieth century. These are the donors and prospects we're working with right now and who will continue to dominate the fund raising scene for the coming twenty-five years. Who are today's and tomorrow's adults? Do we understand their life stages and life styles?

Chapter 6 explains the increasing diversity of our society and suggests we need to widen our prospecting to be inclusive rather than exclusive.

Chapter 7 concentrates on shifting attitudes and how they impact on what people want and support.

The Generations You'll Work With

FUND RAISERS DEAL WITH INDIVIDUALS OF ALL AGES, EITHER DIRECTLY AS PROSPECTS OR BECAUSE THEY INFLUENCE THOSE WHO GIVE. Leaving the very elderly and the very young aside, our beginning point is to understand the generational groupings of the twentieth century as they are the donors of the twenty-first.

VITAL STASTICS ON GENERATIONS

Generation	Year born	Age in 2001	U.S. population (in millions)	% of U.S. population
PRE-WWII			58.7	21.3%
GI Generation	Pre-1930	72+	25.3	9.1
Depression	1930–1939	62–71	17.8	6.5
War Babies	1940–1945	56–61	15.6	5.7
POST-WWII			224.0	78.7%
Baby Boom	1946–1964	37–55	77.4*	28.2
Generation X	1965–1976	25–36	44.9	16.4
Generation Net	1977–1994	7–24	70.7	25.8
Millennials	1995+	6 and under	22.9	8.3

*There were 75,873,000 live births between '46 and '64 in the U.S. But, due to immigration, there are now 77.4 million midlife Boomers.

The dramatically different population numbers tell a story in themselves:

By the early 1920s, American women were turning their backs on childbearing. The decline of births started during World War I. With men at war, births always decrease. Normally, births increase dramatically when wars end, but the Roaring '20s ushered in the age of the "good time girl"—a time of exploration and self-discovery. Births dropped dramatically to just l.8 per woman, the lowest in America's history. The Depression guaranteed continuing low birth rates. World War II simply encouraged the low birth pattern.

With the end of World War II, Americans indulged a pent-up desire for children. Older women had the children they had postponed and younger women had children earlier in their lives. And both groups, reacting to a positive economic climate, had more children than demographers anticipated. The result: *the Baby Boom.*

The Baby Boom couldn't—and didn't—continue indefinitely. The negativism of the 1960s and early 1970s—from assassinations, to the Vietnam War, to double digit inflation, and government and religious scandals—all contributed to a negative attitude towards having children. We call this the *Baby Bust* or *Generation X.*

In the late 1970s, early Baby Boomers began heeding their "biological time clocks." Although Boomers tended to marry later and have children later in life, the higher numbers of boomer women guaranteed that the late 1970s would usher in a *Baby Boomlet* which demographers have named *Generation Y or Net.*

UNDERSTANDING EACH GENERATION'S ATTITUDES,
VALUES, AND LIFESTYLE

■ **Projecting the cycle is a new way of predicting consumer attitudes and lifestyles.** Historians William Strauss and Neil Howe in their book, *Generations: The History of America's Future, 1584 to 2069,* suggest we can read behavior along a "generational diagonal." According to the authors, there are four "generational personalities"—idealistic, reactive, civic, and adaptive—which reoccur in that same order throughout history. To succeed in reaching the generations, your messages will have to pay attention not only to where a generation has been, but also to where it is headed.

According to Strauss and Howe, the following patterns predominate:

- The Missionary Generation (oldest individuals)—Idealistic

- The Lost Generation (born prior to 1901)—Reactive

- The G.I. Generation (born between 1901 and 1924)—Civic

- Silent Generation (born between 1925 and 1942)—Adaptive

- The Boom Generation (born between 1943 and 1960)—Idealistic

- 13th Generation (born in the 1960s and 1970s)—Reactive

- Millennial Generation (born from 1977 on)—Civic

Combining this theory with that of other demographers, I would like to offer my own thumbnail sketch of what people are like—and likely to be—in key adult cohorts:

BOOSTER (MATURE)	BOOMER (MIDLIFE)	BUSTER (YOUNG ADULT)
Security Safety Stability	Identity Personal Growth Meaning Materialism	Identity Relationships Community
"We" the good of the whole	"Me" self fulfillment	"Us" in community
"No Sweat" Worked hard	"No Problem" All kinds of problems	"No Fear" Scared to death

SOURCE: *Share* Magazine, International Resources, The Salvation Army

■ **PRE-WORLD WAR Civics (G.I. or Depression Babies)** are today's activist elderly. Aged 61 and older*, they are 15.6 percent of the American population. Civics came of age during the Depression and many of them fought in World War II. Their shared experiences gave them two key characteristics: frugality and patriotism. They are twentieth-century America's confident, rational problem-solvers, the ones who have always known how to get big things done.

Civics have boundless civic optimism and a sense of public entitlement. Former boy and girl scouts, they volunteer and give because it is part of their inner image. They respect authority, leadership, civic-mindedness, and discipline.

---

*All ages are given as of 2001.

● **Preferred message style:** rational and constructive, with an undertone of optimism.

> "We're quicker to laugh, and not as eager to blame.
> There's time left in this game.
> May we find (along with the inability to tell ourselves
> that we'll keep playing forever)
> A few compensations."
> —Judith Viorst, poet, *Forever Fifty*

● **Financial style:** Shaped by memories of the stock market crash and the great depression, they have cautious spending habits.

● **Key life events:** The Depression and World War II

■ **WORLD-WAR II Silents (often called the "Swing" Generation or Eisenhower Babies)**, aged 56 to 61*, are just 5.7 percent of the U.S. population. War babies growing up during the war "to end all wars," learned to be "seen but not heard." Followers rather than leaders, they will respond to appeals to their other-directed pluralism, trust in expertise, emulation of the young, and unquenched thirst for adventure. Consensus builders rather than leaders, Silents give freely to charity, are inclined to see both sides of every issue, and believe in fair process more than final results. They are organization loyal and value-oriented.

● **Preferred message style:** sensitive and personal, with an appeal to technical detail.

● **Financial style:** Silents were told by their parents the horrors of the previous decade but, personally, they have lived

---
*All ages are given as of 2001.

through the golden economic times of the 1950s and early 1960s. Their financial style is "save a little, spend a little."

● **Key life events:** World War II and the dropping of the bomb on Hiroshima, the Cold War as symbolized by the Berlin Wall, and Senator Joseph R. McCarthy (as well as Marilyn Monroe!)

■ **BABY BOOMER Idealists** were our most wanted generation of children. Born between 1946 and 1964, this is the largest U.S. generation in both size and scope. As of the year 2001, aged 37 to 55, they are 28.2 percent of the American population.

Boomers were told they could do anything. Life is a voyage of self-discovery. They display a bent toward inner absorption, perfectionism, and individual self-esteem. In midlife, they see virtue in austerity and a well-ordered inner life. Also, they are demanding a new assertion of community values over individual wants.

● **Preferred message style:** meditative and principled, with an undertone of pessimism.

> "They're the only generation that ended a war and fired a president," notes Barbara Caplan, vice president at Yankelovich Clancy Shulman, marketing research firm. "To this day, they have a higher level of optimism, a sense that the world is their oyster."
>
> "This will be a much more open and challenging and possibly skeptical set of people."
> —Rena Bartos, marketer,
> on the aging of Baby Boomers.

● **Financial Style:** This is the generation who saw money lose clout. More is worth less. Financial planning is viewed as a sign of status in its own right. However, coming out of the free-spending 1980s, many reevaluated during the 1990s, focusing on non-materialistic values.

● **Key life events:** School Desegregation, Campus Unrest, the Draft, Vietnam, Flower Children, Riots, Kent State, Angela Davis, Jane Fonda, Tom Hayden, Haight-Ashbury, Women's Lib, Free Love, Hippies, the Grateful Dead, Psychedelic, Civil Rights, Freedom Rides, Abbie Hoffman, Berkeley, Timothy Leary, Camelot, Drugs, Sex, Rock and Roll, the Beatles, the Silent Majority, Richard Nixon, John F. Kennedy, Dallas, Jack Ruby, Communes, Folk Music, Sit-Ins, J. Edgar Hoover, Lee Harvey Oswald, Robert Kennedy, Martin Luther King, Malcolm X, Fidel Castro, Che Guevera, Jerry Rubin, SDS, SNCC, Black Panthers, LSD, Bob Dylan, Janis Joplin, Jim Morrison and the Doors—and on and on.

■ **The Baby Bust (better known as Generation X) Reactives,** now 24–36*, comprise 16.4 percent of the population. Following the much-heralded boom, "Busters" could do nothing right. They were the throwaway children of divorce and poverty, the latchkey kids. Reactives weren't trusted nor appreciated as youth and carry the scars into adulthood. They were the most Republican-leaning youths of the 20th century. Generation X will need convincing proof that your organization is reliable and will simplify rather than complicate their lives. They are highly influenced by technology and television.

● **Preferred message style:** blunt and kinetic, with an appeal to brash survivalism. "I want us to be the generation that leads, that votes, that earns, that spends, that doesn't continue to let our parents fight our wars for us," declares Nicholas W. Nyhan, graduating senior, in a commencement speech at the University of Massachusetts at Amherst.

● **Financial style:** Twenty- to thirty-somethings have a different view of the American dream. Only 21 percent say the most important measure of living the good life is financial suc-

*All ages are given as of 2001.

cess, and a scant 4 percent believe that the criterion is owning a home. The rest are more concerned with the acquisition of intangibles: a rich family or spiritual life, a rewarding job, the change to help others, and the opportunity for leisure and travel or for intellectual and creative enrichment.

●   **Key life events:** The crumbling of the Berlin Wall and the opening of Eastern Europe.

COMPARING THE ADULT GENERATIONS

Mature Civics and Silents (56 and older) value duty and tend to be team players:	Midlife Boomers (37 to 55) place a high value on individuality and youth:	Generation X (24–36) approaches life pragmatically:
• Feel they've earned the rewards of life by hard work and careful planning. • See work as an unavoidable obligation. • Look on the future as a rainy day to work for. • More patient about all the time and effort needed to achieve desired results. • Education is a dream, not a birthright. • Tend to trust large, traditional institutions.	• Feel entitled to the rewards of life because they deserve them. • Work is an exciting adventure. • Oriented toward the present tense rather than the future. • Look for tangible, immediate outcomes. • Regard education as a birthright. • Limited trust in large, traditional institutions.	• The defining idea of the generation is diversity, the style entrepreneurial. • Feel entitled to rewards because they are needed. • Work is a difficult challenge, education a way to get where you're going. • The future is uncertain but manageable. • Large institutions are suspect and traditions questionable.

SOURCE: Rocking the Ages: The Yankelovich Report on Generational Marketing, J. Walker Smith and Ann Clurman, HarperBusiness 1997

■ **The Baby Boomlet (increasingly known as Generation "Y" or Net) Civics,** spanning the years from 1977–1994, roughly follow the ending cycle of the early Boomers' years of child-bearing. Aged 7–24*, the Baby "Boomlet" produced 70.7 million children—25.8 percent of the population. While most of Generation Net are still young, *the people who started college in the Fall of 1999 were born in 1982.* They have money of their own AND they influence the buying decisions of their parents, grandparents, and older siblings.

Each year the staff at Beloit College in Wisconsin puts together a list to give its faculty a sense of the mindset incoming freshmen. For the class of 2004 they noted:

- They have no meaningful recollection of the Reagan Era and probably did not know he had ever been shot.

- They were prepubescent when the Persian Gulf War was waged.

- Black Monday 1987 is as significant to them as the Great Depression.

- There has been only one Pope.

- They were 11 when the Soviet Union broke apart and do not remember the Cold War.

- They have never feared a nuclear war.

- They are too young to remember the space shuttle blowing up.

- Tianamen Square means nothing to them.

- Their lifetime has always included AIDS.

- Bottle caps have always been screw off and plastic.

- Atari predates them, as do vinyl albums. The expression "you sound like a broken record" means nothing to them. They have never owned a record player.

*All ages are given as of 2001.

- They have likely never played Pac Man and have never heard of Ping-Pong.

- They may have never heard of an 8 track. The Compact Disc was introduced when they were 1 year old.

- As far as they know, stamps have always cost about 33 cents.

- They have always had an answering machine.

- Most have never seen a TV set with only 13 channels, nor have they seen a black-and-white TV.

- They have always had cable.

- There have always been VCRs, but they have no idea what BETA is.

- They cannot fathom not having a remote control.

- They were born the year that the Walkman was introduced by Sony.

- Roller-skating has always meant inline for them.

- Jay Leno has always been on the Tonight Show.

- They have no idea when or why Jordache jeans were cool.

- Popcorn has always been cooked in the microwave.

- They have never seen Larry Bird play basketball.

- They never took a swim and thought about Jaws.

- The Vietnam War is as ancient history to them as WWI, WWII, and the Civil War.

- They have no idea that Americans were ever held hostage in Iran.

- They can't imagine what hard contact lenses are.

- They don't know who Mork was or where he was from.

- The Titanic was found? They thought we always knew where it was.

- Kansas, Chicago, Boston, America, and Alabama are places, not groups.

- McDonalds never came in Styrofoam containers.

- There has always been MTV.

- They don't have a clue how to use a typewriter.

Generation Net completed the twentieth century by beginning the lifestyle cycle anew, repeating the civic psychographics of their grandparents. Netters believe in science and cooperation, and will be easily persuaded that theirs is a good and special group that knows how to build big things together. Society loves them: considering them smarter, better-behaving, and more civic-spirited than Generation X. They were the "smoke-free, drug-free class of 2000." Netters have heavy influence on parents and relatives, encouraging families to recycle and reexamine values.

A recent study by the Ad Council and MTV, "Engaging the Next Generation: How Nonprofits Can Reach Young Adults," underscores the importance of individualism, community, and contribution to today's youth. Young people are most likely to get involved in issues relating to health (especially affecting children and the elderly), substance abuse, animal rights, the environment, and violence prevention. According to the study, "Young adults today are fiercely individualistic, and are media savvy to a degree never seen before. They are comfortable with—and bombarded by—the abundance of technologies that exist today, from cell phones to beepers to the Internet. As a consequence, they are also extremely stressed in their everyday lives. They also believe strongly that they can make the world a better place—a perfect springboard for getting them involved as volunteers."

● **Preferred message style:** rational and constructive, with an undertone of optimism.

● **Financial style:** for those born in affluent and educated families they are likely to be "financially protected." They will grow up secure in the knowledge that their needs will be met. As a result they are likely to take a balanced view towards spending and saving.

Today more Americans are alive who were born *after* World War II rather than before. Of our adult populations more than:

- 85 percent are not old enough to remember the 1929 stock market crash.

- 70 percent don't remember "before TV."

- 66 percent are not old enough to remember the Korean War.

- 50 percent are too young to remember the assassination of John F. Kennedy.

As a result, we have different points of reference and difference childhood experiences. In *Beyond Mind Games: The Marketing Power of Psychographics* author Rebecca Piirto describes a study by DuPont and Management Horizons that focused on shared experiences. It uses as a starting point an assumption that people are shaped by the events they experience during youth. "People of the same age tend to behave in similar ways because they went through the same formative experiences. During the formative years—between the ages of 7 and 21—core values and attitudes are shaped that will affect an individual for life." As people mature, other influences such as college, marriage, pursuing a career, and/or raising a family take over. Overriding all of these personal influences are the broader events—political, social, international, technological and economic—that shape all of our lives.

■ **Each generation has its own personality.** To understand the differences between generations, we need to ask how they were raised as children, what public events they witnessed in adolescence, and what social mission elders gave them as they came of age.

Here are the five most remembered events for four different adult age groups:

Generation X: 24–36	Baby Boomer: 37–56	Eisenhower: 57–66	Depression: 67+
Oklahoma City bombing	Oklahoma City bombing	JFK assassination	JKF assassination
Challenger explosion	JFK assassination	Armstrong moonwalk	Pearl Harbor
Gulf War start	Challenger explosion	Oklahoma City bombing	End of WWII
Reagan shot	Armstrong moonwalk	Challenger explosion	Armstrong moonwalk
Fall of Berlin Wall	Gulf War start	Martin Luther King assassination	FDR death

Our oldest and youngest adult populations share nothing in common! We must market to and communicate with each generational cohort in terms of their own memories and preferences.[†]

With the help of Ron Zemke, author of *Generations at Work,* here's a wonderful summary chart. Please note that his cohort starting and ending dates differ slightly from mine.

[†]For a more in-depth look at each generation consult *Changing Demographics* or *Global Demographics*—both by Judith E. Nichols, Precept Press.

GENERATIONAL DIFFERENCES

	Defining Events and Trends	Core Values	Generational Personality
The Veterans 1922–1943 (52 million)	• Patriotism • Families • The Great Depression • World War II • New Deal • Korean War	• Dedication • Sacrifice • Hard work • Conformity • Law and order • Respect for authority • Duty before pleasure	Past-oriented and history-absorbed. They believe in logic, not magic. They are conformers.
The Baby Boomers 1943–1960 (73.2 million)	• Prosperity • Children in the spotlight • Television • Suburbia • Assassinations • Vietnam • Civil Rights • Women's liberation	• Optimism • Team orientation • Personal gratification • Personal growth • Health & wellness • Youth • Involvement • Work	Driven, soul-searchers. They are willing to "go the extra mile." They have a love/hate relationship with financial prosperity.
The Gen Xers 1960–1980 (70.1 million)	• Watergate • Latchkey kids • Single parents • AIDS • MTV • Computers • Challenger • Fall of Berlin Wall	• Diversity • Thinking globally • Balance • Technoliteracy • Informality • Self-reliance • Pragmatism	Risk taking skeptics. They seek balance & a sense of family. They think about the job not the work hours.
The Nexters 1980–present (69.7 million)	• Computers • School violence • Oklahoma City bombing • TV talk shows • Multiculturalism	• Confidence • Civic duty • Achievement • Sociability • Morality • Diversity • Street smarts	Both optimistic about the future and realistic about the present. Prefer collective action. They are tenacious.

Understanding generational differences is a key in enabling you to communicate, cultivate and solicit affluent individuals. But there's another, equally important change happening in the United States: we're ethnically and racially diversifying. We'll meet the increasingly diverse population pool of donors and prospects in the next chapter.

CHAPTER SIX

An Increasingly Diverse Pool of Donors and Prospects

THE FUTURE IS HERE—AT LEAST DEMOGRAPHICALLY. The United States population is diversifying, racially and ethnically. By 2010, there will be no "majority." Forty million Americans are multicultural by birth. African-Americans, with substantial buying power, and Hispanics, soon to be the largest segment, are part of most major advertising campaigns. Asian-Americans, the fastest growing segment, have already been targeted by some. Additionally, key segments, such as women and the 50-plus market (including Baby Boomers) are further defined by lifestyles and attitudes. Gays and lesbians and the disabled are already being targeted separately by advertisers.

According to demographer William H. Frey of the Milken Institute, immigrants are reconstructing the face of America. By one estimate, immigrants and their kids will account for more than half of the 50 million people who will be added to the nation's population in the next 25 years.

Nationwide, the Hispanic and Asian populations of the United States surged during the 1990s, with the number of Hispanics growing by more than 35 percent and Asians more than 40 percent, the Census Bureau said. The national Hispanic population is expected to overtake the non-Hispanic black population (with 12.7 percent, or 34.4 million, of the nation's population of 270 million) to become the largest minority group by the end of 2004. Four states—Arkansas, Georgia, Nevada and North Carolina—had their Hispanic populations double. The Asian and Pacific Islander population grew in the 1990s from 3 percent of the overall population to almost 4 percent at 10.5 million.

TOWARDS A DIVERSE AMERICA Percentage of USA Population by Race & Ethnicity			
	2000	2010	2050
Non-Hispanic White	71.8%	68.0%	52.5%
African-American And Black	12.2%	12.6%	14.4%
Hispanic	11.4%	13.8%	22.5%
Asian and Pacific Islander	3.9%	4.8%	9.7%
Native American	0.7%	0.8%	0.9%

U.S. Census Bureau and American Demographics, June 2000

According to Urban Institute projections, the white population (Hispanic and non-Hispanic whites) is projected to be the slowest-growing racial group during the next 60 years, increasing only 29 percent by 2050 (62 million after 1992). The non-Hispanic white share of the population will decline from 75 percent in 1992 to 53 percent in 2050.

The African-American population will increase by 68 percent, and the Asian, Pacific Islander, and Native American populations will increase by 79 percent, the Hispanic population will increase by 187 percent. The Population Reference Bureau has forecasted that by the year 2030, the USA may well be

49 percent white American, 15 percent African-American, 12 percent of Asian ancestry, and 24 percent Hispanic.

The Black, Hispanic, and Asian populations are expected to increase their share of births and immigration, adding 110 million more people than the non-Hispanic white population over the next sixty years:

Meet Generation Z:
Coming to Your Elementary School

Tomorrow's students will defy easy classification. They will come from a wider mix of backgrounds, and will bring different experiences and ideas to their first years of education. Between 2001 and 2010, the number of non-Hispanic white elementary school students will plummet by 2.1 million children, a decrease of 8 percent for children aged 5 to 9, and a decrease of 9 percent for children aged 10 to 14. The number of non-Hispanic black elementary school kids will experience a smaller decline. There will be 400,000 fewer blacks in elementary school by 2010, a decline of 3 percent for the 5- to 9-year olds, and a decline of 10 percent for 10- to 14-year olds. At the same time, the percentage of Hispanic children aged 5 to 9 will increase by 21 percent while the number of Hispanic 10- to 14-year olds will increase by a whopping 29 percent. The number of Asian students aged 5 to 9 will increase by 22 percent by 2010, and the number of Asian students aged 10 to 14 will increase by 31 percent.

Generation Z, Alison Stein Wellner, *American Demographics,* September 2000

● **Blacks are the largest minority except in the West.** *As of June 2000, about 33 percent of the country's 35 million blacks* *are age 18 or younger, compared with 24 percent of America's 193 million whites.* The statistics offer more proof that America's population will become even more diverse in the twenty-first century. According to the Census Bureau, the black population would rise to 59.2 million in 2050, a 70 percent increase. Under this projection, the black share of the total population would increase slightly, from 13 percent to 15 percent.

Today's black population is 27 million, or 12 percent of the U.S. population. It is growing at a rate nearly three times faster than the white population. The black population will grow 94 percent to 62 million in 2050. After 2005, more blacks than non-Hispanic whites will be added each year.

●   Hispanic, a designation that includes people from all four races, will add more people to the U.S. population than any other group. Hispanics are increasing about 3.3 percent per year, or about three times the overall U.S. growth rate. The number of U.S.-born Latinos and Latin American immigrants to the United States doubled from 1980 to 1990, according to U.S. Census Bureau data. Latinos residing in the U.S. total 27 million people, make up nearly 10 percent of the population and are expected to become the largest minority by early in the next century. By 2010, it's estimated that Hispanic-Americans will surpass African-Americans as the largest USA minority group. Noteworthy is the relative youth of this demographic segment: 35 percent are under the age of 18. In 2010, Hispanics are projected to account for 13.8 percent of the U.S. population, up from 11.4 percent today.

California has "tipped."

The most recent census estimates show that the racial balance has shifted in California where the white, non-Hispanic population is no longer in the majority.

White, non-Hispanic	49.8%
Hispanic	31.6%
Asian and Pacific Islander	12.2%
Black	7.5%
American Indian and Alaska Native	0.9%

The Hispanic population will be 81 million strong by 2050 (246 percent growth), representing a total increase of 57 million people after 1992. Within a century, Hispanics could comprise up to 30 percent of the U.S. population, approximately 99,000,000 people.

A total of 2,152 people named Smith purchased a home in Florida in 1999.

The second most common last name was Johnson with 1,486, followed by Rodriguez.

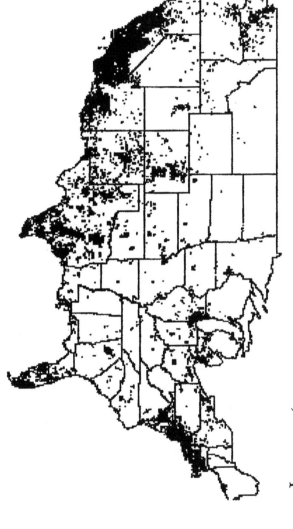

Hispanic Population – 1990 Census

1 Dot = 1,000 Hispanics

Survey Sampling, Inc.

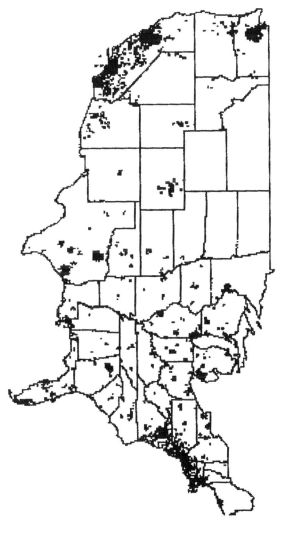

Asian Population – 1990 Census

1 Dot = 300 Asian Households

Survey Sampling, Inc.

● Spurred by the 2.4 million Asian immigrants who arrived in the United States during the 1980s, there has been an 80 percent increase in the number of Asian-Americans. They are the fastest-growing minority group in the United States. The number of Asian-Americans (which also includes Pacific Islanders) grew from 3.8 million in 1980 to an estimated 6.9 in 1989 and onwards to 9 million in 1992. Asians will continue to be the fastest-growing group, increasing from 9 million in 1992 to 41 million in 2050 (356 percent growth).

WHY IS THIS IMPORTANT TO FUND RAISERS?

Today, one in three people in the USA is Black, Hispanic, Asian, or Native American. Fueled by immigration and high birthrates, populations of ethnic and racial minorities in the United States will grow seven times faster than the white, non-Hispanic population over the next decade, according to the U.S. Census Bureau. Fourteen percent speak a language other than English at home. The 1990s became the decade of diversity. And tomorrow's adults are today's youth. Twenty-five percent of California's 4.5 million kindergarten-through-high school students, for example, are Hispanics.

By 2050, "minorities" will make up just under half the United State's population. Non- Hispanic whites will decrease to 53 percent of the population from 75 percent today. By 2050, the projected population of 383 million will be: 21 percent Hispanic, 15 percent black, 10 percent Asian, and 1 percent Native American. In California, New York, and Florida "minorities" are already the majority.

IS DIVERSITY A CONCERN FOR PHILANTHROPY?

Although non-Hispanic whites will be the majority of Americans for at least the next 90 years, the share is steadily shrinking and the number of non-white and Hispanic Americans is

rapidly growing. As our population continues to diversify, so must our base of prospects, donors, and volunteers.

Minorities of all colors and ethnic backgrounds are philanthropic. *Minority donors are generally motivated to "give back" to the community after achieving success in their own lives* observes a study by the Council on Foundations and the Association of Black Foundation Executives. Many start scholarship funds to improve the likelihood of young people pursuing higher education. A study conducted by Hide Yamatani at the University of Pittsburgh demonstrates that financial aid to African-American college students brings a healthy return to society. The tracking of 13,000 recipients of aid shows that they contributed back nearly 20 times the $7 million invested in them including $91 million in taxes and approximately $40.4 million in financial and volunteer contributions. More than 76 percent of them volunteered for nonprofit organizations, compared with the national average of 45 percent.

● *African-Americans have been documented as among the nation's most generous donors of time and money.* According to Independent Sector, the proportion of black respondents reporting household contributions increased from 61 percent in 1989 to 64 percent in 1991. In 1991, blacks also gave the highest percentage of household income (2.7 percent) compared with whites (2.2 percent) and Hispanics (2.1 percent). Black Americans say the church is the primary beneficiary of their giving. Forty-seven percent of African-Americans volunteered in 1998, a 12 percent increase from 1995.

● *Similar to their white counterparts, affluent blacks have often been accused of being "BUPPIES" (Black Urban Professionals), worshiping status and possessions above all else.* However, data refutes the idea of an indifferent black middle class. "The black middle class has always been concerned about and involved with uplifting other blacks," says Dr. Alvin Thoreton, a professor of political science at Howard University. "It's a historical attribute." In recent years, Oprah Winfrey's philanthropy has been an inspiration to Americans of all backgrounds.

● Furthermore, economist Emmett D. Carson, author of *The Hand Up: Black Self-Help in America*, says that charitable contributions from the black middle class are on a par with those of their white counterparts. "In some areas of giving, we give more, but the difference is small," observes Carson, a program officer in governance and public policy at the Ford Foundation.

Blacks with incomes over $40,000 gave at least $500 to charity, the same percentage as white Americans. Informal philanthropy remains the most prominent way that African-Americans display their giving and serving traditions. In general, African-Americans demonstrate reluctance to make donations to open-ended funds and charities.

SOURCE: *African American Traditions of Giving and Serving: A Midwest Perspective,* Cheryl Hall-Russell and Robert H. Kasberg, Indiana University

---

● *While blacks have gained economic ground since 1967, and their household income has grown at a faster rate than that of non-Hispanic whites, only 2.7 percent of black households have incomes of $100,000 or more, compared to 8.9 percent of white households.* That means you need to use some creative means to enable them to be part of bigger gift and endowment campaigns.

- Let donors make monthly payments.

- Pool gifts under a common fund or goal either at your organization or at a community foundation.

Asians and Hispanics also give far more to charity than previously indicated. Several studies in cross-cultural ethnography involving Asian and Hispanic communities have examined cultural dimensions of gift-giving, sharing, and the distribution of income and wealth, as well as the philanthropic impact of religion, mutual benefit associations, godparent-hood, and kinship. The conclusions: while Asian- and Hispanic-Americans may not send a check to United Way or the American Cancer Society, they share with extended family and ethnic members of their community as well as needy relatives and friends in their home countries.

● *Hispanic giving is made up mostly of one-to-one donations to relatives, gifts to the church, and to causes in their native countries.* This giving is informal, mostly through non-institutional means, and tends to be sporadic and uneven. Although cash is often scarce, the giving of in-kind service is very common. The idea of giving through organized philanthropic structures outside of the religious institution is new. Forty-six percent of Hispanics volunteered in 1998, a six percent increase since 1995.

While there is vast diversity in the Hispanic population groups in the USA, which represent 21 countries, Hispanics do share many important and widely accepted values that relate to philanthropy and fundraising. According to Jesse Miranda, president of the Aianza de Ministerios Evangelicos Nacionales (AMEN) and consulting editor of *Christianity Today,* these include:

- Familialismo (significance of family)

- Personalismo (good character)

- Espiritualidad (spirituality)

- Fatalismo (fatalism)

- Colectivismo (collectivism)

- Confianza (trust)

- Orgullo (pride, dignity)

- Respecto (respect)

- Simpatia (congeniality)

● *Generally Asians consider the family first, followed by spe-cific causes that benefit the Asian community.* Like the U.S. Hispanic population, the Asian-American population repre-sents a diversity of ethnic populations such as Chinese, Japan-ese, Filipino, Korean, Pacific Islander, Vietnamese, Cambodian, Laotian, East Indian, Thai, and Samoan with separate tradi-tions, cultures, and languages. This makes a single approach difficult. At this time, few studies have been done on philan-thropy among specific Asian-American populations.

A major impediment to giving for Blacks, Hispanics, and Asian-Americans is that, simply put, they are least likely to be asked. However when asked, the percentage who contributed were two and a half to three and a half times greater than the percentages of those who were not asked!

At the beginning of the 1990s, only 65 percent of Black Americans and 56 percent of Hispanic Americans indicated they were asked to give compared to 74 percent of white, non-Hispanic Americans, according to the *Giving and Volunteer-ing 1992 Survey* conducted by Independent Sector. While awareness improved through the last decade of the 20th cen-tury, the *Giving and Volunteering 1996 Survey* showed that 31 percent of Hispanic people surveyed about philanthropy said they are "not asked" or "not asked by someone they knew," when questioned about why they give or do not give.

- Minorities are asked to give less often than whites, yet minorities are more likely to con-tribute when asked for a donation: Gallup sur-vey.

- In families with household incomes of $25,000 or more, black women are more like-ly to give to charity than white women: "To the Contrary" study, commissioned by PBS-TV program and funded by the W.K. Kellogg Foundation.

Changing demographics have important implications for philanthropy. Our vision of an "ideal" donor must change.

THE "IDEAL" DONOR

Used to be:

- White

- Male

- Happily Married/Widowed

- Protestant

- 50–64 years of age

- Highly educated

- A Corporate Executive or Professional

Today and Tomorrow, Will Be:

- White, Asian, Hispanic, Black

- Male or Female

- Married, Widowed, or Single

- Any Religion

- Any Age

- Highly Educated

- An Entrepreneur or Professional

The changing demographics will provide us with more fund raising opportunities but will require more understanding on our parts: who are our donors and prospects and what are they like?

Indeed, this increasing diversity—both by age and ethnic/racial backgrounds—is reshaping American attitudes. In the next chapter, we'll explore these dramatic psychographic changes and see how they impact philanthropy.

CHAPTER SEVEN

Understanding Changing Attitudes: How Do they Impact the Raising of Major Donor Dollars?

DEMOGRAPHICS EXPLAIN *WHO'S WHO IN AMERICA,* but you also need to understand how our goals have changed and what we are seeking. Why people give is a function of their values, attitudes, and lifestyles.

The second half of the twentieth century was a time of vast change. We moved from the 1960s—a time of boundless optimism—through the 1970s—a time of experimentation—to the 1980s—a time of disillusionment and selfishness through the 1990s—a time of reconciliation.

According to George Barna, president of Barna Research Group which studies cultural trends:

"In the '60s, a group of upstarts made it fashionable to question many of the basic assumptions about life. When their probing revealed the ability to radically reshape views and practices related to culture, it was only natural that we then encountered some creative and bold responses to the foundations and traditions regarding attitudes and life-styles.

But the '60s proved to be mostly a time when we were simply testing the possibilities. Deep in the recesses of the minds and hearts of a few hearty souls was the notion that we could redesign this world to truly exploit the untapped opportunities for fulfillment that it possessed. But it would take some time for the masses to catch the vision.

In the '70s, that vision was more completed articulated and pursued. The pace of experimentation exploded. People began to think more critically about the boundaries of their personal reality.

The tone changed a bit in the '80s, as the unquenched thirst for experience, adventure, the good life, and security in the midst of chaos turned inward. Beyond being a 10-year span of wanton selfishness, the '80s also set the stage for a new era. The '80s saw people realize they could redesign their world according to their deepest personal desires and fantasies regardless of the societal consequences. The theme of the decade may have been, 'It is better to ask for forgiveness than permission: Act now, plead later.'

The 'Me Decade' clearly reflected the utter self-deceit and deep-seated greed and cruelty of humans. But it was a decade that also drove home the reality of all forays into new territory and all attempts to create the world come with a price tag. There really is no such thing as a free lunch, but it took Americans the better part of 15 years to reach that simple conclusion.

The '90s, then, were a period in which the pursuit of priorities and socially acceptable goals were returning to vogue. Fatigued by nearly two decades of taking on the world, many adults were admitting they could not truly mold the entire world in their own image. Pragmatic realists, they were instead scaling back their goals to seek a smaller, more comfortable world in which they could see their imprint on that designer reality."

Ahead for the twenty-first century—a growing understanding of our increased longevity. As we enter the twenty-first century, the Baby Boom generation (those born from the mid-1940s to mid-1960s), and perhaps some of its parents, can expect to live healthy, active lives that stretch to between 110 and 120 years. We've reached a median longevity of nearly 80 years for women, more than 72 years for men. Increasingly, those now in mid-life and younger understand that they have been blessed (or cursed) with the ever-increasing probability of living 90, 100, 110, 120 years or more.

According to evolutionary biologist Michael Rose, a professor at the University of California at Irvine, medical and scientific advances are paving the way so you could live to be 250 years old. Maybe even 300. It's just a question of time!

●   Living longer, post–World War II Americans will be more concerned with the quality of life than were the generations born before World War II. Their interests may be very different than their parents and grandparents and the causes they support will change as well. Many people are questioning how they want to spend their bonus years. They are asking the questions, "Who are we?" and "What matters?".

●   Adulthood is stretching out, comprised of three stages: first (learning and experiencing), second (growing and refining), and third (maturing and reevaluating).

As a result of our increasing longevity, a powerful wave of soul-searching and uncertainty has swept across this country, bringing dramatic, long-term changes to the marketplace.

●   **Many Americans—people who believed and behaved as if abundance would never end—are now, in many cases for the first time, coming to grips with limitations.** Today, Americans are experiencing doubts about their collective and individual futures.

- People feel the scale and pace of change is overwhelming.

- Many have lost faith in basic truths.

- Many have had their confidence in religious truths shaken.

- Many feel that their nation no longer feels a commitment to reduce poverty.

- Technology is a nearly universal concern.

- Many find their personal values and identities challenged.

●   **We are turning from an expectation that government will lead and find solutions.** Instead, we are entering the era of "big citizenship," as Will Marshall of the New Democrat Progressive Policy Institute calls it. The thrust of this new arrangement is, according to Marshall, to "equip citizens and communities to solve their own problems."

● **As large corporations continue to undergo restructuring, the traditional leaders of community stability are being bought out and consolidated.** It is a time of discovery, a time for courageous conversations. The old social contract didn't have a clause for introspection. You gave loyalty. You got security. But now that the old contract has been repealed, people are examining both its basic terms and its implicit conditions. In America and the Netherlands, for example, nearly 29 percent of the workforce is already on its own. As a result, we are living through the closing chapters of the industrial age, and we are in the opening chapters of the purpose age with a new challenge to reinvent work and the workplace.

● **Add to a changing social contract, an increasingly high-tech world.** The global community will be a place where it will be simultaneously easier to reach out to humanity and easier to become isolated. Superficial communication with everyone can lead to meaningful impact on no one. Residents of the global community will need to be inspired and educated in the value of trying to benefit the world, not just themselves. The acceleration of technological progress has created an urgent need for a counter-ballast of high-touch experiences. High touch is about getting back to a human scale. High touch recasts the terms of an organization's interaction with its donors.

The world and the people in it will continue to change at an accelerated pace in the next century, for we are only at the early stages of the transition to the information and communications era.

● **Tomorrow's older individuals will be better educated and more affluent.** They will have fewer relatives, two or more incomes, multiple pensions, better retirement plans, and better health. Their increasing longevity will mean:

- Giving up the notion of a traditional retirement at or before age 65.

- Increased savings for the future.

- Retiring in stages.

- Creating alternative living arrangements.

As we begin a new century Americans are living by a new set of values. People who believe in environmentalism, feminism, global issues, and spiritual searching are scattered across the country and found in all social groups. They comprise nearly one-fourth of American adults, or 44 million persons. Often called "Cultural Creatives," they tend to be affluent, well-educated, and on the cutting edge of social change. Six in 10 are women. They want to walk their talk and are the most altruistic and least cynical of the three major American subcultures.

WHAT DO AMERICANS WANT NOW?

People are building (and rebuilding) their lives on a more stable footing. Grey Advertising calls this **downshifting.** It is a conscious, considered effort to make everyday life manageable and secure.

● **There is a continuing emphasis on family, friends, and community.**

Percentage of Americans who agree that:

"The simple jobs in life are what
matters today"   88%

"Current conditions have made me
more aware of the importance of family"   87%

"I'm looking for more meaningful values"   81%

SOURCE: "Downshifting in America," Grey Matter Alert No. 4

● **There's a move away from judging success in terms of economics and material assets and towards "quality of life" evaluators.** Trend forecasters see that more people are willing to give up as much as 40 percent of their income to lead a better, more quality lifestyle, where in the middle of the day they could play with their kids if they wanted to.

Faith Popcorn, head of BrainTrust—a think tank for marketing forecasting—asserts that, "in their desire to avoid the harsh realities of the outside world, and their mile-a-minute, almost schizophrenic lives, Americans are 'digging in' and 'cashing out.'" Other trends Popcorn identifies include:

- They're nostalgically looking for the "good old days," or trying to escape to a real world "fantasy island" without even leaving the comfort of home.

- They can no longer afford every new luxury, so they're rewarding themselves with "smaller, more affordable indulgences."

- They're no longer willing to settle for just being a "number," and they're demanding more personalized attention.

- A new social conscience is stirring. Ethics, passion, service, compassion, and basic honesty are "in"; hype, glitz, and moral bankruptcy are "out."

● **Control of time, not money, is what Americans want most.**
Americans' Use of Time Project and *National Recreation and Park Association* surveys indicated that more than one in three Americans (38%) says they "always feel rushed." This compares with 22 percent in 1971 and 32 percent in 1985. In a survey conducted by Hilton Hotels, 50 percent of 1,010 people polled said they would sacrifice a day's pay for an extra day off each week. Today, many are rethinking their use of time. In a recent survey, 25 percent of Americans say they think work and leisure are equally important. That's about double the level of 1975 (13%). Maybe you can't have it all, they say, but that should not stop you from trying.

Important goals begun in the 1990s and continuing strong into the new century include:

- Spending time with family
  and friends   77%

- Improving oneself intellectually,
  emotionally, or physically   74%

- Saving money   72%

- Having free time to spend any way
  you please   68%

WHAT DOES THIS MEAN AND HOW DOES IT AFFECT PHILANTHROPY?

The 1990s were labeled and relabeled: "the decency decade," the "we decade," the "new community," and the era of "a thousand points of light." These varying labels point to the same impulse: the impulse to give.

Americans are giving more. In 1999, charitable giving reached $190.16 billion, 9.1 percent higher and well ahead of the 5.7 percent growth in gross domestic product, according to the AAFRC Trust for Philanthropy. After inflation, donations increased 6.7 percent making 1999 the fifth year in a row they rose in real dollars.

Americans can do more. The truth is that it is the poorest who give the largest percentage of their income—5.2 percent in 1998. This compares with just 2.2 percent for those earning $100,000, according to Independent Sector.

● The affluent can give substantially more—it's really a question of what are our priorities. Amy Dacyczyn, founder of the *Tightwad Gazette* states that: The average American consumes twice as many goods and services as did the average American in 1950; 10 times as many as the average American in 1928. In addition,

- The average American spent $403 a year on hobbies and home recreation in 1950; nowadays—adjusted for inflation—the average American spends $1,149.

- Of every food dollar spent in 1950, 21 cents went for restaurant meals; the amount had doubled by 1990.

- The average family today is smaller than the average family of the '50s, but the average new house is twice as large as the average post-World War II house.

● **Increasingly, as individuals, we are taking charge.** Our bonus years plus the personality of Baby Boomers (today's midlife adults)—committed to change, impatient with the status quo—add up to a new formula for civic leadership. An individual who wants to help the poor and rebuild community institutions and who is prepared to be as exacting in his or her charitable activities as in other domains of his or her life. Such individuals want to help the poor and rebuild community institutions, but take a different approach than traditional charitable giving. We've begun calling such individuals "Civic Entrepreneurs."

Edward McCracken, chairman and CEO of Silicon Graphics asserts that, "civic entrepreneurs are the new links between the economy and the community." He sees that "understanding the importance of collaboration, they are driven to achieve results." Acting as an investor, not a passive check-writer, this new donor can help guide the charity s/he partners with and work with it to deepen its impact in the community. This type of donor can keep watch on what works—and what does not—in helping the poor and under served. And the true civic entrepreneur welcomes the opportunity to serve as a sounding board for new projects.

● **Americans are reaching for personal control in response to overwhelming change:** a new emphasis on human relations—the desire for a sense of belonging—extends right out the front door and into the community; 90 percent of Americans believe we should do more to help the homeless, and 87 percent are now "more interested in playing a role in protecting the environment."

- Sixty-three percent of Americans say they want to be rich in order to give to charity. Not worrying in an emergency (81%) and college for children (79%) were the only reasons to outscore philanthropy. (Gallup Poll)

- If money were not a problem, Americans choose charity. Twenty-seven percent of Americans would make charity their first priority if they were given unlimited money to fulfill "their wildest dreams." Next in desire came travel (22%), followed by purchasing real estate (19%), and paying bills (11%). (Roper Poll)

> "Should 20-something generation be ignored?"
>
> Blake E. Evans, *The Oregonian*
>
> My generation is facing the most difficult challenge of any generation before us: to solve all of the problems left by our foreparents. Global warming, destruction of the rain forests, pollution on an epidemic scale, depletion of resources and nuclear proliferation—our ability to deal with these issues may determine the quality of life on this planet for the next millennium... We must redefine the American Dream as a vision of hope, rather than wealth."

● "Charity and social consciousness are finding a renewed importance across the country," notes Kitty Mountain, vice president and publisher of *Victoria* magazine. Fifty-seven percent of those polled said they do more charitable work now than five years ago. What's more, almost one-third cut back on or forewent their own gift giving to donate more to charity.

● **Americans' charitable giving has become less "self-directed" and more "altruistic."** Groups devoted to the environment, human services, public or social benefit (such as civil rights and community development), and international aid have been gaining a larger share of donors' total contributions since 1987.

- Human service organizations continue to dominate the top spots on the NPT 100, America's Biggest Charities, a special report of the *NonProfit Times.* According to *Giving USA,* human service donations grew by over 20 percent in 1998, followed by an increase of 8 percent in 1999.

- Although contributions to public/society benefit organizations only grew by 0.8 percent in 1999, this follows two years of double-digit increases.

- Contributions to international affairs organizations increased by 9.3 percent in 1998 and by 23.6 percent in 1999.

- Contributions to environment/wildlife organizations increased by 28.3 percent in 1998 and 11.1 percent in 1999.

● **Value positioning is the best strategy.** As people live longer, healthier lives, they are increasingly looking to give back to their communities and expand in new ways. With life expectancy growing from 47 in 1900 to mid-seventies today, and with many people living until well past 85, society must create meaningful roles for older adults. Many social commentators are beginning to view retirement as an open vista rather than a cliff.

Remarks syndicated columnist Ellen Goodman: "Living well is no longer the best revenge, but a sign of profligacy and proof of shortsightedness. It may even be a warning sign that sends you to a twelve-step program. To put it simply, spending is out and sacrifice is in."

Values positioning involves appealing to people's values—their beliefs and priorities—when marketing a product or service. A good example: Ben & Jerry's. Notes a marketer, "Though there's nothing particularly good for you in their ice cream—in fact it's the richest around—it is popular with the healthy, back-to-basics, politically correct, environmentally aware crowd in part because the company donates a percentage of its pretax profits to charity. Doing good is not only included in the company's corporate culture, it's also become part of its marketing strategy."

But attitudes towards charitable organizations are more critical. Asked about the value to society of a dozen top philanthropic organizations, the public's highly favorable opinions have declined each year since 1974.

Groups such as Easter Seals (53 percent say it is "very important," down 15 points) and the March of Dimes (56 percent, down 13 points) are less apt to be viewed as "very" important and increasingly considered only "somewhat" important to society. Only the Red Cross (66 percent "very important," up 6 points) has shown any significant improvement since 1974.

An Independent Sector survey has found that concerns over United Way and other not-for-profit scandals have taken a toll on our confidence: 31 percent of people had "quite a lot" or "a great deal" of confidence in federated campaigns such as United Way, compared to 52 per cent in a 1990 survey.

- 31 percent of those surveyed believed that charities were not more effective today than they were five years ago.

- 34 percent said charities "make very little difference in dealing with major problems."

- 36 percent had a "low degree of trust" in charities compared with 28 percent in the 1990 survey.

In fact, less than half of all Americans surveyed by Independent Sector expressed a "great deal" or "quite a lot of confidence" in charitable organizations. Leading the list were:

- Private higher education (49%)

- Youth development or recreation (48%)

- Religious organizations (47%)

- Public higher education (47%)

- Private elementary or secondary education (44%)

- Public elementary or secondary education (43%)

- Health organizations (40%)

Accountability is the new key to consumer (and donor) satisfaction. Even more so than in earlier years, Americans want to trust your organization. They are looking for substance, performance, informativeness, access, and organizational responsibility. While the good news is that religious and other not-for-profit organizations lead the list when Americans are surveyed as to the level of confidence they place in demographic institutions, there has been a serious—15 to 20 percentage point—erosion of that credibility.

● **More people are questioning how charities use funds.** Only 47 percent of the public, down from 55 percent in 1974, think half or more of the money raised for charity actually goes to the designated cause, and 30 percent think under a quarter of the funds reach the cause. More than one in three people interviewed thought charities were wasteful, and more than one in four thought that groups were not "honest and ethical" in their use of money.

A survey by NPT/Barna Research reveals that Americans do not find nonprofit leaders overly trustworthy:

- only 8.3 percent found them very trustworthy.

- 57.9 percent found them "somewhat" trustworthy.

- 29.3 percent found them "not too" trustworthy.

- 8.2 percent found them "not at all" trustworthy.

In recognizing their fears and doubts, Americans have moved from an attitude of invincibility to a deep and unsettling sense of vulnerability. Fifty-eight percent of adults now say religion is "very important" to them, up from 53 percent in 1987. Another 29 percent term it "fairly important." Nationally, church attendance has grown five percent since 1980. Utah tops the church-going at 79.8 percent; Nevada ranks lowest at 32.1 percent. Forty-two percent of adults now attend church or synagogue each week, a 2 percent rise over the last year. About a fourth of present-day church members have switched denominations at least once from the domination in which they were raised.

HOW CAN YOUR ORGANIZATION GAIN CREDIBILITY WITH DONORS AND PROSPECTS?

In charitable giving, as in other areas of consumer decision making, the twenty-first century may well be the decade of the "smart shopper." Americans are focusing on quality rather than quantity. Many are cutting back on the frequency of purchases and/or postponing or cutting out discretionary items. In charitable giving this means choosing a few priorities and funding them more heavily.

Tracey Gary, author of *Inspired Philanthropy,* has argued that regardless of how much or little donors have to give, they must create a giving plan that makes their charitable giving "catalytic." Because individuals are choosing their charitable purchases more carefully, more communications, rather than less, is being demanded.

The results of a poll conducted by the Roper Organization suggest that "rather than merely telling potential donors that their money is going towards 'fighting' a particular disease, for instance, groups should lay out in no uncertain terms precisely how, and in what proportions, funds are being used—and they must be prepared to prove it." Notes Roper, "Before charities can expect people to part with hard-earned dollars, they must provide them with critical information about where their money is going—and what it is doing."

● **Use hard news rather than vague promises** or unspecific claims in your promotion. A simpler, more straightforward tone and a more down-to-earth attitude that reflects their new, more traditional values.

● **Provide practical information** about your organization. Today's donors and prospects are information gathers. Upfront they want to know exactly what type of organization they are dealing with. You can be clever, but you must always be direct with them. They know the ad game and are sensitive to media/marketing manipulation.

● **Use testimonials carefully.** Who do we most admire today? In 1898, 78 percent of Americans surveyed chose politicians, moral leaders, and generals. George Washington, Clara Barton, and Christopher Columbus headed the list. In 1948, 33 percent chose historical figures, 23 percent chose sports figures, 14 percent entertainers, and 1 percent religious figures with Franklin Delano Roosevelt and Clara Barton heading the list. In 1986, with the exception of Ronald Reagan, all leading figures were entertainers such as Bill Cosby, Molly Ringwald, and Arnold Schwartzenegger.

Hero-Less Society

According to the Institute for Technology Development, 38 percent of people cannot name a hero. Most of those who do name a hero chose someone in one of four categories:

Politicians	22%
Religious/humanitarians	12%
Military persons	12%
Family members	7%

In conclusion: All signs point to a twenty-first century in which we focus on selectivity, accountability, and interactivity.

● *Selectivity*—the ability to reach an individual based on knowledge of his/her background, interests, and habits.

● *Accountability*—the ability to trace the individual's response to a particular communication/appeal.

● *Interactivity*—the ability to cultivate a rapport with, and loyalty of individual consumers. The years ahead will be interesting and challenging ones for charities who understand the implications of a changing world.

PART III

FINDING AFFLUENT PROSPECTS DEMOGRAPHICALLY AND PSYCHOGRAPHICALLY

To capture their philanthropic dollars, you will need to understand how to find the real affluents, interpret their needs, analyze their past giving behavior, and know how and where to reach them.

Who are our donors? They tend to fit the profile of affluent Americans! According to Bruce Campbell in *Successful Direct Mail & Telephone Fundraising,* our *"donors tend to have a higher marriage rate, be better educated, and a higher level of household income than the general U.S. population ($44,000 vs. $35,000)."*

●   For the typical donor file, 72 percent are married, 10 percent are single, 5 percent are divorced or separated, and 13 percent are widowed. In general, donors to religious organizations have a higher marriage rate (75%) compared to donors to nonsectarian organizations (48%). Also, donors to family- or children-focused organizations have an even higher marriage percentage (83%) than donors to other types of nonprofits (72%).

● Over half the donors (56%) have completed their college degree or have gone to graduate school, compared to the general U.S. public which is less than half as likely to have completed college or gone on to graduate school (27%). Donors to religious organizations are slightly more educated then typical donors, with 59 percent having a college degree or graduate education.

Now that you understand the rationale for a development strategy focusing on affluent individuals, how will you locate and connect with your best prospects? Obviously, we'd like to increase the number of affluent donors in our files. When prospecting, we can try to find them strictly by income across a broad geographic spectrum. Or look for specific demographic subgroups linking affluence with age, household and gender, ethnicity, and career paths and professions.

Unfortunately, the greater number of affluents in the country has also increased the difficulty of locating them. How do you separate the truly affluent from those who wear the title by virtue of income but lack the ways and means of affluence?

● **We could, for example, look for affluent Americans geographically.** According to the U.S. Bureau of Labor Statistics, in 1997, the average annual pay in the United States was $30,336, but of the country's 296 counties with 75,000 or more employees, 113 recorded pay levels higher than the national average. New York County, comprised entirely of the borough of Manhattan, led the way with an average annual pay of $58,791 followed by Fairfield, Connecticut ($49,867) and Santa Clara, California (48,702).

● **Or, we can group them by a broader variety of common life stage concerns:** We can target to MOBY's (Mommy Older, Baby Younger) and DOBY's (their daddies). We can look at the-once Yuppies (Young Urban Professionals), now their PUPPIES (Poor Urban Professionals) and WOOF's (Well-Off Older Folks). We've got Sandwichers (adults caught between caring for their children and their older parents), SKIPPIE's (School Kids with Income and Purchasing Power), as well as groups based on special interests like Global Kids (kids with strong feelings about the environment **plus** strong influence over family purchase choices); and New Health Age Adults (consumers who consider their health and the health of the planet top priorities).

● **Another way we might look at how the affluent is by how they spend their leisure time.** For example, did you know that active people have more money? A study commissioned by the National Sporting Goods Association reports that the greater your income, the more likely you are to work out and the less likely you are to be inactive!

In this section of *Pinpointing Affluence in the 21st Century,* we move from a more general discussions of the today's demographics and psychographics trends, a deeper understanding of the demographics and psychographics of American affluents. **Chapters 8 through 17** explore the wealth of demographic and psychographic information we can tap to identify affluents.

CHAPTER EIGHT

Pinpointing Affluence Geographically

THERE ARE PLENTY OF AF-FLUENT POPULATIONS THROUGHOUT THE UNITED STATES, MOSTLY IN MAJOR METROPOLITAN AREAS. While the United State's poorest counties are scattered across the country, the top 20 counties for median household income are overwhelmingly located in metropolitan areas.

■ **The heaviest concentrations of wealth are found in and around New York City, San Francisco, and Washington, D.C.** Fifteen of the top 20 counties are on the East Coast, and three of the top 10 are in New Jersey. In fact, 20 of the top 50 counties are clustered around one of these three metro areas—10 in New York City, five in San Francisco, and five in D.C.

● *Targeting may be easiest in the urban corridor stretching from Boston to Washington, D.C.* Of the 20 counties with the highest concentrations of households earning $50,000 or more, 15 are in the northeastern megalopolis. This region also contains the majority of top-20 counties for affluent Black-, Hispanic-, and Asian-headed households, as well as affluent households headed by young, middle-aged, and older adults.

According to the 1990 Census (the last for which complete information has been released):

● Eleven of the 20 counties with the highest share of household incomes of $50,000 or more form a suburban ring around the vast New York-Northern New Jersey-Long Island Consolidated Metropolitan Statistical Area (CSMA).

● Four more are in the Washington, D.C.-Baltimore area.

● The most comfortable county is Fairfax, Virginia. In 1989, 61 percent of Fairfax households had an annual income of $50,000 or more compared to only 25 percent of households nationally.

● The county with the greatest concentration of $100,000 households is Westchester County, New York with almost 18 percent compared to 4 percent nationwide.

● **For all-around affluence, the clear winner is Morris County, New Jersey.** According to a report in *American Demographics* magazine, Morris is found on nine lists: 58 percent of households in Morris County have incomes of $50,000 or more. A high share of minorities in Morris County can be classified as affluent, and its riches are enjoyed by young and old alike. And, unlike most other counties with high concentrations of affluent householders, Morris County's affluent population is still growing rapidly.

■ **While the most affluent Americans are concentrated on the east coast, median household income is higher in the West.** In 1990, it was $31,800 versus $29,900 nationally. The West also counts the highest proportion of executives and professionals—33.4 percent—compared to the national average of 27.8 percent. And, with 45.5 percent of residents having some college background, Westerners are also more educated, exceeding the national average of 38 percent. According to the Roper Organization, this income disparity will grow more pronounced.

U.S. COUNTIES WITH THE HIGHEST PER-CAPITA INCOME IN 2000 AND PROJECTED INCOME FOR 2010, IN 1999 DOLLARS

COUNTY	2000 Per Capita Income	2010 Projected Income
New York, NY	$69,157	$99,088
Marin, CA	$54,608	$85,243
Pitkin, CO	$54,076	$79,455
Fairfield, CT	$53,474	$80,234
Somerset, NJ	$51,605	$81,320
Alexandria (independent city), VA	$50,752	$78,255
Westchester, NY	$50,402	$74,206
Morris, NJ	$49,640	$76,613
Bergen, NJ	$48,137	$72,053
Arlington, VA	$47,252	$71,679
Montgomery, MD	$46,911	$69,648
Teton, WY	$45,758	$69,648
San Francisco, CA	$45,694	$68,942
Montgomery, PA	$45,553	$67,748
Fairfax + Fairfax City + Falls Church, VA	$45,493	$69,378
Lake, IL	$45,218	$69,154
Nassau, NY	$45,176	$68,399
Oakland, MI	$44,767	$69,393
Nantucket, MA	$44,534	$66,055
San Mateo, CA	$43,884	$65,378

SOURCE: Woods & Poole Economics, Inc.

Between 1988 and the year 2000, Western household incomes grew 2.4 percent annually compared to national average growth of 2 percent. California did especially well. Ventura County's proportion of households making $50,000 or more increased from 29 percent in 1980 to 45 percent in 1990.

■ **There are non-metro areas with high wealth—mainly seasonal escapes** such as Pitkin county, Colorado, home to Aspen; Teton County, Wyoming, Jackson Hole; and the island county of Nantucket, Massachusetts.

While not making the top 20, several upscale Florida communities—Sarasota, Martin, Collier, and Indian River—score highly. Southern affluence growth is concentrated in a few rural retirement counties, suburban Atlanta, and south Florida. Many affluent blacks are relocating to Atlanta. The Sweet Auburn Welcome Center, the first African-American welcome center in the South (located at 135 Auburn Avenue, Atlanta) can provide demographics on the influx of newcomers.

■ **Generally, affluent Americans clearly prefer the edges of metropolitan areas.** Many of the top 20 counties for growth in affluence are adjacent to the most affluent counties of the previous decade as more and more people are moving farther and farther from the city without actually settling down on farms. These well-educated professionals drive 30 to 60 minutes one way to jobs in more populated metropolitan areas. Observes Bob Jones, president of BJA Communications, "they moved far enough away to escape the crowds and crime of the city, but stayed close enough to enjoy the city's high-paying jobs and cultural opportunities. Somewhere between the 'burbs and the boonies, you might say."

■ **Meet "RUPPIES": rural urban professionals.** "Ruppies" can be found reading the magazines published by the rural utility companies, buying by catalog or mail, or attending local community events. They consider themselves strongly family-oriented (83%) and committed to their communities (69%).

TRACKING THE "UP AND COMING" AREAS OF AFFLUENCE

In *Where to Make Money: A Rating Guide to Opportunities in America's Metro Areas,* author G. Scott Thomas ranks the nation's 73 largest metropolitan areas (those with populations of 500,000 or more). Each area has been analyzed statistically and graded on a scale which takes into account those indicators that point towards economic opportunity. Thomas' top three areas are:

● **West Palm Beach, Florida:** a thriving high-technology center plus large numbers of retirees. It has the highest score in the business opportunities test and the healthiest retail sector in the country (only Denver has a stronger service sector).

● **Orlando, Florida:** has an expanding job base and the highest score on the job opportunities test. The citrus, aerospace, and tourism industries continue to attract new businesses.

● **Las Vegas:** rapid expansion will continue. The population is expected to increase by 40 percent between now and 2020. Jobs are plentiful.

AFFLUENT PEOPLE ARE MOVING TARGETS

Up to 8.5 million Americans buy new homes or change addresses each year. As their addresses change, their lives change. Throughout the 1990s, moves were most likely to the Southeast and the Midwest. There was substantial out-migration from California, New England, and New York State to such areas as the Pacific Northwest, Colorado, and the South Atlantic states. As the former areas have among the highest real estate prices in the United States and the latter much lower costs, new residents often arrive with hefty bank accounts.

■ **A heavy number of out-migrations are California's equity refugees:** *American Demographic* magazine asked the question "Where do ex-California homeowners live?" Their answer: "Anywhere they want to." In the 1990s, nearly 200,000 outward-bound Californians chose to live instead in:

• Arizona	23,000
• Oregon	21,000
• Texas	21,000
• Nevada	17,000
• Florida	15,000
• Colorado	14,000
• Illinois	13,000
• New York	13,000
• Washington	8,500

■ **Older individuals are often affluent migrants.** Most people don't plan to move from their hometowns after they retire. Those that do are better off, better educated, and more active than those who don't. Fifty-three percent of would-be movers have gone to college, versus 40 percent of non-movers. Forty-seven percent of movers have annual family incomes of $35,000 or more, compared with 31 percent of the non-movers. The typical older migrant household has high discretionary income. And, spending has grown dramatically. Charles F. Longino, Jr. and William H. Crown in researching "The Migration of Old Money" note that spending power is increasing in the typical older migrant household.

Affluent migrants among sixty-something couples of the 1980s favored Hernando, St. Lucie, Collier, and Marion counties in Florida. In the 1990s, newly popular retirement areas include the South Atlantic coastal states (Beaufort County, South Carolina) and the Rocky Mountains (Summit County,

Colorado). Today, Phoenix and Tucson as well as the Pacific Northwest are among the favored destinations.

Mark Fagan, a professor at Alabama's Jacksonville State University advises the Alabama Department of Economic and Community Affairs on ways to attract retirees. He notes that those who pick a community for its lakes or golf are generally between the ages of 55 and 64 and "usually well educated and affluent."

● **Florida tops the list of states benefiting from retirement migration.** This state boasts the largest percent of people over 65—nearly 18 percent in 1989—and is expected to outdistance California's actual number of senior citizens by the year 2000. Florida has gained $6 billion from the elderly migrants it welcomed between 1985 and 1990, compared to just $1 billion it lost at the same time through mature out-migration. Its extremely low tax base means higher discretionary income for retirees.

● **Arizona came second** with a net income gain of $1 billion, followed by ten other states—Texas, North Carolina, Arkansas, Oregon, South Carolina, Nevada, Georgia, Washington, New Mexico, and California—which each had a net gain of $100 million or more from the elderly migrants they received during this same period.

● **The Pacific Northwest is gaining in senior population at a faster rate than the rest of the country.** With mild climates, access to recreation, and relatively low cost of living, many small towns across this region are becoming retirement meccas. While the U.S. population of persons over 65 increased by 18.9 percent between 1980 and 1988, according to the U.S. Census Bureau, the senior population of Washington, Oregon, and Idaho increased by more than 25 percent.

■ **Long-distance movers tend to be writers, engineers, marketers, and lawyers.** According to Barbara Ehrenreich, writing in her book *Fear of Failing,* they are members of the "professional middle class," people whose economic and social status is based on education rather than ownership of capital or property.

■ **America's twenty- and thirty-somethings, change residences far more than older adults, and they cover greater distances in their moves.** "A whole generation of young people see the world as their job market and their playground, and they have a one-way ticket," says Elissa Moses, who completed a massive survey of teen attitudes as vice-president of global marketing for Philips Electronics. This trend will only grow more important as the generation of children born to Baby Boomers comes of age. Among young Americans, ages 15 to 19, the survey found barely half expected to live in the county of their birth, and only slightly more than a quarter expected to live in their hometowns.

Movers are often ready, willing, and able to volunteer and give at a substantial level. Be sure to find out who's new in your area: use contacts with realtors, join the local welcoming organization or acquire recent address changes through a list broker.

REFINING WITH GEO-DEMOGRAPHICS

We now have the ability to quickly analyze massive amounts of data using sophisticated computerized programs that take into account behavior patterns as well as demographic data such as income, home value, education level, etc. Today, fund raisers can use lifestyles plus demographics to target highly affluent potential prospects. This process of segmentation is called geo-demographics.

■ **"Birds of a feather flock together."** The fundamental assumption of geo-demographic systems is that households in a neighborhood share a similar lifestyle and that these neighborhoods repeat themselves across the United States so that similar neighborhoods can be classified into a smaller number of market segments.

Daniel Hansler, president of the Fund Raising Marketing Company, a California-based fund raising consulting firm specializing in geo-demographics asserts that "Your home address (where you live) largely reflects how you live. You are where you live. Since the geo-demographic neighborhoods contain only approximately 361 homes there is a high degree of homogeneity in these neighborhoods. It has also been demonstrated that these neighborhoods are replicated all over the country. In other words, a certain type of upscale suburban neighborhood near San Francisco has the same demographics and exhibits similar behavior to certain other upscale suburban neighborhoods near Chicago, Dallas, Atlanta, etc."

■ **Fund raisers can use demographic tools to do a better job of identifying, screening, and researching who your donors are and who your most affluent prospects are likely to be.** Several geo-demographic systems are available. Some have been adapted by consulting firms specializing in not-for-profits. In considering use of such systems you may want to know which methodology it is based upon.

To help with those types of decisions, here are brief examples of three of the consumer geo-demographic systems—Claritas: PRIZM, National Demographics & Lifestyles: Cohorts, and EQUIFAX/National Decision Systems: VISION.

■ **Claritas: PRIZM (Potential Rating Index for ZIP Markets) sorts the USA's 36,000 zips into 40 'lifestyle clusters,' each with distinct boundaries, values, consuming habits, and political beliefs.** The most affluent clusters are giving descriptive names: Blue Blood Estates, Money & Brains, Furs & Station Wagons, and Urban Gold Coast account for only 6 percent of the American population, but the majority of the wealth.

ZIP QUALITY RANKINGS, BY PRIZM CLUSTER

Zip Quality is based on income, home value,
education, and occupation:

Zip Quality\Cluster	Median Income	Median Home Value	% College Grads
Blue Blood Estates	$70,307	$200,000+*	51%
Money & Brains	$45,798	$150,755	46%
Furs & Station Wagons	$50,086	$132,725	38%
Urban Gold Coast	$36,838	$200,000+*	51%
National median	$24,269	$64,182	16%

*because the upper census limit for home values is $200,000+, these figures are estimates.

Let's review PRIZM's most affluent clusters:

● **Blue Blood Estates:** the zip codes of Beverly Hills, California; Palm Beach, Florida; Scarsdale, New York; and McLean, Virginia are all part of "Blue Blood Estates." According to PRIZM, here is where you find the few, the proud, and the rich. They make up only 1.1 percent of the population, but they hold one-third of the private wealth, 60 percent of corporate stocks, and almost 10 percent of the nation's real estate. One in 10 American millionaires resides here.

■ **Many of today's most affluent are not old money.** They are the college-educated, corporate leaders and white-collar professionals (including heart surgeons and entertainment lawyers) who worked long, hard days to reach this pinnacle of success.

● **Money & Brains:** Just 0.9 percent of U.S. households, this demographic group is closest to the "Yuppie" profile beloved by the media. These Americans worship conspicuous consumption. They display both possessions and their bodies proudly.

● **Furs & Station Wagons:** 3.2 percent of U.S. households, these are career-oriented households who—unlike Money & Brains—save for the future.

● **Urban Gold Coast:** 0.5 percent of U.S. households, they are major consumers of all forms of culture—plays, theater, books. While situated in metropolitan areas, Gold Coasters spend much of their time away from home for both work and play.

■ **COHORTS: National Demographics & Lifestyles' market segmentation system defines 33 Cohorts, statistically cohesive groupings of adult Americans based on not only demographic and lifestyle characteristics, but also consumer behavior.** All 33 Cohorts are designated by given names to help you know them better:

● **Margo & Elliott:** Composed of 8.1 percent of U.S. households, they are affluent empty-nesters, comprising close to two-thirds of all households over age 45 with incomes over $75,000. Over 40 percent of all U.S. households reporting an income over $75,000 are found in this Cohort.

● **Jacqueline:** Representing 0.8 percent of U.S. households, she is a career women with a median income of $50,014 and a median age of 36. Almost two-thirds of this cohort are never-marrieds; over three-fourths are employed in professional, management, or sales occupations.

● **Stephen:** Comprising 0.7 percent of U.S. households, he is Jacqueline's counterpart among males: a young, extremely affluent, professional male heavily involved with his career. One in four is divorced or separated. Median income is $69.667; median age is 34.

■ **EQUIFAX: National Decision Systems uses Vision™ to classify every household in the United States into one of 48 market segments based on the demographic, socioeconomic, and housing characteristics of its neighborhood block group**. Each market segment is defined so the consumption, purchasing, and financial behavior is very homogeneous within the market segment but very different from the other segments. Households are segmented, then clustered, first by residential area, then by level of general affluence. The result is 12 categories, three dealing with our target market:

1.   Suburban Wealthy
2.   Urban Affluence
3.   Suburban Affluence

Like PRIZM, VISION gives each of its 48 segments a descriptive label or nickname, e.g., "Urban Gentry," "Young Urban Professionals," "Carports and Kids," and "Prairie People."

"QUICK AND DIRTY GEODEMOGRAPHICS"

Reverse or criss-cross directories are backward telephone books, of sorts. Here you'll find listings arranged by street address followed by telephone number and name. This handy tool allows you to canvass specific neighborhoods.

SOURCE: Power Calling, Joan Guiducci

Using geo-demographics can help fund raisers to answer four key questions:

● Who are my best prospects?

● Where and how do they live?

● What do they read, listen to and watch?

● How can I reach them most effectively?

Large portions of this section are based on the 1990 Census as information from Census 2000 has not been fully released at this time. Additional information on Geo-Demographic systems can be found in my books, *Changing Demographics* and *Global Demographic* (Precept Press).

CHAPTER NINE

Pinpointing Affluence by Age

*T*ODAY, AFFLUENCE CAN BE *FOUND IN **ALL** AGE GROUPS.* Never before have so many households enjoyed such affluence. Jerry Huntsinger, fund raising's direct mail authority, reminisces that "it used to be when a single person or a husband and wife reached the peak of their career, their children were grown and educated, and their homes paid off—suddenly they had discretionary income. Today, discretionary income exists just as soon as an individual or a couple starts earning their own salary, often in their early 20s. Even though young people today think that they are never going to get ahead, they actually make an awesome amount of money and they can choose whether to make a down-payment on a house or buy a car or buy a new television set or take a vacation or go on a fishing trip or—yes—make a gift to a non-profit. It is a question of what is referred to today's jargon as 'lifestyle.'"

COMPARISON OF MEDIAN NET WORTH
OF HOUSEHOLDS BY AGE,
1989 AND 1998, in 1998 Dollars

AGE OF HOUSEHOLDER	1989	1998	% CHANGE 1989–1999
Under 35	$9,900	$9,000	−9.1%
35 to 44	$71,800	$63,400	−11.7%
45 to 54	$125,700	$105,500	−16.1%
55 to 64	$124,600	$127,500	+2.3%
65 to 74	$97,100	$146,500	+50.9%
75 or older	$92,200	$125,600	+36.2%

SOURCE: *American Demographics* Magazine

YOUR BEST PROSPECTS: MATURE AMERICANS

Let's start with the very best affluent prospects: mature Americans. There are now more than 75 million people over age 50 in the United States—nearly 28 percent of the total population—among them, the advanced edge of the Boomers. Some 45 million people (16.5 percent of the U.S. population) are already over age 60. Older adults are the most rapidly growing age group in America—and, because of the fact that Baby Boomers can only get older, the current number will more than double by the year 2030.

■ **Older Americans are the most charitably inclined of all individuals.** Both in total dollars and in percentage of income, they give generously.

MATURE AMERICAN CHARITABLE GIVING PATTERNS

	All House-holds	Total Older House-holds	Age 55–64	Age 65–74	Age 75+
Total Giving	$706	$791	$874	$681	$800
Religious	$259	$303	$343	$294	$241
Educational	$13	$20	$15	$ 7	$ 5
Political	$ 7	$12	$16	$ 9	$ 7
Other	$73	$83	$79	$78	$96

SOURCE: Bureau of Labor Statistics

■ **Older Americans have both assets and income to give.**

Two particular facts are of special interest to fund raisers, looking to raise major dollars:

• Mature Americans control half of America's discretionary income.

• Mature Americans control 77 percent of America's assets.

● **Older Americans enjoy 42 percent greater disposable income.** In fact, though they account for just 35 percent of the adult population, 30 percent of all households with incomes exceeding $50,000 are headed by persons over age 55. Because most older people live alone or with just a spouse, per capita discretionary income is high for these households although average discretionary income per household declines after age 59.

● **The golden generation: Americans from their mid-fifties through late sixties.** At $14,584, average household discretionary income peaks among households headed by those aged 55 to 59. The proportion of households with discretionary income also peaks in this age group, at 35 percent. Called the New Elders by some, this particular cohort is better educated and more affluent than their parents were at the same age. The one-third of mature Americans with discretionary income are found mainly in this group. Ken Dychtwald, author of *Age Wave,* points out that men and women now in this age group are, in many ways, at the high point in their adult lives. The children are grown, the mortgage is paid, and they have the highest disposable income of any age group. They are the first generation to benefit from substantial pension plans and generous hikes in federal benefits for the elderly.

● **The financial security of older middle-income Americans now stretches well into retirement.** From 1976 to 1986 (the last year for which figures are available) the inflation-adjusted median income of married couples over age 65 rose from some $9,800 to over $20,520. While retirees still rely principally on inflation-indexed Social Security checks, pensions and savings are becoming ever more important. In the mid-1980s, 46 percent of employed Americans worked for companies offering pension plans, and just over half were fully vested. By 1990, nearly 90 percent of these individuals were vested. For the 40 percent who are 65 and over and draw private pensions, the bullish stock market of the late 1980s/early 1990s lifted their total asset value dramatically: from $795 billion to $1.4 trillion over six years. And finally, the proportion of elderly collecting interest payments and dividends from savings and other assets has risen from 56 percent to 67 percent since 1976.

Per capita discretionary income is highest among households headed by individuals aging from 65 to 69, at $6,280. Twenty-five percent of these households have discretionary income. The share of affluent elderly households is not insignificant. Eleven percent of households headed by someone aged 65 or older had 1989 incomes of $50,000 or more, and 4 percent had incomes of $75,000 or greater.

● **Older women make up an increasing share of well-off pensioners,** says Emily Andrews, a pension expert who is senior economist at the Fu Associates consulting firm in Washington, D.C. She projects that the proportion of married women who retire with pensions will nearly double, to 56 percent, by 2010. Thus, the poverty rate among elderly widows should fall—they now make up almost 60 percent of all low-income elderly. The second pension will also make retired families more prosperous—keep in mind their ability to give more especially through planned gifts.

● **Americans over age 65 hold 40 percent of the nation's personal financial assets—such as savings and real estate.** The over age 55 group accounts for 80 percent of all funds in savings and loan banks, 77 percent of America's financial assets, and 70 percent of the net worth of all U.S. households, or nearly $7 trillion. Seven out of 10 older adults own their homes and 80 percent of those are without a mortgage.

● **The New Elders (mid-50s through mid-60s)** "had the benefit of an extremely good economy, and that makes them unique," acknowledges Charles Longino, former director of University of Miami's Center for Social Research on Aging. He reminds us that these Americans' careers prospered with the longest economic boom of the 20th century. "They've reaped big economic benefits from the postwar boom. In the more difficult 1970s and 1980s, their homes, savings, and investments still appreciated handsomely."

● **The "elderly": lighter in income, but heavy in assets.** Those aged 65 to 74 receive 80 percent more income than average from estates, trusts, dividends, and rentals. The value of their assets is almost 21 percent greater than average. Households headed by people aged 75 and older receive income from estates, trusts, dividends, and rentals at more than twice the average.

● **Home ownership, generally, has created significant assets for older Americans.** The median value of a single-family home rose from $23,000 to $89,300 between 1970 and 1988.

The overwhelming majority of older homeowners over age 62 own their homes debt-free.

● **Nearly half of all American millionaires are over age 65.** Some 1,000 older Americans each worth $100 million or more are expected to die within the next 10 years. Says Peter Goldmark, president of the Rockefeller Foundation, "I personally know five donors who could each create Ford Foundation-sized foundations tomorrow."

PINPOINTING AFFLUENT OLDER AMERICANS

How do you pinpoint the geographic clusterings of the more affluent older Americans? Although affluence is a reality for growing numbers of older Americans, approximately half of elders struggle from day to day. As with all age groupings, there is tremendous variation. There are many older persons living in or near poverty just as their are pockets of mature adults who have very high levels of wealth and income. The majority are in the relatively comfortable middle range.

The top five states with the greatest percentage increase in households aged 65 and over, 1990–1998 are:

1.	Nevada	56.6%
2.	Alaska	50.1%
3.	Arizona	28.3%
4.	Hawaii	27.7%
5.	Utah	21.9%

SOURCE: U.S. Census Bureau

Charles F. Longino, Jr. has researched the key questions: how many retired people are affluent and where do they live? Longino suggests that there are two key groups of relatively affluent retired Americans: the "comfortably retired" and the "pension elite." While the comfortably retired are probably best approached for the more modest, annual gifts, the pension elite are the group we need to approach for major and planned donations.

■ **The pension elite** are clustered in the 65-to-74 age group, with 12 percent falling into this category. Nine percent of those aged 75 and older and only 5 percent of those aged 55 to 64 are members of the pension elite.

● **There is definite geographical clustering.** There are several million Americans among the pension elite. By the year 2010, 3.2 million persons from the Northeast—primarily retirees—will migrate with billions of dollars in investment portfolios to South Florida. In addition, California, New York, Connecticut, Pennsylvania, Michigan, Arizona, Oregon, and Washington have the highest proportion of retired who are in the pension elite in all three age groups. Fully 18 percent of 65- to 74-year olds in Connecticut and Washington, for example, are in the pension elite. Florida, Maryland, New Jersey, and Wisconsin also have large shares of the pension elite in two out of three retired age groups.

There are also important concentrations of upscale retirees at the county and metropolitan level, such as Fort Lauderdale and Palm Beach in Florida, and San Diego and Palm Springs in California.

● **There is also "psychographic" clustering.** In *The Maturing Marketplace: Buying Habits of Baby Boomers and Their Parents,* author George P. Moschis suggests that the mature market can be clustered in to one of four segments of life stages with Healthy Indulgers the most affluent:

1) Healthy Indulgers (18 percent of the 55-plus population) have experienced the fewest life events such as retirement, widowhood, and chronic conditions that contribute to peo-

ple's psychological and social aging. They are the group most likely to behave like younger consumers. Their main focus is on enjoying life rather than trying to "make it."

2) Healthy Hermits (36%) are likely to have experienced life events that have affected their self-concept and self-worth, such as the death of a spouse. They tend to respond to these events with psychological and social withdrawal. Many resent the isolation and the fact that they are expected to behave like old people.

3) Ailing Outgoers (29%), on the other hand, maintain positive self-esteem and self-concept despite life events, including the onset of chronic health problems. Unlike hermits, outgoers accept their "old-age" status and acknowledge their limitations, but are still interested in getting the most out of life.

4) Frail Recluses, who make up 17 percent of today's mature population, have chosen to cope with detrimental changes in later life by adjusting their lifestyles to reflect physical declines and changes in social roles and by becoming spiritually stronger.

● **Affluent grandparents, typically aged 45 to 64, are an outstanding market for not-for-profits.** Today, over 35 percent of Americans will be grandparents. In addition, more than one in 20 children—four million nationally—lived in their grandparents' homes in 1997, according to the U.S. Census Bureau. The figure has grown steadily, from 3.2 percent of all children in 1970 to 5.5 percent in 1997.

According to Data Group Inc. of Plymouth Meeting, Pennsylvania, affluent grandparents spend about $819 annually per household on their grandchildren. And their spending is directly relevant to not-for-profits. For example, 41 percent of the customers for the National Geographic Society's book series for 4- to 8-year-olds are grandparents. Between 20 and 25 percent of the subscriptions to the Society's *World* magazine are bought by grandparents. Thirty-one percent have bought investments (stocks, bonds, US Savings Bonds, or coins) for their grandchildren.

"Establishing a Trust Fund," a FREE MetLife brochure, explains how a trust can help to provide peace of mind for the grandparent by contributing to a grandchild's financial well-being. According to the brochure, it is important to determine the purpose of a trust before establishing it. Options include:

A spendthrift trust—a beneficiary receives small amounts of money at specified intervals.

A life insurance trust—used to give your estate liquidity.

A bypass trust—allows a married couple to shelter more of their estate from estate taxes.

A charitable trust—used to make donations and realize tax savings for an estate.

You might look for affluent grandparents by promoting an intergenerational vacation. Grandtravel, a Chevy Chase, Maryland travel operator, offers tour packages for grandparents and grandchildren traveling together. Their Kenya safari for 15 days costs over $4,255 per adult and $3,725 per child.

APPEALING TO AFFLUENT MATURE AMERICANS

Five key values determine the likely behavior of older individuals:

- autonomy and self-sufficiency

- social connectedness

- altruism

- personal growth

- personal revitalization (Revitalization includes the need for play, the need for change of pace and change in activities, and the need for rest and relaxation.)

MARKETING TO MATURE AMERICANS

Avoid age-ism and negative myths:

- Myth 1: People over 65 are old.

- Myth 2: Older individuals are unattractive.

- Myth 3: Older individuals are unproductive.

- Myth 4: Older individuals are inflexible.

- Myth 5: Older individuals are in poor health.

- Myth 6: Older individuals are all the same.

Segment by Age:

- 50–64: In transition, pre-retirees

- 65–74: Traditional givers and volunteers

- 75+: Asset rich, concerns about outliving $$$

Market positively:

- Communicate in length/depth

- Use appropriate age models

- Watch signage, type size, color usage

Be value oriented. Match your organization to their niches of concern:

1) home   2) health care   3) leisure

4) education 5) personal & business counseling

6) aging   7) financial products and services

Because by the time people turn 12, they develop the value systems, morals and attitudes that are carried through their lifetime, we need to break the mature market into categories: 55 to 64, 65 to 74, and 75 and over. (Some marketers prefer to subdivide the last group into 75 to 84 and over 85.) There are distinctly different patterns with differing emphasis on wants and needs.

Frank Conaway, president of PrimeLife Advertising, notes that "the 'older' population, 55 to 64, generally have grown children and are taking a serious look at retirement. They lead a pre-retirement lifestyle more like that of a 45-year-old rather than that of a 70-year-old."

Because economic conditions differed, we find that the 75-plus group is different than the 55-plus group. The older group remembers trying to raise families during the depression when they were young. Their children, now in the 55 to 64 group, were able to realize a quality of life and living standards after World War II that far exceed anything their parents and grandparents ever thought possible.

■ **The pre-retirement group:** ages 55–64, 32 million, 13 percent of the U.S. population. They spend an average of 13 percent more than the national average in contributions. Volunteerism is at a high.

● **Many of these individuals are "possession" experiencers**, people whose satisfaction comes from establishing their status. They are purchasers, not ready to give up the opportunity to own more material objects. They consider themselves to be "in transition." Not quite sure where retirement will take them, they may be reluctant to make or to continue commitments (both financial and as volunteers) to your organization. It's especially important that you not lose contact with these affluent prospects but be patient until they move to the next psychographic level.

■ **The newly retired:** aged 65 to 74, 20 million, 8 percent of the U.S. population. While spending is about the same as for the pre-retired, the emphasis shifts. For many individuals, this is what they hoped retirement would be all about. Decreased costs and/or different priorities have left them with the ability to free up substantial discretionary money for what now matters.

The consumer behavior of older individuals, especially in terms of discretionary spending, is influenced far more by levels of maturity than by a person's age, asserts marketing consultant David Wolfe. While some retirees will remain "possession"-focused, many of our affluent, older prospects will turn heavily toward either "catered" or "being" experiences, described below.

● **"Catered" experiencers:** have developed a greater interest in experiences such as travel, education, or sports. They are willing to pay for intangible experiences as well if you package philanthropy as part of a membership club.

● **"Being" experiencers:** have reached an anti-materialistic state, says Wolfe, when people derive the greatest satisfaction from simple pleasures and human contact. More inner-directed than are "catered" experiencers, they are less interested in recognition and formal appreciation.

■ **The elderly:** 75-plus, 13 million, 6 percent of the U.S. population. Spending becomes more concentrated on health-related areas. Discretionary spending drops off. Often, with fear of outliving assets, persons return (or remain) as "possession" experiencers.

● **Older individuals are cautious spenders:** While the available statistics indicate that many older Americans have significant discretionary income, they are not quick to spend it.

- Older people are concerned with outliving their assets because of unexpected major expenses (e.g., health care, nursing home).

- Because they retire early and live longer today, older people need to finance a longer post-retirement, often a lifestyle similar to the one they were accustomed to before retiring.

- Older people have a money personality which has conditioned them to be thrifty and careful with money.

● **They are value oriented.** The elderly are more willing to try something new if they perceive it as adding value to their lives. Remember, we're talking about people who have experienced more profound social change in their lifetime. Images and text will more successfully invoke values if they are indirect.

When marketing to older adults of any age, remember, the eyes change first. By age 42, most people can't read 8 point type. Check your brochures as well for light against dark and bright against dull to increase visibility.

THE LARGEST ADULT GROUPING: BABY BOOMERS

In 1991, the first of 77 million Baby Boomers joined the 45-plus group. Between 1990 and 2000, the age 45–54 segment alone increased by 46 percent, versus overall population growth of only 7 percent!

● By 2030, when the oldest Boomers are 84 and the youngest have turned 65, there will be an estimated 65 million Americans 65 and older—more than twice as many as today.

● By 2040, we could have more people aged 65 or older than we have persons under 20 years of age.

As they mature, the much-aligned Baby Boomers are demonstrating a commitment to philanthropy that outpaces that of other age groups. More adult Americans born between 1946 and 1964 give to non-religious charities than did people in any other age group. The results of surveys contradict the view the members of the Baby Boom generation are selfish or unwilling to be loyal to causes or institutions. The Russ Reid Company, for example, has found that while Boomers are 42 percent of all adults, they are 47 percent of all donors to nonprofit charities. And, researchers believe that Baby Boomers are likely to become even more generous as they grow older and more affluent.

America has a new ruling class, argues author David Brooks in *Bobos in Paradise: The New Upper Class and How They Got There* (Simon and Schuster 2000). Primarily Boomers, these are well-educated men and women who scored well on their aptitude tests and who flourish in a world that prizes merit over heredity. They have toppled the WASP establishment that dominated postwar American life. What makes this new elite unique is that its members have blended the mainstream and the countercultural, bringing together bourgeois values and bohemian attitudes.

Bobos:

- Sip Starbucks coffee from Pottery Barn mugs while sitting on peasanty but pricey throw rugs writing an Internet business plan on their iBooks.

- Seem to turn life into one long stint of graduate school.

Having been told all their lives that they are the generation to change the world, only lack of money has prevented many of them from participating fully in charitable giving. "The dramatic increases in donating time and money among the Baby Boom generation is good news for today and may suggest even better news for the future as this very large population group assumes community responsibility," says Brian O'Connell, former president of Independent Sector, a coalition of more than 750 corporate, foundation, and voluntary organizations. In middle age, Boomer idealists are positioned to move from "active" philanthropy—marching, protesting, physical involvement—to "passive" philanthropy—check writing.

WHAT FACTORS ARE CONTRIBUTING TO INCREASING BABY BOOMER AFFLUENCE?

Today, Boomers rule the world. The 10 years loss of income *Fortune* magazine noted as a consequence of their being always in competition for resources, has been addressed. Some have finally moved up the corporate ladder; some have moved on to their own businesses, some have made do with less, and many are waiting to inherit from parents.

■ **As Boomers enter mid-life, their large numbers have been absorbed into society.** Because most Baby Boomers married later, often divorcing and remarrying for a second (and third) time, many are just leaving their high cost, child rearing years behind. As we enter a new century:

● **Boomer "nests" are emptying.** These households will gain almost $7,000 per year in discretionary income when children leave the home. Boomers FIND/SVP Inc., which has tracked boomer trends since the 1980s, estimates the disposable income of Boomers over 50 is $930 billion, and projects that figure will swell to $1 trillion by 2003.

● **The older half of the Baby Boom is solidly in its peak earning years.** The medium income of Boomer households was $47,261 in 1994, higher than that of any other age group and well above the national median of $32,264. Twenty-three percent of households headed by 45-to-54 year olds earn $75,000 or more. Of the 8.3 million American households with incomes of $100,000 or more, 63 percent are headed by Boomers.

● **Baby Boomers are two-earner households.** And, much more so than in previous generations, we may be seeing Double Income, Plural Pensions. Dippies can accumulate substantial future retirement resources through plural streams of future retirement income. They can look forward to two Social Securities, two occupational pensions, and, perhaps, two individual retirement accounts, in addition to their other savings and investments.

■ **As Boomers age, they will accumulate wealth through property ownership, investment, and inheritance.** In 1986, the net worth of householders under the age of 35 was negligible, according to the Federal Reserve Board's Survey of Consumer Finances. However, it increases dramatically: while the average net worth of householders aged 35 to 44 was over $100,000, those aged 45 to 54 averaged nearly $175,000. And householders aged 55 to 64 averaged over $200,000 in net worth.

● **Older Boomers rode the heady housing market of the 1970s,** often buying first homes at modest rates, then driving up the prices as the demand kept increasing. These older Boomers have substantial assets, though they may not have the cash for current giving. However, their concerns—retirement and educating children—lend themselves to planned gifts. And the older Boomers' psychographics: focusing on the experiences that money can buy should encourage exploration of real estate gifts.

● **Boomers are about to come into their inheritances,** delayed by the increased longevity of their parents and grandparents. Estimates to the amount vary wildly: in the next 20 years, between $6.8 and $43 trillion will be passed from a senior generation, famous for making money and babies, to its children the Baby Boomers. Whereas once, only the top 10 to 15 percent of families had significant wealth to bequeath, today the parents of Boomers between the 50th and 80th percent wealth brackets have amassed relatively large nest eggs of $70,000 to $225,000.

"People are inheriting more and more money every year," says Alexander Bove Jr., a Boston tax lawyer. "My father, a machinist in a shipyard, left a $150,000 estate. In my kids' generation, because of what's happened in terms of parents' real estate appreciation, profit sharing, pensions, and life insurance, we're going to see millionaires created just by the parents dying off. It's nothing now to have half a million dollars' worth of life insurance. If my wife and I dropped dead, my son and daughter will get $1 million *each*."

POTENTIAL ESTATES THROUGH 2011	
Years	TOTAL ESTATES in billions of 1986 dollars
1987–1991	$ 778.9
1992–1996	$1,098.8
1997–2001	$1,464.8
2002–2006	$1,707.0
2007–2011	$1,771.6

SOURCE: FORTUNE Magazine

FIND/SVP's *The Insider's Guide to Marketing to Boomers* notes that the Boomers' parents needn't have been super-wealthy to leave jumbo inheritances.

● Boomers will inherit the highly appreciated, paid off homes of their parents. The medial value of a single family home rose from $23,000 to $89,300 between 1970 and 1988.

● Life insurance, pensions, profit sharing plans, and stock portfolios will add to the stock of inherited wealth. Millionaires will be created overnight, sometimes even if parents' cash savings do not amount to more than $150,000.

● Tax reform, if left alone, will add to the windfall. Reagan's 1981 tax law more than tripled the amount two parents can bequeath without incurring estate taxes from about $350,000 up to a staggering $1.2 million for a married couple who plans carefully.

The majority of Boomers will not inherit until they reach their late fifties, if not their sixties and seventies. For many Boomers, inherited money will not be used for necessities of life. By that point, they will be comfortable. Many are guessing the money will go to philanthropy. Even if only a few percent of Boomers' potential inheritance went into private foundations, the amount would nearly double the $94 billion now on hand.

How Do You Find Pockets of Affluent Boomers?

State-by-state there's considerable variation in the percentage of Boomers in the population. Maine's share of Baby Boomers is the same as the national average, 32.5 percent. There is a difference of over 10 percentage points between the state with the highest concentration of Baby Boomers (Alaska, 39%) and the state with the smallest percentage of Boomers in its population (Utah, 29%). The top five states with the greatest percentage increase in households aged 45–54 between 1990 and 1998 were:

1. Colorado		72.9%
2. Nevada		72.3%
3. Alaska		66.8%
4. Arizona		64.3%
5. Oregon		61%

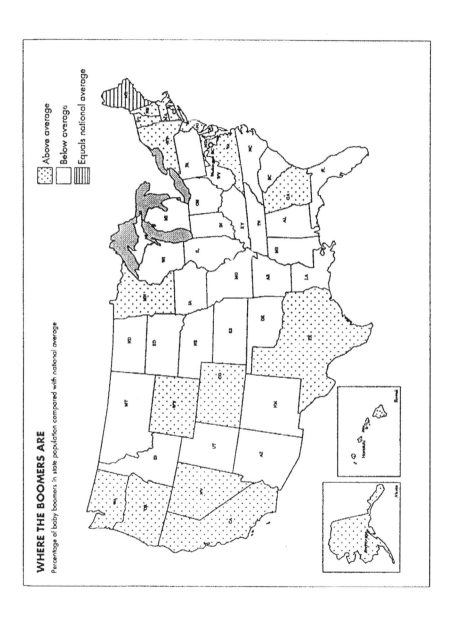

WHERE THE BOOMERS ARE

Percentage of baby boomers in state population compared with national average

Above average

Below average

Equals national average

The Boomer Report, September 15, 1992

According to calculations by the U.S. Census bureau and FIND/SVP, 20 states have boomer populations within one percent of the national average. Fourteen of these are east of the Mississippi River. The states with the largest percentages of Boomers are concentrated primarily on the east and west coasts. Besides Alaska, the other four states most favored by Boomers are Colorado, Maryland (near Washington, D.C., which has an even higher percentage of Boomers), New Hampshire, and California. Two states in the boomer top 10 are the two non-continental states: Alaska and Hawaii.

Boomers prefer urban environments: 64 percent live inside urban areas, 24 percent live in rural areas and 12 percent live in the suburbs. The top 10 cities, based on the proportion of boomer households, are Houston, Denver, Washington, D.C., Atlanta, San Francisco, Dallas, Albuquerque, Salt Lake City, Baton Rouge, and Portland.

Finding affluent Baby Boomers can be a challenge, because many Boomers aren't in the traditional structures of society. Baby Boomers are less likely to be employees of large corporations than their fathers were, since more are starting their own businesses, says Virginia Hodgkinson, vice president for research at Independent Sector. Baby Boomers are less likely than their parents to go to church, although some are starting to return, and they are less likely to belong to organizations.

Generally speaking, we find early Boomers (those born between 1946 and 1956) are more affluent than later Boomers. They got into the market first, both for jobs and homes. Many bought their homes before mortgage rates soared and benefited from the demand for entry-level housing as they traded up. In addition, you can look for more affluent Boomers:

■ **Demographically,**

● **Segment by education and employment.** The Superclass is often known as "Yuppies." According to Landon Jones, author of *Great Expectations: America and the Baby Boom Generation,* the boomer superclass "is most visible on the two coasts. In New York and Boston and in San Francisco and Los Angeles—and their capital is Washington, D.C. They are the professional-managerial working couples who command more discretionary income than any other group."

● **Focus on boomer singles.** Boomers are often a singular generation: they delayed marriage in record numbers. Create an event for boomer singles tied into the dating scene. Upscale Boomers will pay several thousand dollars for membership in dating services or matchmaking organizations. Any type of workshop, combining a subject of interest with the chance to meet people, is a good draw.

● **Reach them through their kids.** If you run a public service announcement in *Child* magazine you'll reach 500,000 people with incomes of over $50,000. *Working Mother* gives you dual-income families—another big target.

■ **Psychographically,**

● **"Satisfied Selfs" have the financial edge.** Based on a study by N.W. Ayer Advertising, Boomers have been segmented into four attitudinal groups. The "Satisfied Selfs," the largest group of Boomers, are the well-educated and well-paid professional managers. They have positive self-images and are optimistic about life and themselves. These men and women are innovative, risk takers, frequent travelers, and leaders of change. They are receptive to new ideas and new technology.

● **Identify those in mid-life crisis.** The collective cultural past of the Boomers abounds with motorcycle images, from songs by Steppenwolf and Springsteen to the classic film "Easy Rider." As affluence meets mid-life crisis, **RUBs (rich urban bikers)** are ringing up sales of Harley Davidsons and upscale biker accessories.

● **Find early purchasers of new technology.** Boomers can't get enough of gadgets. Cellular phones, pagers, and beepers. It's a sign of status for many upscale Boomers as well as a tool of the trade for boomer physicians, stockbrokers, and salespersons.

Appealing To Affluent Baby Boomers

Often compared to "a very large mouse going through a very small snake," Baby Boomers will continue to have a major impact on our society at every stage of their maturation.

■ **As the oldest Boomers pass 50, they are changing the image of aging.** Boomers look, act, and feel younger at 50 than previous generations did. "Fifty will be like 40," says UCLA gerontologist Fernando Torres-Gil, who predicts that this generation won't confront "old age" until well into their 70s. When the American Board of Family Practice asked a random sample of 1,200 Americans when middle age begins, 41 percent said it was when you worry about having enough money for health-care concerns, 42 percent said it was when your last child moves out, and 46 percent said it was when you don't recognize the names of music groups on the radio anymore.

■ **They make a lot and they spend a lot more than they make.** These are the twin truths about Baby Boomers upon which the world has been able to depend. This "Gotta have it" attitude makes Boomers a different generation then their parents. The Depression was just an idea to them—a fable passed down by their parents. And, skepticism and the persistent individuality that are part of the Boomers' very make-up makes them difficult to address.

Today, Baby Boomers increasingly define the "upscale" market. They are very different from the luxury consumer of the 80s and 90s. That typical upscale consumer was very image-conscious, status-oriented, and ostentatious. Upscale Boomers continue to appreciate excellence and the finer things in life. However, they are less interested in status symbols and seek recognition from their friends and peers rather than society as a whole, expressing quieter luxury. Baby Boomers are very comfortable with who they are and what they have accomplished—they have "arrived." Now that they are where they want to be, they want to keep that status, enjoy it, find balance in their lives, and, most importantly, stay young. The attitude of the luxury Baby Boomer consumer is summed up as: "At 50, my father was 60. At 50, I am 40."

■ **For the majority of Boomers, life is made up of three inter-connected elements: work, personal relationships, and family.** They are a unique combination of traditional and nontraditional values. In many ways their primary concerns are the same as their parents and grandparents: home, marriage, family, and work. But, there are four important new themes: globalism, unisexism, individualism, and instant gratification.

■ **The trick in marketing to Boomers is in combining the traditional and nontraditional in your appeals.**

BOOMER TURN-ONS:

- Straight talk

- Personal Development

- Meeting New People

- Change

BOOMER TURN-OFFS:

- Authority

- Materialism

- Anonymity

As the "me generation" has matured, many have moved to a new "ethic of commitment," remarks Daniel Yankelovich in his book, *New Rules.* Tending to be more inner-directed than previous generations, Boomers are committed to a search for self-fulfillment through superpersonal relationships and more enduring commitments to the world of work and the business of common survival. Boomers have become less concerned about showing their wealth. Conspicuous consumption of jewelry, furniture, and new cars is down. Experiences such as travel or sports are considered more valuable, states Walker Smith of Yankelovich Partners.

Comments Donna Schuurman, executive director of The Dougy Center in Portland, Oregon, herself a Baby Boomer: "Many of us do not have the sense of community that used to be a common factor of American life. We're looking for new communities, places where we can belong, contribute, and make a dent. We're not as likely to respond to mailings as people used to be. We're more cynical about fund raising, for good reasons, and need to be convinced. We want to care and get involved, but aren't always sure how or where. Here's a biggie: we're waiting to be asked."

When marketing to Baby Boomers, remember they:

- Have been held back 10 years economically. *Created networking as a way of life.*

- Not donor/customer loyal. *Encourage pledges, multiple connections.*

- Grew up being told they were special yet were overwhelmed by their numbers. *Concentrate on recognition and instant gratification.*

- Don't trust anyone. *Looking for outcomes and accountability.*

- Very nostalgic for "the good days." (*Prior to 1963.*)

- Key concerns for gift planning:

  Their own retirements

  Quality education for their children

  Their parents' aging

AMERICA'S YOUNGER ADULTS: GENERATION X

Younger adults are often overlooked by fund raisers searching for the affluent. There are currently 45 million Generation Xers—Americans between the ages of 25 and 36. They're generally better educated (particularly the women) and more ethnically diverse than the Boomers. Gen Xers hold $125 billion in spending power. They spend more money on technology, exhibit extraordinary brand loyalty, and are much more savvy when it comes to making purchases.

■ **The incomes of householders under age 35 have grown since 1990.** The median income of households headed by people under 35 increased 2 percent after adjusting for inflation, while hose headed by people age 35 to 44 fell by the same amount. Households headed by people aged 45 to 54 had stable incomes during the decade, while the median income of householders aged 55 to 64 rose 4 percent.

● **Because of its smaller size (approximately 45 million versus 77 million Boomers), the "bust" will create a new income environment.** Sought after by businesses, the competition for qualified Busters will drive up wages and benefits. Fewer young adults means fewer young adult households. This equals more affluent young households.

The number of affluent young householders—those with annual incomes of $50,000 and above—nearly doubled, from 2.4 million in 1986 to 4.2 million in 2000. In the following chart, households are in thousands; income is for previous year and is in 1985 dollars.

HOUSEHOLDS HEADED BY PERSONS
UNDER AGE 35, BY INCOME: 1986–2000

	1986	1990	1995	2000
All household	25,913	26,785	25,380	23,853
Less than $10,000	4,734	4,574	3,985	3,446
$10,000–$19,999	6,574	6,308	5,441	4,652
$20,000–$29,999	5,904	5,909	5,338	4,738
$30,000–$39,999	4,103	4,423	4,278	4,001
$40,000–$49,999	2,237	2,575	2,747	2,836
$50,000–$59,999	1,137	1,323	1,467	1,590
$60,000–$69,999	736	948	1,116	1,266
$75,000 and over	488	724	1,008	1,324
Median income	$22,790	$24,250	$26,120	$28,080

SOURCE: *American Demographics* magazine

■ **There are increasing numbers of young adults who either never left or have returned to live in a parent's home.** While their current career earnings are lower than those of more mature persons, their family responsibilities are fewer and their economic prospects are bright. Over 60 percent of the under-35s have gone on for education beyond high school, versus 39 percent for the adult population as a whole. Asserts Conference Board chief economist Fabian Linden: "This longer period of financially independent young adulthood amounts to an economic, social, and psychological revolution."

● **The number of Gen X Nesters, grown children age 18 or older who live in the parental or family home because they have postponed leaving or have returned, is on the rise.** Nesters often prefer to stay at home to enjoy a more affluent lifestyle for as long as possible. In fact, young people from the highest-income families are most likely to stay at home. The percentage of people in their 20s in Spain, Greece, and Italy still living with their parents far exceeds American levels. In 1994, 91 percent of men 20 to 24 and 81 percent of women in these three countries were still rooming with the folks. Meanwhile, 52 percent of their male counterparts and 37 percent of young women in the U.S. lived with their parents. Young adults living at home or on college campuses have their basics paid for by parents. Thirty-nine percent spend more than $50 a week on entertainment—the same money available for charitable giving.

Generation X continues to influence their parents' charitable choices as well as demonstrate a charitable intent of their own. Twenty-five percent of adults, they are already 13 percent of donors, according to a study by the Russ Reid Company. And, they give just $20 less annually than do their philanthropically minded civic grandparents!

More practical, less idealistic than Baby Boomers, Xers express more confidence in charities and other major institutions, according to a study by George Barna. Busters demonstrate a 36 percent confidence level in nonprofits compared with just 23 percent for all adults. There have been some signs that "quality of life" issues will predominate for Busters and this could bode well for volunteerism and philanthropy. Concerns for AIDS, the environment, and abortion, as well as parenting and positive self-issues, and ongoing education are "hot."

REACHING GENERATION X (BABY BUSTERS)

You have two goals in marketing to Generation X:
1. *To begin their identification with your organization at a modest level of giving.*

Although Baby Busters are quite philanthropic they see themselves as having only small amounts of disposable cash (their priorities include sharing with a large extended family of friends and concerts) to give to charity. Their gift fulfillment needs to be structured to allow for a constant stream of extremely modest gift amounts.

2.   To begin identifying the few who currently can, in fact, make significant gifts. A Yale University president gave this advice: "Always be kind to your A and B students. Someday one of them will return to your campus as a good professor. And also be kind to your C students. Someday one of them will return and build you a $2 million science laboratory." Many of the latter are part of the new wave of "Civic Entrepreneurs" profiled in Chapter 16.

Understand their attitudes, values, and lifestyles. Generation Xers are "the New Pragmatists." Growing up in the Reagan years, they have a sense of diminished expectations. Maintains Lilian Maresch, whose Minneapolis consulting firm, Generation Insights, tracks generational trends, "the Busters have decided that you can't have it all, that the American dream is not your birthright." The Busters are trying to find stability in an unstable world. As a result, they're focused on quality rather then trendiness.

Those still living at home are often referred to as "boomerang kids." Many see themselves as having been forced back home by societal problems and are eloquent about the need for change. Boomerangers feel they were born into a society with lots of room for improvement...and it's up to them to fix it.

●   **Give them a sense of community.** Much more so then to Baby Boomers, Busters believe in the importance of friends and family. They move as a "tribe." You need one buster to endorse your cause and then sell it to his or her peers. Consider creating a named fund that a group can contribute towards for a common goal.

●   **Give them a specific role to play.** Post-boomers are not trying to change things. They want to fix things. Active projects—planting trees, cleaning up the beaches, painting lower-income houses—are very attractive to them. Many are unwilling to make financial contributions without a hands-on knowledge of the organization. That's why Habitat for Humanity does so well with this age group.

● **Find and involve the trendsetters.** There's a trendy sub-group of Generation Xers that Yankelovich Partners calls "Friend-zied Xers." Younger, more often never married, they live in higher income households. They see themselves as ambitious, daring, intelligent, fun-loving, and out in front of the pack.

● **Remember that younger persons grew up in a different world.** Highly computer literate, they prefer the cashless society: using credit cards, standing bank drafts, and electronic transfers. An increased use of electronic newsletters, videos, e-mail, and computer bulletin boards should be in your organization's future.

● **Let them go shopping for charity.** It's one of the twenty-somethings' favorite leisure activities. Offering merchandise through a catalog (online, of course!) that benefits your not-for-profit is a good way to attract a strong list of upscale Busters.

MARKETING TO GENERATION X

- America's second largest adult population grouping.

- Currently, have high disposable incomes: postponing marriage and children.

- Grew up in the "shadow of the Boom."
  Cautious   Conformist   Pragmatic
  Anti-intellectual/pessimistic
  Often fearful, frustrated, angry

- Key Concerns are "quality of life"
  - The Environment   - Parenting
  - Positive Self Issues   - Ongoing Education

- Tribal in nature: Friends first

Introducing Generation Net: Today's Affluent Youth

Born during a baby bulge that demographers locate between 1977 and 1994, they are as young as seven and as old as 24, with the largest slice still a decade away from adolescence. And at 80 million strong—nearly twice the size of Generation X—they're the biggest thing to hit the American scene since the 77 million Baby Boomers.

While the majority of your time and effort should be spent finding, cultivating, and appealing to our three adult populations—our traditional pre-World War II audiences, middle-aging Baby Boomers, and the young adults of Generation X—fund raisers should be aware of opportunities among our youngest population, the Baby Boomlet, often called Generation Net or Yers.

■ **The first wave of "Netters," one-third of the 3.3 million born in 1978, received college degrees in 2000.** Starting salaries are inching up. JobTrak.com reported that average starting salaries for 2000's graduates rose, on average, by $4,271.

Average starting salaries for college graduates in February 2000:	
Computers & Information Science	$44,722
Engineering	$43,740
Education	$38,898
Sales & Marketing	$35,746
Business & Management	$34,452
Accounting & Finance	$35,104
Public Affairs & Social Services	$29,535
Communications/Media	$28,446

SOURCE: *American Demographics,* May 2000

● **Generation Net tends to be wealthier in their own right than previous generations.** EdVenture partners, a consulting firm in Berkeley, found that 31 percent of the students they polled had money invested in the stock market.

● **The children of affluent parents are optimistic about their future.** Fifty-four percent expect to be wealthier than their parents; one in five expects to earn $40,000 or more.

● **A key source of Generation Net affluence is "leapfrog legacies."** Many grandparents are by-passing well-to-do children and leaving money directly to their grandchildren. A recent study by Columbia University found that 25 percent of all college prepayment plans were being funded by grandparents rather than parents. Also, 14 percent of private school tuition is being paid by grandparents.

■ **It's especially important for charities to understand Gen Net or Y teens: destined to be the largest teen population in U.S. history.** They are currently some 31 million kids between the ages of 12 and 19 and projected to grow to 34 million by 2010.

● **The average 13- to 17-year old today has 51 percent more pocket money than a comparable youth in 1995,** according to the 1999 Roper Youth Report. In particular, tech-savvy teen males, who earn and spend more than their female counterparts (and comprise 51 percent of the total U.S. teen population), are fast becoming an attractive market all of their own. On average, teen boys earn $88 per week compared to the $75 teen girls make, according to Teenage Research Unlimited. And 69.9 percent of teen males have a savings or checking account, while 16.2 percent own a credit card or have access to one in a parent's name.

> *Ohio State University researchers say the*
> *$5 allowance is long gone.*
>
> Half of teens get nothing. But of those who do, some report getting more than $200 a week. While teens in households earning less than $20,000 get $14; teens in $100,000 households say they get $175. Teens in the Great Lakes region get $75 a week, while teens in the south get $30 to $38.

● **Teens strongly support cause-related marketing.** Over half (55%) would switch brands and two-thirds (64%) would switch retailers to one associated with a good cause, when price and quality are equal. Three times as big as Generation X, Generation Y will have buying power of $156 billion by 2002. Teen buying power comes to $1 billion a week.

● **The fastest growing youth segment in America—Hispanic Teens.** By 2001, 18 percent of all babies born in the USA will be of Hispanic origin. In addition, the number of Hispanic teens will grow at more than three times the rate of the general teen population within the next six years. The Hispanic teen population is projected to grow 25.8 percent by 2005, according to the U.S. Census Bureau, while the overall teen population is projected to grow 7.3 percent during that time. By 2005, Hispanic youth will be the largest ethnic youth population in the USA. At 13.6 percent of all teens—4.3 million—by 2005, they'll comprise 16 percent, the largest minority teen group. Hispanic teens spend an average of $375 a month., 7.8 percent more than the average teen does.

■ **And, it's not just older kids.** Last year, 6- to 11-year-olds, as the kids market is generally defined, spent $25 billion of their own money and influenced another $187 billion of spending.

MARKETING TO GENERATION NET AFFLUENTS

Young Americans have a heavy influence on the philanthropic choices of their families. Raised by Baby Boomers and Gen Xers who encourage them to participate in family decisions and exposed to media from all sides, kids are becoming active and sophisticated consumers at an extremely young age.

Generation Net kids have had a totally different life experience than did people who are in their late twenties. They have distinctive buying habits that likely will follow them as they enter the high-spending years of young adulthood. By the time teens hit high school, their brand preferences are beginning to set. Changes in family composition, elevated expectations, and the accelerated delivery of information all have made this generation more self-reliant and more discriminating of messages directed at them.

● **Generation Net has grown up in a world saturated with advertising and they're turning into consumers at a high school near you.** Generation Net teens are coming of age during one of the hottest domestic economies in recent memory. They are being raised in a society where consumerism runs rampant. Their parents are earning more than ever, and they are sharing it with their kids. The kids are, in turn, spending like never before. The average teenager has about $90 a week to spend, and teens, unlike their parents, don't have to worry about paying bills and mortgage payments. Their disposable income is truly disposable.

● **Generation Net children are following in a pattern of values, attitudes and lifestyles we know as Civics** (review Part Two, if needed). This is America's drug-free, smoke-free generation. They encourage us to "just say no to drugs including tobacco," urge us to "get out and vote," and remind us that "we borrow the earth from our children." They grew up living the values many Boomers aspired to: 73 percent have friends of another race and 63 percent would welcome someone of another race as a neighbor. Financially protected, affluent Boomlets would gladly share with others: 61 percent would give up some pocket money to help feed kids and more than half would go without some presents at Christmas.

What matters to the young?

In a survey of 20,000 students in 45 cities, fourth-graders gave a clear mandate on their concerns:

- 18% said cleaning up the environment should be the first priority

- The three biggest problems facing the USA:

  23.6% cite drug use

  17.3% note crime

  16% say it's AIDS

SOURCE: Eastman/Kodak Survey

A CAUTION: Ethically, you should not be marketing to members of Generation Net directly. Unless they seek you out (i.e., via the Internet or by joining a community service project or special event their families participate in), you should not be marketing to this young demographic group, *at this time,* for contributions. Your goal is to educate them for the future. Educational messages about volunteerism and the role your charity is playing in making their community a better place can be tastefully done.

● **Find tie-ins with their studies.** The vast majority of Generation Net are still in school. The importance of incorporating volunteerism and philanthropy into school cannot be overemphasized. Students are also reached through several out-of-home media vehicles, like wall boards, kiosks, and ads placed on campus newspaper stands.

● **Find companies trying to market to Generation Net and make a case for support.** Young people are overwhelmingly likely to buy products from companies that support a charitable cause. According to a survey by Roper Starch Worldwide for Cone Inc., "when price and quality are the same, nine out of 10 teenagers say they would switch brands to one associated with a cause they care about." This response is up from 55 percent who said they would switch a year ago.

● **Read what they read.** Create public service advertisements that emphasize volunteerism and community participation.

- **Become familiar with your community's college and high school newspapers.** About 60 percent of students report reading four or five of the last five editions. Many sell advertising at extremely low rates.

- **The top five general audience publications among students are *Sports Illustrated, Newsweek, Time, Rolling Stone,* and *People.*** Several magazines have teen versions as well. Special interest magazines—focusing on "in" sports such as wind surfing and skateboarding—are also good choices.

- **Reach Hispanic teens in *Latingirl, SuperOnda,* and *Latina*—**magazines specifically targeted to this demographic group.

MARKETING TO GENERATION NET

Like grandparents, have "civic" personalities.

They enjoy volunteerism and embrace membership in organizations.

Have grown up with technology—will be proactive in researching charities.

When children of educated and affluent Boomers, they are financially "protected."
    61% would give up some of their allowance
    50+% would give up some of their holiday presents
    27% would give up their back-to-school clothing allowance

CHAPTER TEN

Pinpointing Affluent Households

MEDIAN INCOMES ARE IN-CREASING IN ALL HOUSEHOLD CATEGORIES:

- Young householders (under age 25) married or living together and childless often have high disposable incomes

- Younger Baby Boomers (aged 25 to 34) prior to entering primary years of family-building

- Householders aged 35 to 44, entering their prime earning years, will have the second highest average incomes

- Householders aged 55 to 64 will have more time and money to spend as children leave the home

- Older householders aged 65 and up will experience the largest rise in per capita household income, partially due to shrinking household size because of the death of a spouse

In this chapter we'll identify a variety of versions of American households and look at where the truly affluent ones can be found.

"COUPLED IS BETTER"—FOR AFFLUENCE, THAT IS

By a slim margin, the majority of American adults are in traditional marriages. According to *Marital Status and Living Arrangements: March 1998,* a U.S. Census Bureau report, 56 percent of all American adults were married and living with their spouses in 1998 (111 million people). California, Texas, New York, Florida, and Nevada were the top five states, respectively, for marriage in 1996.

Boomers marry, divorce, and remarry versus Generation Xers, many of whom are holding off on making that big commitment for the first time. As a result, the current median age at the time for first marriage for Gen Xers is 25 years for women and 26.8 years for men in 1997. Boomers, by contrast, were marrying young: In 1970, the median age for marriage for women was 20.8 years, and for 23.2 years men.

■ **Married couples are the nation's richest households.** The median net worth of married-couple households was $57,134 (according to data from the U.S. Census Bureau based on a 1988 survey). This compares to $13,571 for women-maintained households and $13,053 for those maintained by men.

● **Married men earn more money than single men.** According to a University of Michigan study by Robert F. Schoeni, even when age, race, education, and work experience are similar, the income of married men in the U.S. is 30.6 percent higher than that of unmarried men.

● **Dual earners comprise two-thirds of all married couples.** Of the 45.1 million married couples drawing paychecks in the U.S. today, 29.44 million—or 65 percent—are dual-income pairs. Although we still have a "gender gap" in pay, increasingly both partners work, significantly raising household incomes. Roughly 80 percent of the $50,000 and over income bracket households are made up of two or more wage earners.

● **High-earning men and women, like birds of a feather, flock together.** Among two-career couples, fully 79 percent of wives with earnings of $25,000 or more have husbands with equivalent or higher earnings. Twenty-one percent of full-time working wives earn more than their husbands.

AFFLUENCE VERSUS DISCRETIONARY INCOME

> A reality check for fund raisers:
>
> **Few of our donors are saints. They won't sacrifice the essentials of life to make a gift.**
>
> What matters for fund raising is how much is left after prospects pay for taxes, groceries, housing, and other essentials.

■ **Some 26 million American households have discretionary income: after-tax income that is left over after expenditures 30 percent greater than the average for households of similar size, age, and region of residence.** While this group represents only 29 percent of all households, it receives fully 53 percent of all consumer income before taxes. The average after-tax income of households with discretionary income was $42,000 in 1987, versus just $17,000 for households without discretionary income. The amount of discretionary income for households that have it averaged $12,330, or about 30 percent of after-tax income.

> The typical household with discretionary in-
> come is headed by a two-earner couple, aged 35
> to 59, with at least some college education and
> professional or managerial jobs. They are sub-
> urban homeowners in New England, the South
> Atlantic, or Pacific states, and they are twice as
> likely to be white as black.

■ **While two-earner, married couples are the most affluent, there are dramatic differences in which couples have the most discretionary income.** Regardless of how much we love them, children (or the lack of them) can make the difference in how much discretionary income is available for luxury purchases—among them charitable giving. Although married householders aged 45 to 54 have among the highest average household incomes, they also often have two or more kids per household reducing what they have to spend after the necessities of life.

● **Child-rearing cuts discretionary income.** Typically, Full Nesters, Crowded Nesters, New Parents, and Young Families are **not** good choices for gifts of affluence:

- Full Nesters—two-earner couples with children aged 6 to 17 only—are the largest segment accounting for one-quarter of all two-earner couples.

- Crowded Nesters—with children aged 18 to 24 at home—are in second place.

- New Parents—with children only under age 6—are third in size.

- Young Families—with children both under the age of 6 and aged 6 to 17—rank sixth in size.

AFFLUENCE AND THE CHILDLESS HOUSEHOLD

**Because having a single child eats up 30 percent of the house-
hold budget, look to affluent households without kids for big
discretionary budgets.** The best audience are those who are
married, aged 55 to 60, well-educated, white, two-earner family, husband and wife pursuing careers, in good health, and
planning to retire soon.

■ **When we think of families, most of us think of the traditional
family with a working father and a mother who stays home
with the children, at least until they go to school.** *In reality,
only 14 percent of our families are this way.* Family demographics have changed radically since the 1970s, when less
than 13 percent of all families were headed by single parents.
By 1990, 30 percent of all families were headed by single parents. (Mothers are the parents in 90 percent of single-parent
homes). The "Dick and Jane" era of households (two children
and a dog named Spot) is vanishing. Less than seven percent of
American families now fit that profile. The majority of American households are now without children.

■ **Only 34 percent of American households now have children
under 18 living at home.** Couples without children are not by
any means all "young marrieds." The majority have heads who
are 35 and older. And almost 4 in 10 are "empty nesters," headed by someone 50 to 64. Childless couples include the Empty
Nesters, Honeymooners, and Just A Couple groups.

● Empty Nesters—the fourth-largest segment—are householders aged 50 to 64.

● Honeymooners—the fifth-largest group—are householders
just under the age of 35.

● Just A Couples—are the smallest two-earner group with
only 2 million couples—are aged 35 to 49.

● **There are more "empty nesters" than honeymooners among those dual-earner couples without children.** America's 3.5 million Empty Nesters are the parents of Baby Boomers. This group represents 13 percent of all two-income couples. Interestingly, 15 percent of all Empty Nester households have no earners at all: they are early retirees. The income distribution of this group is decidedly upscale: 47 percent make more than $40,000 a year. And for those who have children? A large number (84.5%) of affluent Empty Nesters (household incomes of $50,000 or more per year) report that they have 10–20 percent more money when their children leave home. However, about one third (33.7%) of Empty Nesters have experienced boomerang children, those who leave home for a brief period but return at some point thereafter.

Consider segmenting your marketing to Empty Nesters by age:

- **Empty Nester Households headed by people age 45 to 54** have a before-tax income 67 percent greater than average; their spending is 45 percent greater than average. These are the people with the bumper stickers "I'm spending my children's inheritance."

- **Empty Nester Households headed by people age 55 to 64** have before-tax income 22 percent greater than average; their spending is 12 percent above average.

- **Empty Nester Households headed by people over 65** have both income and spending below average (by 23 percent and 14 percent, respectively). However, as empty nesters age, they spend a higher share of income on cash contributions.

● **Just-A-Couples' high income offset their relatively small numbers.** Dual-income no-kids households (DINKS) are concentrated in the $100,000+ income range and tend to be older, married, and have college backgrounds.

● **Mature "DINKS" are the very best affluent prospects.** They are 7 percent of all two-income couples. Over half bring home more than $40,000 a year.

● **Today couples often chose to be childless as a lifestyle decision.** In a recent New York Times article entitled "Your Kids Are Their Problem," Lisa Belkin points out that child-free couples have formed groups of their own and the trend is growing. An organization called No Kidding! which schedules social events for those who remain childless, had just two chapters five years ago; today it has 47. And there is no way to count the number of "child free" sites online (with names like Brats! and alt.support.childfree/moderated), but together they make up a parallel and expanded universe where the printable names for children include "anklebiters," "crib lizards," and "sprogs."

In this world, couples in which one parent stays home are called SITCOMS (Single Income, Two Children, Oppressive Mortgage). Those enlightened enough not to have children are THINKERS (Two Healthy Incomes, No Kids, Early Retirement). Childless by choice or chance, they have the time and inclination to live for themselves. Quality is a guiding principle in their lifestyle.

● **A CAUTION: Honeymooners lack discretionary income.** While they have an average before-tax income of nearly $46,000, these mostly younger Baby Boomers spend 22 percent more than the average for all American households. They are postponing children to gather money for the things they crave. They do, however, have discretionary time and are good volunteer prospects.

NOT ALL AFFLUENT HOUSEHOLDS ARE MARRIED COUPLES

Demographers have been tracking a continued decrease in the proportion of households made up of married couples. For many Americans, women in particular, marriage will be only one of many household types they will experience as adults.

The number of never-married men and women in America is rising—a lot. Between postponement of first marriage, higher levels of divorce, and other societal changes, the percent of adults who are unmarried substantially rose between 1970 and 1996. In 1970, unmarried people represented 28 percent of the adult population, according to the Census Bureau. In 1996, 40 percent of all adults were unmarried. Today, overall, the number of never-married adults of both sexes has almost doubled in the past 24 years, from 21.4 million to 44.2 million.

■ **A big part of the increase in single adults is the result of the continuing delayed marriage trend.** The median age at first marriage is higher than ever before. In 1994, the median age for first marriage was 26.7 years for men, 24.5 years for women, about 3.5 years higher than the median ages in 1970. Nearly half of U.S. adults aged 25-49 are single, with 55 percent of them without a significant other.

● **Many in their twenties are postponing marriage to achieve financial independence.** And it is not cynicism that holds people in their 20s back from marriage. According to The National Marriage Project at Rutgers University led by family experts David Popenoe and Barbara Dafoe Whitehead, Gen Xers describe marriage as a union between soul mates, with a lifelong best friend or a kindred spirit. They see marriage as such an important step that they want to be absolutely sure that their intended is right for them in every way.

● **Because of the Baby Boom, the demographics of who lives alone have changed.** While it used to be that we thought of singles in terms of two polarized groups—college-aged kids at one extreme and widowed elderly ladies at the other, by the turn of the century 35- to 54-year-olds will comprise the fastest-growing segment of Americans living alone. And, these households—without spouses or children—are more likely to be affluent.

GAY AND AFFLUENT

■ **The "gay market" is a seriously neglected and very wealthy segment.** They're single, with plenty of disposable income and usually without children. "Almost recession-proof," is how Andy Schmidel of RSVP Cruises describes the gay community. The Simmons Gay Media Survey verifies that the gay consumer has a very high income level, a very high educational level, usually no dependents, and, consequently, very high discretionary income. According to recent Simmons Market Research Bureau figures, the tangible financial assets of the gay and lesbian community in the U.S. exceed $800 billion.

● **Gay households have a median income of $55,670.** Of American homosexuals, 28.5 percent have an annual household income in excess of $50,000; 21 percent of household incomes surpass $100,000. About 70 percent of gays have at least a college education and work in professional or managerial jobs, and 89 percent say they are more likely to buy a product if its advertising is targeted at them, according to Simmons Market Research. They are especially interested in financial services.

● **Male gay households do better than lesbian households.** Just over 54 percent of gay male households earn annual incomes above $50,000; 29.7 percent of lesbian households earn annual incomes above $50,000.

GAY MARKET STATISTICS

	Gay Men	Lesbians
Median age	37	35
Average household size	1.7	1.9
Average household income	$51,624	$42,755
Median household income	$42,689	$36,072
College graduate	58.0%	58.0%
Advanced degree	26.8%	25.6%

SOURCE: Overlooked Opinions, Chicago, Illinois

● **However, lesbians with a live-in partner earn significantly more on average than their married, heterosexual counterparts,** according to researchers from Syracuse University, Carnegie Mellon, and the University of Maryland. Partnered lesbians earned $23,433 a year on average, in 1990, compared with married women, who brought home $15,981.

Average annual earnings by education and age, 1990

Age	Education	Partnered lesbians	Married women
25–34	H.S. Graduate	$17,473	$11,988
	College Graduate	$24,265	$21,348
	Graduate Degree	$26,028	$26,580
35–44	H.S. Graduate	$18,961	$13,567
	College Graduate	$28,387	$21,448
	Graduate Degree	$34,427	$29,633
45–54	H.S. Graduate	$21,698	$14,351
	College Graduate	$30,653	$21,927
	Graduate Degree	$43,106	$31,090

SOURCE: *Demographics of the Gay and Lesbian Population in the United States*

■ **How big is the gay market?** The standard estimate is 10 percent of men and 4 to 6 percent of women, or 13 to 14 million adults. Although it's hard to get firm statistics, John Knoebel, president and CEO of Liberation Publications, estimates that there are probably 4 to 6 million gay men and a smaller number, 2 to 4 million lesbians, who have an openly gay and lesbian lifestyle and participate in such things as reading the gay and lesbian press, belonging to gay and lesbian organizations, and have a shared lifestyle and a point of view that means that being gay or lesbian has something to do with how they live their lives, where they live, and what they purchase. This is the group we call active gay consumers.

■ **What are gay consumers like, psychographically?** They are trend-setting; they purchase new products ahead of society at large. They are responsive to targeted advertising in their own media, and they have proven to be socially motivated consumers—they vote with their pocketbooks. Given products of comparable quality, an astounding 87.7 percent of gays and lesbians surveyed indicated that they would buy products and services marketed directly to them, suggesting a very brand loyal audience.

■ **How do you reach affluent gays?** The gay market can be a good prospecting source for charities. If you contemplate targeting this market you should do two things. First, conduct a market research of the gay market in the cities where you are considering the development of a marketing strategy. Second, perform demographic and psychographic analyses of your existing donors to determine some of their key social characteristics. If your donations depend predominantly upon donors who hold very traditional gender role attitudes toward women and gays, then consider carefully whether to market.

● **Use Geo-Demographics.** According to analyses done through PRIZM, the Claritas/NPDC segmentation analysis model on 40 neighborhood types, affluent gay and lesbian households have very high indices in urban gentry neighborhoods as well as in the affluent and elite urban areas. There is high incidence in university towns, but almost no incidence in rural areas at all.

● **The largest marketing organization in the gay and lesbian community is *The Advocate,* a national gay and lesbian news-magazine** founded in 1967 and headquartered in Los Angeles. *Advocate* readers are young, professional, and highly educated. In 1990, the average household income was $62,100 with 40 percent having household incomes of over $60,000, and a small household size of only 1.79 persons. Education level is distinctly high, as is employment in a professional or managerial area.

● **Gay men and women are three times more likely than the general population to be online.** Gay.com—a news, culture, and chat site—now draws 1 million hits per month. Sixty-two percent of the American gay and lesbian population own personal computers versus 38 percent of the general U.S. population. Of this total, there are 4.8 million online users, with 1 million of these people online for 20 or more hours in the last 30 days.

MEET MALAS—MIDLIFE AFFLUENTS LIVING ALONE

■ **There are more unmarried and never-married women than ever before.** The Baby Boom is the first generation in history to see a "tsunami" of single women. The average age of a bride in 1998 was 25, nearly five years older than in 1970. An estimated 20 million never married or divorced women are moving into their most productive earning years.

As the third millennium unfolds, it has given rise to a powerful new consumer: the liberated single female. According to a revealing new report from Young & Rubicam's Intelligence Factory, educated, professional single women are exercising serious purchasing power and social influence as we head into the twenty-first century. Factors contributing to the prevalence of and newfound sense of empowerment among single women in modern societies include greater educational and career opportunities, longer life expectancy, delayed marriage—or no marriage at all—cohabitation, and higher divorce rates, all of which mean that women are more likely then ever to live alone at some point in their lives (and may do so more than once).

● There are fewer unmarried men (37.6 million) than unmarried women (44.3 million) in the U.S., reports the U.S. Bureau of the Census.

● Because in our society we expect women to marry older men, there is a shortage of male partners available for early boomer women.

■ **Contrary to popular perceptions, the majority of single women are not young twenty-somethings waiting to get married.** Rather, there is a growing movement around the world toward marriage delay and avoidance.

● **In the U.S., Europe, and Japan, the average age at which a woman marries is now the mid-to-late 20s.** In the U.S., the number of women living alone has increased more than 33 percent in the past 15 years to 30 million, and marriage rates are now at the lowest point in history. Similarly, in Japan, the percentage of women in their late 20s who are single has risen from 30 to 50 percent over the past 15 years. In the U.K., the number of first marriages is the lowest it's been this century. Meanwhile, in Scandinavia, marriage rates have dropped by more than half since the 1950s. And Australia's marriage rate is the lowest it has been in 100 years.

● **As many six out of 10 women over age 43 will be never married or unmarried.** The number of women aged 35 to 54 who live alone increased from 2.6 million in 1990 to 3.4 million in 2000. That's a 30 percent rise for the Boomer years, compared to 24 percent for all women living alone. In addition, since 1960, the number of unmarried women in their late 20s has tripled.

■ **Around the world, solo women are developing an enormous amount of spending power.** Affirms Marian Salzman, president of The Intelligence Factory: "The results make it clear that women living alone increasingly comprise the strongest consumer block—in much the same way that Yuppies did in the 1980s. Marketers vying to reach this segment will need to understand what makes these women tick and how to appeal to their interests and ideologies."

And, despite their diversity, a global culture of young, single females is emerging. From a marketing standpoint, this consumer has three identifiable characteristics: she is info-savvy; she is a relationship-seeker who remains loyal to trusted brands; and she is strongly influenced by her confidants. In targeting this demographic, advertisers are beginning to appeal to single women's aspirations of freedom and independence. Single women respond to advertising messages that respect their intelligence, honor a myriad of lifestyle choices, and affirm their self-esteem and independent spirit.

Research suggests these women are cultivating a new attitude towards money and money management: more aggressive than previous generations. And today's single women make more money—single women make 92 percent of men's wages today. But, MALAs are not necessarily Yuppies. They're not into conspicuous consumption nor are they compulsive acquisitors. Some points to keep in mind:

● **They're not passing through on the way to another stage.** Many see being single as a way of life. They are involved in their communities, look to put down roots, and often choose volunteerism as a way to meet people. A Long Island, New York group—Singles for Charities—has actually been formed for singles who want to do good while networking.

● **They're home-proud.** MALAs have not put buying a home or condo on hold. They invest in their apartments. As a result, they have an investment in the neighborhood around them and the greater community. Not-for-profits who create positive economies or provide cultural opportunities will find MALAs receptive.

● **They're into convenience.** These are busy people. And, they can afford to pay for it. Catalog and internet shopping, for example, is big. Not-for-profits can tap into this. And, not just art museums: a Rockland County, New York domestic violence not-for-profit has scored big with its catalog, *A Company of Women*, which showcases products manufactured or created by or with women in mind.

● **They're into entertainment and leisure activities.** Although affluent singles work hard, they also play hard. Whether it's vacations, cultural or sporting events, or hobbies, they are generous to themselves. (See Chapter 16 for some examples of the hobbies of the affluent.)

TARGETING AFFLUENT HOUSEHOLDS BY ATTITUDES

As you can see, affluent households have a variety of demographic profiles. Once you have found an appropriate group of affluent prospects, you may want to consider using psychographics—values, attitudes, and lifestyles—in deciding how to approach these individuals.

■ **It is "America's New Grown-ups who are the pace-setting heart of marketing,"** according to Grey Advertising, which regularly conducts probing, extensive interviews with American households. Projected to include all U.S. households, America's New Grown-Ups add up to 57 percent of all households— some 52 million of the nation's biggest spenders. Grey warns that "any marketer who fails to understand the dreams and goals of this enormous group risks being shut out of the most important marketing opportunities of the 1990s."

America's New Grown-Ups transcend demographic categories—their agenda is a matter of attitude. For example, while 63 percent are in the household-forming 25-to-44 age group (Baby Boomers); a surprising 27 percent are 45-plus. Eighty-six percent of these householders are married, and more than half have children. Three-quarters of these householders are employed, and 27 percent earn $50,000 or more a year. Some 27 percent of New Grown-Ups are college graduates, and 35 percent have professional or managerial careers.

■ **The New Grown-Up population includes two attitudinal segments: Vanguards and Rear Guards.** The differences between the two groups is largely a matter of degree. While both Vanguard and Rear Guard Grown-Ups are taking on the demands of

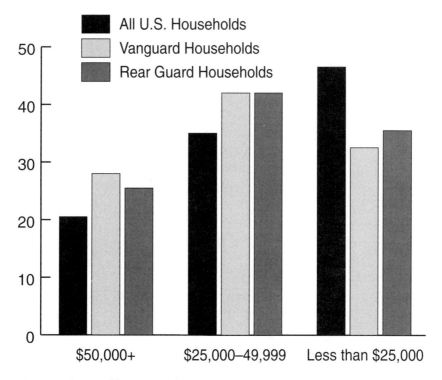

SOURCE: U.S. Dept. of the Census and Grey Strategic Services

jobs, families, and self-fulfillment, the Vanguard want even more. They are the inspiration; they lead the way.

New Grown-Ups differ from all grown-ups before them in two special ways. First, their expectations of life far surpass any agenda that has previously been attempted. Second, the determination to realize those expectations is leading them to a revolutionary new outlook on problem-solving and the day-to-day management of time. They want to feel satisfied with their lives and to make those lives the best they can possibly be. For an impressive 37 percent of New Grown-Ups, protecting the environment is a major goal.

■ **How can you reach New Grown-Ups?** Generally, Grey suggests the following:

● **Indicate we're in it together:** community, family, and connections are keys to this audience

● Home is the emotional center of the New Grown-Up universe: relate to their personal concerns.

● **Respect their intelligence:** they don't want a lecture, just information.

● **Reflect diversity:** show you respond to all kinds of households—single parents, childless career couples, working parents with day-care kids, families of every ethnic and racial origin, same sex couples.

● **Time is precious:** respect their need to find the best use of this limited commodity. Make volunteering satisfying. Send materials that can be skimmed. Always include reply envelopes.

● **Make it real:** show honest emotions, candid conversations, lifelike situations, and streetwise repartee.

● **Keep in close contact:** give these householders a chance to talk with you. Ask them for their opinions, questions, and ideas. Make each contact personal. Make it count.

● **Understand they know it's the only world they've got:** show them they can make a difference. Help them feel like good citizens.

CHAPTER ELEVEN

Pinpointing Affluent Women

THERE ARE TWO OVER-WHELMINGLY PRACTICAL REASONS WHY YOUR ORGANIZATION SHOULD FOCUS A GOOD PART OF ITS EFFORTS TO PINPOINT AFFLUENCE DIRECTLY ON WOMEN.

● Women aren't asked for major donations in the numbers they should be.

● Women philanthropists often don't receive public recognition.

Most Americans have misperceptions regarding charitable giving by women. Women have consistently demonstrated that they have both the money and the inclination to give. Yet not-for-profit organizations seeking significant gifts often ignore female prospects.

- **Women—on average—donate twice as much to charity as men do.**

- **Women take philanthropy seriously.**

■ **Women are more philanthropic than men.** Although they typically earn less than men, women save more and make three times the number of donations as men make.

● According to *Women's Philanthropy,* the newsletter of the National Network on Women as Philanthropists, an investigation conducted by Southwestern University in Georgetown, Texas revealed that the largest single gift to the university was made by a woman—saving that institution from going under!

● Recently, five women with Harvard ties, in partnership with the university, established a $15 million matching fund to encourage other women to make significant gifts to the university.

● Over half of the members of The Committee of 200 (C200), an organization of business women who own companies with revenues in excess of $15 million or manage divisions of U.S. corporations that generate a minimum of $100 million annually, donate $25,000 or more annually to charitable organizations while 19 percent donate $100,000. Largest support went to education (45%), women-related (42%), and arts (1%).

In addition, according to a study, commissioned by the PBS TV program "To the Contrary" and funded by the W.K. Kellogg Foundation, 71 percent of American women (compared with 65 percent of men) donated to charities in 1995.

● Women are more likely to volunteer than men: 62% to 49%.

● In estates worth $5 million or more, 48 percent of female decedents, versus 35 percent of male decedents, made a charitable bequest in 1986. Men who inherit wealth are more likely to invest it in business endeavors.

An analysis of Federal Reserve Board data show that women control 51.3 percent of personal wealth in the United States.

But the survey accompanying the study shows that three-fourths of Americans believe men to be in control of the country's wealth.

■ **It used to be that the only way women became wealthy was by inheriting, but today they are as likely to have earned it themselves.** Two major trends contribute to an increasing female affluence—especially among boomer and buster working women:

● **Higher Educational Attainment:** a quarter of today's female workers have college degrees versus one in 10 a generation ago and over half of all college students today are female. The number of women earning four-year college degrees has surged 44 percent over the last two decades; on the other hand, the number of men earning four-year degrees has actually fallen by 6 percent since 1993. As fewer men obtain bachelor's degrees, women will make further inroads in the managerial and executive ranks as the job candidates of choice.

● **Later Marriage and Child Bearing:** in 1960, 72 percent of women ages 20 to 24 were married. Today, 61 percent are not. The drop among those having babies is greater yet: 54 percent were mothers 30 years ago; now just 28 percent are.

A GROWING FEMALE AFFLUENCE

Women's incomes have grown while men's have stagnated. The real median income of married-couple families which has increased by a whopping 150 percent between 1970 and 1998, according to the US Census Bureau, is largely due to the earnings of women! Women's median income is at a record high, while men's median income is below the peak it reached in the early 1970s. Women's incomes have grown rapidly because of women's growing attachment to the labor force. During those years, the median incomes for women increased by 63 percent, but decreased by 6 percent for men.

■ **Women in the workforce are emerging as an increasingly powerful economic force in today's society.** Seventy-five percent of women are now employed, and as a group, share over $1.6 trillion in income in 1995. The gap in wages earned by men and women is narrowing with, in 1998, women earning 76.3 percent as much as men. That's up from 74 percent in 1996 and compared to wages in 1979, when women earned 62.5 percent of men's wages and salaries. That's progress.

● **Fifty-five percent of employed women account for half or more of household income.** *In families where both spouses work full time, wives earned more than their husbands in 22.7 percent of the households,* according to the Census Bureau's latest figures. From 15.9 percent in 1981, the percentage of homes where the wife is the bigger breadwinner rose steadily through the 1980s. Among upper-income women, three-quarters of the married women out-earn their spouses.

● **Sixty percent of women now work.** As of 2000, women account for two-thirds of new entries into the workforce.

● **The number of women who make at least $75,000 a year annually more than quadrupled from 1980 to 1995** and the wage gap between women and men has been shrinking.

■ **As today's senior (male) executives retire, 50 percent of the next group of managers are women.** According to John A. Challenger, CEO of Challenger, Gray, and Christmas, Inc., an international outplacement-consulting firm, companies have an increasingly difficult time finding qualified individuals to fill the growing number of highly skilled positions, and college-educated women will be the biggest benefactors, ultimately leading to the disappearance of the glass ceiling. The National Network on Women as Philanthropists notes that 43.6 percent of all executive, administrative, and managerial positions in the United States are held by women.

● **Women top earners have more than doubled since 1995— growing from 29 women (1.2 percent of all top earners) in 1995 to 77 (3.3%) in 1999—though the numbers remain relatively meager.** Companies with two or more women officers increased 28 percent, from 220 (44%) in 1995 to 282 companies (56%) in 1999. For the first time, all of the top 20 female executives in corporate America earned more than $1 million. (However, there are only three jobs generally where women earn more than men. Female vice presidents of marketing earned $129,000 on average, $2,000 more than men in the same jobs. Women engineers with 10 to 14 years experience earned $64,108, slightly more than the $63,520 earned by men. Women pharmacists at chain stores earned $53,600 ($1,400 more than men in a similar position). While the infamous gap between men's and women's earnings persists and the glass ceiling that blocks women's rise to senior management remains stubbornly shatterproof, nearly 90 percent of the 3,100 women the Conference Board surveyed said their prospects were better than those of their mothers. Two-thirds said they were *much* better.

● **Women now hold over 11 percent of the seats on Fortune 500 company boards,** according to Catalyst which tracks women's progress. Women represent 11.9 percent of corporate officers (1,386 out of a total of 11,681) in America's 500 largest companies as of March 31, 1999, an increase of nearly 37 percent since 1995, according to the 1999 Catalyst *Census of Women Corporate Officers and Top Earners.*

■ **Entrepreneurial boomer women are growing their own businesses in record numbers.** The increasing education and experience of women, their frustrations at hitting the corporate "glass ceiling," and continued restructuring are important factors in the proliferation of women-owned businesses. Today, one-half of all sole proprietorships are owned by women. Overall, women now own one in three small businesses in the U.S.

The number of women-owned businesses in the U.S. has more than doubled since the late 1980s, and today women own more than one-third of all U.S. companies, employing some 27 million people in the process. The 9.1 million women-owned companies today represent 38 percent of all businesses. Georgia, Arizona, and Washington are the fastest growing states for women-owned businesses. According to the National Association of Women Business, 40 percent of women business owners have been in business for 12 or more years. And, women-owned businesses employ more people than the Fortune 500 firms.

Women Entrepreneurs by Telephone

The Business Woman's Global Network lists approximately 7,500 women in more than 70 occupations, including accountants, architects, bankers, and entrepreneurs of all sorts.

For information call 1-800-847-2946.

Keep in mind the following *Megatrends for Women* noted in the book of the same name by Patricia Aburdene and John Nasbitt:

● Women are developing businesses in the $50-to-$100 million a year category. Eventually there will be billion-dollar women-owned businesses.

● More than 5 million women today lead small-to-medium-sized growth businesses that will become the top companies of the future.

■ **Changing family patterns give women more control of family money.**

● **The female half of married couples represents an equal partner in long-term financial decisions.** Today, women have an equal financial say in 75 percent of U.S. households and a 1999 SRI Consulting survey reveals that four in 10 homes are managed by women.

● **Older couples are the most likely to keep their finances separated, while younger ones are actually the most likely to combine their money.** According to the General Social Survey conducted by the National Opinion Research Center at the University of Chicago, 40 percent of couples under the age of 30 pool their finances, but the share drops to a third for couples aged 70 and older. And while just 4 percent of couples aged 18 to 29 keep their finances separate, that percentage rises to 10 for couples aged 70 and older.

● **Women are inheriting in record amounts.** Baby Boomers will inherit $7–$41 trillion in the next 20 years, and as women outlive men by an average of seven years, much of that money will end up in their hands.

TAPPING INTO WOMEN AS PHILANTHROPISTS

Many organizations don't capitalize on the charitable intents of their female prospects by researching their capabilities and publicizing their gifts to others. That's bad for charities: Reports indicate, among other points, that many women have tended to contribute significant volunteer time and service to the institutions about which they care but have not been asked to consider significant gifts of money. Often, women are interested in not only how their gift benefits a specific institution, but also how it benefits society in general. Women often rely not on formal relationships with institutions, but on their perceived value of the institution's goals and impact.

■ **Follow the "Six C's of Women's Giving,"** suggested by Sonda Shaw and Martha Taylor in *Reinventing Fundraising: Realizing the Potential of Women's Philanthropy:*

● **Create:** Women want to help fund initiatives that serve society beyond the life of the donor. And rather than give to established institutions, women prefer to create new programs and institutions.

● **Change:** Women want to target a program and see an impact rather than give unrestricted gifts.

● **Connect:** Women want a personal connection with the recipient organization. They want to know how the project is going and how their donation helped.

● **Collaborate:** Women like to be part of a larger effort which is why giving circles and focused funds find favor with women donors.

● **Commit:** Women have a commitment to volunteerism.

● **Celebrate:** Historically, women have raised money through events. Honor this tradition.

■ **Understand that there are definite gender differences in giving.** According to Sondra Shaw-Hardy: "The traditional pleas for bricks and mortar and athletics have not motivated women in the past. Women have generally not responded well to fund raising appeals based on maintaining the status quo, competition, status, peer pressure, or public recognition. Women want their gifts to address the needs of children, opportunities for women, diversity, the arts, education, economic opportunities for all, health issues, and the environment."

The W.K. Kellogg Foundation's 1999 survey on women as donors found that although issues drive giving—both men and women believe that helping to address an issue is the most compelling reason to give money—among affluent adults, twice as many women as men make their largest cash contribution to a social service organization.

● **Education and the arts receive the greatest share of major gifts from both men and women.** But the largest donations from women are evenly distributed among social services, education, and culture while men favor education and culture with their largest contributions far more frequently.

● **Generally, men give for recognition while women give more for reasons of the heart.**

WOMEN:	MEN:
• A personal response to need	• Give for recognition
• Give to specific needs	• Giving is reciprocal
• Give time and money	• Give to network
• Give because of personal impact	• Give for practical, tax-related reasons
• Personal involvement in organization	• Give for business reasons
• Want to make a difference	• Have a longer tradition of giving big $$

SOURCE: Survey conducted by the University of California, Los Angeles

Other gender differences to note:

● Women have less security about finances than do men and, as a result, often make smaller gifts.

● Men are more likely than women to also be concerned about their involvement in the group and the group's financial accountability.

● American women are more concerned about privacy issues than men (58 percent compared to 33 percent).

With the increasing cultural diversification of our society, not-for-profits need to have their donor and prospect bases reflect the audiences they serve. Increasing numbers of Blacks, Hispanics, Asian- and Native-Americans are affluent. Our next chapter looks at where to find possible prospects.

CHAPTER TWELVE

Pinpointing Affluence by Cultural Diversity

WHILE THE INCOME GAP BE-TWEEN WHITE, NON HISPANIC AND OTHER AMERICANS REMAINS, THERE ARE DEFINITE POCKETS OF AFFLUENCE THROUGHOUT OUR POPULATION. Households earning $50,000 and above quintupled their numbers during the 1980s. Currently, 8 to 10 percent of Black, Hispanic, and Asian-American households earn more than $50,000 a year: this compares to an 11 percent affluence level among white households.

These are the newly wealthified working. They will be saving more according to a Mendolsohn Media Research report. Many are capable and willing to give generously to charities if asked.

LOCATING AFFLUENT MINORITIES

Affluent whites pretty much dictate the overall geography of affluence. Blacks, Hispanics, and Asians who have money tend to reside in the same communities as affluent whites. The 158 counties where households are the most racially diverse and affluent are concentrated on the East Coast, in southern California, and in Alaska.

---

*According to the 1997 U.S. Census, released in 1998, the median American family income is $40,611. However, it differs by ethnic and racial background. It's $42,646 for white, non-Hispanic families; $25,970 for black families; and $24,570 for families of Hispanic ancestry.

Forty-three percent of U.S. counties have above-average concentrations of affluent black, Hispanic, and Asian-Americans. But only 5 percent of counties have above-average concentrations of affluent minority households for all three of these groups. Say Judith Waldrop and Linda Jacobsen in *American Demographics* magazine, "through a combination of settlement patterns and segregation, affluent minorities don't often mix."

THE LARGEST MINORITY: BLACK AMERICANS

Forget the term "emerging" black middle class. Blacks are gaining in economic power. According to the US Census Bureau, between 1994 and 1995 the median income of African-American households rose 3.6 percent, in real terms to $22,393, while the median income of white, non-Hispanic households increased 2.2 percent.

According to "The State of Black America 2000" survey, the National Urban League's annual overview, blacks continue to better economically:

● For many black families, the median income has increased to $29,404 in 1998 from $6,279 in 1970.

● Black homeownership is at an all-time high of 45 percent.

● The poverty level for blacks has recently declined to 23.4 percent in 1998 from 29.3 percent in 1990.

In fact, the number of affluent African-American households increased 360 percent between 1967 and 1987.

● Today, nearly half of black married-couple families (48%) report incomes of $50,000 or more.

● Since 1990, buying power among African-Americans has surged 66 percent to nearly $500 billion in 1998.

● Today, half of all black households with annual incomes of $50,000 or more (5.6 percent of the population) have brokerage or mutual fund accounts, according to a survey by Ariel Mutual Funds and Charles Schwab.

Like Hispanics and Asian-Americans, Blacks are clustered geographically. Affluent blacks are often a small minority in their affluent, mostly non-Hispanic, white neighborhoods. Some 275,000 affluent black households, the largest group of black affluents, appeared to be dispersed throughout non-black America. In Somerset County, New Jersey, for example, half of black-headed households have annual incomes of $50,000 or more, compared with 13 percent nationwide. But only 4,400 of Somerset's 88,300 householders are black.

● Claritas-NPDC, Inc. tracks black affluence, mixing government and private marketing information to build its multidimensional model of where such individuals live and how. In 1980, a "Black Enterprise" Cluster emerged: half of these households have yearly incomes above $36,000 and 29 percent make more than $50,000; 39 percent have been to college, 19 percent for four or more years. The 645,243 Black Enterprise households represent about five percent of all black households. (The racial composition of a Black Enterprise neighborhood is 70 percent black; 11 percent Hispanic, Asian, or foreign-born; and 19 percent white.)

Sixty percent of the "striving seventh" live in big cities: in Chicago between 102 South at the lakeshore and Western Avenue and Dearborn Park (zip 60605); Detroit's Palmer Woods and Sherwood Forest (48221); Roosevelt, New York (zip code 11575); Englewood Cliffs, New Jersey (07631); and Alameda, Texas (with zips 77053, 77045, and 77085).

The oldest neighborhoods of black affluence are in Chatham (60619) and Pill Hill (60617) in Chicago, Seven Oaks in Detroit (48235), Baldwin Hills and View Park (90008) in Los Angeles, and Baychester (10469) in the Bronx, New York.

Today 27 percent of all blacks and 40 percent of the most affluent live in suburbs like Cheverly, Maryland (20785), Harvey, Illinois (60426), South DeKalb, Georgia (30034), Upper Marlboro, Maryland (20772), and Carson, California (90746).

Surburban blacks tend to have greater educational attainment and more disposable income than do blacks who live in cities. In metropolitan areas with a population of 1 million or more, black families who live in the suburbs have an average income of more than $32,000, according to the 1990 census. That is 55 percent higher than the average income of black families living in the central cities of those metropolitan areas.

● **Six metropolitan areas have black populations greater than 500,000 (Washington, D.C., Philadelphia, Detroit, Atlanta, Baltimore, Houston) and three have populations of over one million (New York, Chicago, Los Angeles/Long Beach).** The states with the wealthiest African-American populations in 1997 were New York, California, Texas, Illinois, Georgia, Florida, Maryland, Michigan, North Carolina, and New Jersey.

- **Of the 20 counties with the greatest concentration of affluent black households, seven are in New York and New Jersey.** Six more are in the Baltimore and Washington, D.C., metro areas. Eight non-Southern metropolitan areas—Chicago, Washington, D.C., Detroit, New York, Los Angeles, Philadelphia, Newark, New Jersey, and Nassau and Suffolk counties on New York's Long Island are home to 47 percent of Black Enterprise residents.

- **The highest concentration of affluent black households (almost 16 percent of the total) is in the Washington-Baltimore corridor.** Among blacks in Maryland, the median household income was $30,746, higher than in any other state with a black population of more than 200,000. Blacks also did well in Washington.

- **Atlanta and other smaller metropolitan areas in the South hold the most attraction for the growing black middle class.** Even though almost half of all black Americans live in the South, currently no counties in the Deep South are listed among the top 20 centers of affluence.

- **Many of the affluent black individuals are moving back South from states like California.** They moved out in the '40s seeking jobs. Now, in retirement, they're taking the houses they bought in 1950 for $30,000 and selling them for $400,000. According to UCLA demographer Leonardo F. Estrada, quality of life issues will continue pulling blacks who moved from California to Connecticut back to cities all across the South. "There will always be some reason for some African-Americans to stay in California," says Estrada. "But the home base of black culture will shift back to the South, back from Chicago and New York to Houston, Dallas, and Atlanta."

THE EMERGING MAJORITY: HISPANIC-AMERICANS

There are more than 22 million Hispanics in the United States (only four Spanish-speaking nations have more). Nationwide, the Hispanic population is estimated at 11 percent, but that number is expected to increase to 25 percent by 2025. The Bravo Group, an integrated Hispanic communications agency in New York, estimates Hispanic buying power at $365 billion nationally, a figure that is expected to double by 2010.

The number of Hispanic households with an income of at least $50,000 a year doubled in the past decade, a rate of growth faster than that of the general Hispanic population. An increasing share of Hispanic households have annual incomes in excess of $75,000—9.1 percent in 1997 compared to 6.0 percent in 1980. Another affluent trend: home ownership for Hispanics between 1993 and 1996 increased by 16 percent compared with 7.5 percent for African-Americans and 4.5 percent for Anglos.

In each of the top 20 counties for affluent Hispanics, at least one in three Hispanic households is affluent. But, as in the affluent black community, Hispanics are often still a small number of affluent householders. In the top 4 counties, for example, Hispanics are less than 5 percent of all householders. An affluent Hispanic middle class is asserting itself—especially in California, Florida, and the Southwest.

● **Hispanics account for 34 percent of the population in California.** The state, always a trend leader, began acknowledging the increasing economic power of its Hispanic population in late 1988. *Los Angeles* magazine profiled the "Brown Elite"— Mexican Americans who have made it big. The *Los Angeles Times* magazine, in an article entitled "New Prosperity, New Power," told "tales of the Emerging Elite."

> • **San Mateo County, just south of San Francisco, has the largest number of affluent Hispanic households.** Twelve percent of all households there are Hispanic, and fully-one-third of these—almost 10,000 households—have incomes of $50,000 or more.

● **The most affluent suburban Hispanics live in older, elite neighborhoods along the east coast.** The most affluent of them all live in the suburbs of Newark, New Jersey, where the 1989 household income is $47,172, followed by the suburbs of Washington, D.C. and Bergen-Passaic.

> • **Many affluent Hispanics live in large metropolitan areas where there are sharp class divisions between central cities and suburbs.** In Philadelphia, for example, the per capita income of Hispanics in the suburbs is nearly twice that of the central city.

> • **The most affluent Hispanic center of all? Maryland.** Hispanics who make up only 2.6 percent of Maryland's population fared better there than in any other state with a median household income of $37,300.

Reaching affluent Hispanic Americans can be difficult as the term means many different things depending on where you are. In New York, the dominant Hispanic group is Puerto Rican; in Texas, California, or other parts of the Southwest, it's Mexican; in Florida, it's Cuban. And, there are also Hispanics from the Dominican Republic, Colombia, and other Latin American countries, as well as Spain.

Many affluent Hispanic Americans are not very visible. "You don't see the Puerto Ricans who are married to Anglos," notes Rodolfo de la Garza, a professor of community affairs in the government department at the University of Texas in Austin. "You don't recognize them as Puerto Ricans. A man has gone to college and married an Anglo woman. He's successful, and you don't think of him as Puerto Rican, even though his last name is Diaz."

ASIAN-AMERICANS: AFFLUENTS GROWING EXPONENTIALLY

Asian-Americans are the fastest growing ethnic group in America*, and they are the wealthiest ethnic-origin group in the U.S.—wealthier than whites. Impact Resources, in profiling consumers with incomes of $75,000 by ethnic background (U.S. index = 100) finds Asians have an index rating of 131, and East Indians have an index of 200 compared to blacks at 55, Hispanics at 47, and whites at 107.

● The median income of Asian-American households is $45,248, compared to the median income of all U.S. households, $37,004.

● Thirty-one percent of Asian households bring in $60,000 or more annually, compared with 4 percent of all households.

● Disposable income of Asian-Americans hit $229 billion in 1999, a rise of 102 percent in nine years.

The affluence of Asian-Americans isn't surprising:

● **Asian-Americans are the most highly educated of all ethnic populations.** About 39 percent of Asians and Pacific Islanders aged 25 and over had completed four or more years of college in 1991. This rate was almost twice that of white, non-Hispanics (22%).

● **Another factor in Asian-American affluence is the composition of the family unit.** About 78 percent of Asian and

---

*However the much larger number of Hispanics will offset the higher Asian growth rate assuring they will be our largest population grouping by the year 2050.

Pacific Islander households are family households, compared with 70 percent of white households. And, 63 percent of these Asian and Pacific Islander families consist of two or more wage earners in contrast to 60 percent of white families. Nineteen percent (compared to 14 percent of white families) have three or more wage earners.

Asian-Americans are geographically clustered. Twelve states (California, Hawaii, New York, Illinois, New Jersey, Texas, Massachusetts, Pennsylvania, Virginia, Florida, Michigan, and Washington) have over 100,000 Asian-Americans—five times more than in 1980. There are 38 metropolitan areas with Asian populations of at least 9,000. These are home to about 75 percent of all Asian-Americans.

● **The greatest concentration of Asians and Pacific Islanders is on the West Coast** (fully 56 percent compared with 21 percent of all Americans), except for Asian Indians, who are concentrated in the Northeast. Nearly four out of 10 (39%) Asian-Americans live in California, while about one out of 10 (11%) lives in Hawaii.

● **However, 14 of the top 20 counties for affluent Asians are in New York, New Jersey, or Connecticut.** Asians in New Jersey had a median household income of $52,846, the highest level for any group in any state. In Nassau County, New York, nearly two-thirds of Asian households are affluent.

Similar to Hispanic households of affluence, there is great diversity within the Asian-American community. The demographics of Asian-Americans more properly are subgrouped in at least ten distinct ethnicities: Chinese (32 percent of the total Asian/Pacific Islander population), followed by Filipinos (19%), Japanese (12%), Asian Indians and Koreans (11% each), and Vietnamese (8%). Each Asian subgroup is widely separated by language, culture, and history.

All are above average in affluence. The U.S. has 1.2 million Filipinos, who are more likely than natives to have a bachelor's degree or higher, and to have incomes over $35,000. China-born

Americans are older than the national average, and they are more likely than natives to have incomes over $50,000. Indians are very well-educated, with 29 percent holding graduate or professional degrees and 52 percent holding a four-year college degree. Heavily middle-aged, Asian Indians have incomes over $50,000. As with Black and Hispanic households of affluence, the dilemma for targeting is the small size of the group.

MARKETING TO AFFLUENT MINORITIES

If your organization is committed to diversifying its base of volunteers and donors, you'll need to be proactive in identifying persons of color. A key to being successful is to know where to find the resources.

REACHING INDIVIDUALS

■ **Start by locating individuals who are already prominent with organizations focusing on their own ethnic backgrounds:**

● *Minority Organizations: A National Directory* is the largest single source book on the subject. It contains listings over 7,500 minority organizations and covers all minority groups.

● *Who's Who Among Hispanic Americans* is a biographical guide listing more than 6,000 prominent Hispanics. The book includes geographic, occupational, and ethnic/cultural heritage indexes.

● *Notable Hispanic American Women,* published by Gale Research Inc., is the first biographical guide devoted exclusively to Hispanic women. It features nearly 300 individuals with profiles highlighting their professional accomplishments and personal, family, and career details.

● *The Asian Americans Information Directory* lists more than 5,200 resources concerned with Asian-American life and culture.

● *SuccessGuide,* a yearly black business directory, lists the names, titles, phone numbers and affiliations of black executives, community leaders, and entrepreneurs in the metropolitan areas it covers. The first edition, published for Cleveland, listed 3,000 black executives, lawyers, and doctors in the area. Issues have since been added for Atlanta, Baltimore, Chicago, Cincinnati, Dallas, Detroit, Los Angeles, Memphis, New York, Philadelphia, and Washington, D.C.

■ **Read what successful minorities read.** The national, ethnically-targeted magazines regularly run articles with biographical information on upwardly-mobile men and women in a variety of communities. Several publications run yearly lists of individuals who are doing well in a variety of occupational areas. Most have regular features such as a newsmakers column which list accomplishments and promotions. Regularly read such national publications as *Black Enterprise, Emerge, Jet, Ebony, Minority Business Entrepreneur, Hispanic, Hispanic Business,* and *Minorities and Women in Business,* as well as your local Black, Hispanic, and Asian media.

● Each year, *Hispanic Business* magazine features the 500 largest Hispanic-owned companies in the USA. In 2000, the list spans all states—with California (124 entries), Florida (117), and Texas (66) leading.

● Each issue of *Ebony,* for example, contains a column "Speaking of People" which profiles newsmakers. *Ebony* also runs annual lists of "The 100 Most..." A yearly feature is the May issue's "100 Most Influential Black Americans." An issue featuring "100 of the Most Promising Black Women in Corporate America" provided thumbnail profiles with company affiliations of those in high-powered positions.

● Articles and regular features in *Black Enterprise* magazine are useful prospecting tools for fund raisers: recent issues contained special reports on "The Most Powerful Black Executives in Corporate America," "Powerful African-American Directors on Corporate Boards," "The Franchise 50 Report," "America's Leading Black Law Firms," and "The 25 Hottest Blacks on Wall Street." A regular monthly feature, "On the Move," tells who's moving on and up.

● Don't forget to check out the Internet. Visit BlackVoices.com, an online virtual community catering to African-Americans, as well as the websites for the various media mentioned above.

■ **Consider minority publications for placement of public service ads.** Or, you might inquire about use of their subscription lists for a direct mail appeal. Your list broker can handle such inquiries.

● **African-American magazines are part of the general trend in publishing towards niche marketing.** *Code,* for example, reaches a half-million readers (mostly male) whose median age is around 35, who are professional, educated, and have an income near $45,000. Other publications include: *Ebony* (general lifestyle), *Essence* (women's), and *Emerge* (news and public affairs).

● ***Black Enterprise,*** with a circulation of over 256,000 per issue, is a business publication targeted to upscale black professionals, managers, and entrepreneurs. Its subscribers have:

- an average household income of $69,400

- an average individual employment income of $48,600

- an average net worth of $227,300

- an average investment portfolio worth $59,300

- an average life insurance policy worth $155,500

- 84.2 percent own mutual funds or stocks

- 72 percent own their own homes

■ **Seek out executive recruitment, search and professional organizations which specialize in minority job placement.** *Black Enterprise* magazine, for example, publishes a yearly list of the nation's black-owned executive recruitment firms.

■ **Network at the meetings of professional organizations that emphasize ethnic or racial heritage.**

● **Women of Color:** Women, especially women of color, are at the forefront, of the new wave of affluence: entrepreneurism. More than one-third of all Hispanic-owned companies are held by women and Hispanic women are starting businesses at four times the national average. Leading states are California, Florida, and Texas.

> • The *National Women of Color Organizations,* a report from the Ford Foundation (Office of Communications, 320 East 43rd Street, New York, NY 10017, (212) 573-5169) profiles 23 societies and clubs.

> • *MANA,* the *Mexican American Women's National Association* (1101 17th Street NW, Suite 803, Washington, D.C. 20036, (202) 833-0060) is the nation's largest volunteer membership organization for Hispanic women with members in the majority of states and active chapters across the country.

> • *Contact one of the many organizations for Black professional women.* Among them: the National Association of Negro Business & Professional Women's Clubs, 1800 New Hampshire Ave, NW, Washington, D.C. 20009, (202) 483-4206; The African American Women's Conference, P O Box 15819, San Diego, California 92175, (619) 236-87509; or the International Black Women's Congress, 1081 Bergen St, Suite 200, Newark, New Jersey 07112, (201) 926-0570.

● **Minority capitalism is on the rise.** Look for more minorities in franchising, including starting their own. Certain businesses attract minorities. For example, black Americans are most heavily represented as auto dealers and in the food and beverage industries. Attend the professional meetings, offer to be a speaker, or sponsor or provide refreshments for an event.

- *There are associations of Black and Hispanic MBAs with chapters in your community.* National MBA Associations provide a national network of business executives working in a broad variety of industries. Find out when their meetings are and participate. The National Black MBA Association is located at 180 North Michigan Avenue, Chicago, Il 60601, (312) 236-2622.

- *Find the professional associations.* The National Society of Black Engineers (Alexandria, Virginia), the National Association of Urban Bankers (Silver Spring, Maryland), the National Association of Real Estate Brokers (Washington, D.C.), the National Insurance Association (Chicago, Illinois), the National Association of Minority Automobile Dealers (Oak Park, Michigan), the National Bar Association (Washington, D.C.), the Black Entertainment and Sports Lawyers Association (Chicago, Illinois), the National Association of Black Accountants (Washington, D.C.), and the National Dental Association (Washington, D.C.) are but a few of many occupational associations you can contact.

- *Mingle at trade shows.* In Oregon, for example, OAME—the Oregon Association of Minority Entrepreneurs—holds a yearly conference, with an exhibitor's fair open to the general public. The National Brotherhood of Skiers meets in January in Vail, Colorado.

● More general, ethnic segmentations are also possible through list purchases.

- *TRW Target Marketing Services offers more than 38 million names,* categorized within its Ethnic Markets Performance Data System in 35 categories including Chinese, French, German, Irish, Italian, Japanese, and Jewish surnames.

- *Claritas-NPDC, an Alexandria, Virginia market re-search firm, has identified over 650,000 households within "Black Enterprise Zones,"* representing 5 percent of all black households. Another 210,000+ are found in downscale urban Claritas clusters, like "Emergent Minorities," and another 180,000 reside in "Downtown Dixie Style," adjacent to Black Enterprise zones in Southern metropolitan areas like Nashville, Tennessee and Little Rock, Arkansas. Some 275,000 affluent black households appear to be dispersed throughout non-black America.

- *Find new movers.* African-American, Asian, Latino, and other minority households represented 42 percent of the 4 million people who bought a home for the first time from 1994 to 1997. Recent studies by Harvard and other universities have shown that immigrant and minority households will achieve many of the social, cultural, and economic benefits associated with home ownership. These include reduced crime rates, higher education levels, greater family stability, and increased family wealth.

■ **Once you've identified affluent minority prospects, be sensitive to "psychographic keys."**

● **African-Americans in general yearn for a sense of acceptance and belonging,** and are, therefore, very image conscious, says Pepper Miller, president of a Chicago-based research firm. She notes that blacks want to be accepted by mainstream society, not singled out. To effectively reach black individuals, your organization must embrace the values held by the black community. You must be seen as personally inviting blacks to partake of your programs and services; you must create communication vehicles and appeals that blacks see as relevant, realistic, and positive.

Like many newly affluent, they are conspicuous spenders: they spend heavily on expensive clothes and are two and a half times more likely than the national average to buy a convertible car. They purchase imported brandy and own sailboats in larger numbers. According to Claritas/NPDC, they are far more likely than the average American to own an American Express card.

If you want to attract affluent blacks to your cause, Eugene Morris, president of E Morris, Ltd. in Chicago, suggests you might want to take the following into account:

- *When planning meals:* Blacks and whites have different preferences in taste. Although blacks drink less coffee than average, they are much more likely than other Americans to use large amounts of sugar, cream, or nondairy creamer. And, most blacks want something sweet with their meals: candy, cookies, sweet snacks, and desserts are an important part of the black diet. Blacks are also much less likely than whites to eat rare meat.

- *When planning entertainment:* Country-western is the least favored music genre among blacks. Urban contemporary music featuring black talent is perceived positively.

- *When planning a travel event:* Blacks are 50 percent less likely than whites to have taken a trip abroad in the last three years, according to Simmons Market Research Bureau in New York City. When they do travel outside the U.S., blacks prefer destinations that are both "language comfortable" and "color comfortable," like the Caribbean.

  They heavily concentrate their vacations in the summer and prefer to travel in groups, not as individuals, with a preference for tour packages. Blacks are far less likely than whites to go camping or hunting, however, and are less likely to engage in adventurous or risky activities. They prefer to relax and see the sights, shop, or party with friends.

● **Hispanics—although from diverse backgrounds—have many shared characteristics.**

- Hispanics tend to be Spanish-speaking. More than 75 percent of Hispanics are Roman Catholics.

- Hispanics are extremely loyal.

- They are outer directed, looking for signals of acceptance by society.

- They are very family- and community-oriented.

- Hispanics put great emphasis on the importance of higher education.

The *Hispanic Monitor* has identified four Hispanic consumer clusters in the population: Hopeful Loyalists, Recent Seekers, Young Strivers, and Established Adapters. Established Adapters, primarily native-born Hispanics, (18 percent of the Hispanic Market) show above average incomes and higher levels of education. Unfortunately, due to the proprietary nature of this study, information on the nature of the segments is limited.

● **Asian-Americans' attainments outstrip all other ethnic groups as well as the white majority.** Their cultures include:

- Higher expectations: Asian-Americans are hopeful and believe in an excellent future for themselves, if they succeed in their education.

- A historical tradition of honoring the intellectual elite, with a sense of learning as a worthy pursuit.

- Parental involvement and interest in the child's learning begins very early: It is sustained throughout all the school years.

- Fear: Asian families and heritage instill a fear of failure to rise in society, so Asians are more driven than others.

- Asians are often uncomfortable with direct eye contact.

■ **If you don't follow the rules of sensitivity, you might find your organization one of the Nominees for the Chevy Nova Award**—given out each year in honor of GM's fiasco in trying to market this car in Central and South America. In Spanish, "No va" means "it doesn't go."

1. The Dairy Association's huge success with the campaign "Got Milk?" was initiated in Mexico and it was quickly brought to their attention that the Spanish translation read "Are you lactating?"

2. Coors Beer put its slogan, "Turn It Loose," into Spanish, where it was read as "Suffer From Diarrhea."

3. Clairol introduced the "Mist Stick," a curling iron, into Germany only to find out that "mist" is slang for manure. Not too many people had use for the "Manure Stick."

4. When Gerber started selling baby food in Africa, they used the same packaging as in the US, with the smiling baby on the label. Later they learned that in Africa, companies routinely put pictures on the labels of what's inside, since many people can't read.

5. Colgate introduced a toothpaste in France called Cue, the name of a notorious porno magazine.

6. An American T-shirt maker in Miami printed shirts for the Spanish market which promoted the Pope's visit. Instead of "I Saw the Pope" (el Papa), the shirts read "I Saw the Potato" (la papa).

7. Pepsi's "Come Alive with the Pepsi Generation" translated into Chinese reads as "Pepsi Brings Your Ancestors Back From the Grave."

8. The Coca-Cola name in China was first read as "Kekoukela," meaning "Bite the wax tadpole" or "female horse stuffed with wax," depending on the dialect. Coke then researched 40,000 characters to find a phonetic equivalent "kokoukole," translating to "happiness in the mouth."

9. Frank Perdue's chicken slogan, "It takes a strong man to make a tender chicken" was translated into Spanish as "it takes an aroused man to make a chicken affectionate."

10. When Parker Pen marketed a ball-point pen in Mexico, its ads were supposed to have read, "It won't leak in your pocket and embarrass you." The company thought that the word "embarazar" (to impregnate) meant to embarrass, so the ad read: "It won't leak in your pocket and make you pregnant."

SOURCE: Chevy Nova Awards 1999

● **For audiences that don't use English as their first language,** Marcy Huber, president, Center of Language Training, advises:

- Speak slowly and enunciate well. But be careful not to talk down to people. Chances are good that they're well-educated in their own language although they may take more time to process what they hear in English.

- Avoid idioms. People whose first language is not English tend to take them literately.

- Humor doesn't translate well. Puns are especially ineffective.

- Sarcasm is often misunderstood.

- People from different cultures often show little reaction to speakers.

It's especially important for fund raisers to consider the ethical implications of targeting minority affluence. Before our organizations can expect Asian, Black, or Hispanic Americans to support our organizations financially, we must ask ourselves how well our organizations support their communities:

- How relevant are our organizations to meeting the needs of the Asian, Black, and Hispanic American populations in our geographical area? Do we serve in a way that acknowledges our similarities yet benefits from the differences among us?
- How welcoming have we been? Are our boards, volunteers, and staffs truly embracing cultural diversity? Chapter 22, dealing with volunteerism, may be especially helpful to you in looking at this concern.

We cannot expect people to give if we are only taking. In this case, "doing the right thing" will mean the right things will get done.

CHAPTER THIRTEEN

Pinpointing Affluence in Corporate America

WHO'S HEADING FOR THE CORNER OFFICE? During the 1990s, Baby Boomers took over the leadership of corporate America. According to *Business Week,* the typical CEO of America's largest companies takes power at age 51. That means that that today CEOs of even the biggest, most conservative companies are being drawn from the ranks of the postwar Baby Boom.

Within the Baby Boom, new demographic leadership is emerging including:

● **Women.** Within the next five years, women will get to the corporate top asserts Lester Korn, chairman and cofounder of Korn/Ferry International—the world's largest executive recruitment firm. He notes that "surveys show two-thirds of all senior male executives really don't want the top job in their companies. But there certainly are a lot of women who do."

● **Minorities.** Judith Waldrop in *The Seasons of Business* says that between 1970 and 1990, the number of black-owned businesses more than doubled, the number of black managers and administrators nearly tripled, and the number of black lawyers increased more than sixfold. The gains have continued through the 1990s and, at the threshold of a new century, we can anticipate increased diversity in corporate leadership.

How Do You Locate Who's Got The Most?

■ **Find the corporate categories with the most.** Dr. Thomas Stanley, author of *The Millionaire Next Door, The Millionaire Mindset,* and several books dealing with the affluent, runs the Affluent Market Institute at the University of Georgia. His research suggests that there are several corporate categories which, because they have higher positive income than the majority of businesses, are good prospects.

Stanley recommends:

- Manufacturers of specialty apparel/accessories.

- Manufacturers of optical, medical, and ophthalmic goods.

- Manufacturers of meat products.

- Manufacturers of industrial machinery.

- Wholesalers of farm products and raw materials.

- Manufacturers of dairy products.

- Accounting, auditing, and bookkeeping services.

- Wholesalers of motor vehicles and automotive equipment.

■ **Read what corporate leaders read.** Business publications are outstanding sources for prospects. Regularly, issues contain lists of the stars and top contenders for the industries and/or market segments they cover. A good way of finding out when they are available is to request the media kits from the publications that interest you.

● ***Forbes* Magazine may very well lead the field in tapping the affluent executive market** with *The Forbes 400* in which the richest Americans are profiled annually. In addition, Forbes provides a host of directories and reports aimed at the corporate market. Among these are:

- ***The Forbes 500s:*** The Annual Directory for America's Corporate Leaders provides a multidimensional evaluation of America's largest companies. It also contains the Forbes Super 50 list of absolute leaders.

- ***The 800 Best-Paid Executives in the U.S.:*** Analyzes the total compensation package, including salary, bonus, stocks, and other awards. Forbes also provides a background report on each CEO and highlights the year's stellar performers.

- ***The Forbes International 500 Survey* and bonus report on the world's billionaires:** With a shrinking world, prospects are everywhere. This issue presents an insightful look at the world's most successful companies in these key areas: The 500 largest foreign companies; the 100 largest foreign investments in the U.S.; the 100 largest U.S. multinationals; the 100 U.S.-traded foreign stocks. In addition there's a bonus report on the world's richest people—capitalists all, no royalty or dictators.

- ***The 400 Largest Private Companies:*** All U.S. owned and headquartered, these companies have too few common shareholders to file with the SEC or, if they do, their stocks are not available to the general public. As a rule, company information is hard to find. Forbes does this for you, determining sales revenue and number of employees.

- ***The Annual Report on American Industry:*** This report serves as scorekeeper for U.S. business, highlighting over 1,200 companies. This special issue profiles 20 industry groups and 70 subgroups, revealing who is prospering, who is breaking even, and who is falling behind.

● *Fortune* **magazine also offers several useful issues:**

- *The Fortune 500,* profiling the largest U.S. industrial corporations.

- *The Fortune Service 500* provides an in-depth look at the service sector, now accounting for over 60 percent of the gross domestic product.

- *The Fortune Global 500 and Fortune Global Service 500* recognize the importance of international companies, both industrial and service.

- *The Billionaires* profiles the individuals and families around the world that control the largest fortunes.

- *America's Most Admired Corporations* rates the reputations of more than 300 companies.

● **And don't forget the "niche" magazines, specializing in the Hispanic, Black, Asian, and women's business markets.** *Hispanic Business, Black Enterprise,* and *Working Woman* magazines, for example, all run a number of lists. On a local level, the "People on the Move" sections of the weekly business journal—as well as a similar column in the business section of the daily newspaper—provide vital information.

■ **Find where they network and be there.** For example, the Young Presidents' Association is open only to persons who are presidents of million-dollar corporations before they reach age 39. And the "old standbys," the Lions, Chamber of Commerce, Rotary, etc. are still good sources for both entrepreneurial and corporate stars.

HOW DO YOU DETERMINE COMPENSATION?

There's no need to guess at salaries. Use these reliable sources:

● JobStar (www.jobsmart.org/tools/salary/sal-prof.htm) offers links to more than 300 salary surveys. Click "Executives," and you find links to surveys of executive compensation in everything from high-tech start-ups to casinos.

● Wageweb (www.wageweb.com) provides salary data for over 150 common positions that's regularly updated.

● U.S. Bureau of Labor Statistics (www.bls.gov/compub.htm) is organized regionally and includes information on benefits.

Research stock options and executive perks as well. They may amount to much, much more than yearly salary.

● **EDGAR-Online may have that information.** The Web site carries required corporate disclosure filings to the Securities and Exchange Commission. There's a $9.95 monthly fee for more in-depth searches at the site, which allows users to search through SEC filings by an executive's name. Its search engine can access various details including company position, corporate board memberships, stock ownership, and executive perks.
A Partnership Data system allows users to search third party data from leading companies such as PC Quote, Big Charts, Hoover's Inc., Zacks Investment Research, Wall Street Research Net, and Company Link.

● **And don't forget the "standard":** Standard & Poor's *Register of Corporations, Directors, and Executives*!

EXECUTIVES ARE NOT THE ONLY GROUP IN CORPORATE AMERICA WHO ARE DOING WELL

The Futurist magazine predicts that "occupations traditionally stereotyped as moderate-to-low-paying will experience a boom in the twenty-first as standard job skills are adapted to meet specific corporate needs. 'Occupational Synthesis' will result in workers with more varied yet specialized skill sets that command higher and higher pay. Two occupations likely to benefit: public school teachers and auto technicians."

Workplace 2005 will be very different. There will be more older workers and, conversely, more teens. There will be fewer men and, for the first time, more Latinos than African-Americans. Employers may have to get by with fewer workers overall because the labor market will only get tighter.

The tight market is benefiting workers. Today's skilled workers are highly sought after and well compensated. The U.S. Department of Labor says median weekly earnings last year topped $780 for a tool-and-die maker and $749 for someone who repairs and installs telephones. That's more than the median earnings of biological and life scientists ($739), psychologists ($679), insurance salespeople ($629), and computer operators ($513). Higher salaries suggest that many well-paid line and middle-management employees could be giving more to your not-for-profit!

Increasingly, corporate America is only one of many workplaces. Chapter 14 looks at today's independent professionals.

CHAPTER FOURTEEN

Pinpointing Affluence in Professionals and the Self-Employed

*T*ODAY, SELF-EMPLOYED PRO-FESSIONALS LEAD THE AFFLUENT LIST. In the twenty-first century, most people are going to have to treat themselves as self-employed and not hitch a ride into the future with one employer, predicts Carol D'Amico in the *Workforce 2020: Work and Workers in the 21st Century* report released by The Hudson Institute, New York.

This is a world-wide phenomenon. According to *The Free China Journal,* 17 percent of Taiwan's total work force now works independently in small or home offices, approaching the popularity of such arrangements in the USA (20%).

About 85 percent of all men and 78 percent of all women are self-employed before age 40. Fifty-six percent of all new businesses are formed by people between 25 and 40 years of age with the 30 to 34 age group the single most productive five-year interval. Money is not the biggest attraction to owning their own businesses: most are concerned, rather, about issues of independence and power.

PROFESSIONALS

In the sixties through the eighties, parents hoped their sons and daughters would be doctors. But, today's physicians are not your best donors. First of all, they're over prospected. Secondly, although the average salary for physicians in the U.S. is $164,300, more than half earn less than $95,000 a year. Finally, most have low net worth. Of course, there are clusters of affluence: surgeons are the highest earners ($236,400 in 1990) followed by cardiologists, psychiatrists, internal medicine specialists, radiologists, and doctors with multiple outlets.

■ **Rather, cultivate professionals who put deals together: attorneys, marketers, agents.**

● **Attorneys have the largest concentration of upscale professionals in America.** In fact, the United States has the heaviest concentration of lawyers in the world: one million, or more than one lawyer for every 300 Americans, asserts the *ABA Journal*. There are just over 600,000 physicians and barely 300,000 certified public accountants.

The ABA Journal proudly proclaims its readership to be "one of the most affluent groups in America." They're relatively young and predominantly male: 4 in 5 are men, average age is 42, with 7 in 10 between the ages of 25 and 44. Most are married, and nearly half have children. *ABA Journal* readers have an average household income of $133,800 compared to the general U.S. population's $36,400. Forty-five and a half percent of its readership claims household incomes of over $100,000. Nearly 42 percent have personal investment portfolios of over $100,000. And 80 percent own homes with the average value being $260,900.

● **Top producing sales professionals are on the upswing.** The growth of incentive compensation for employees has created strong pockets of affluence. As more and more smaller and mid-sized businesses offer substantial bonuses to employees who perform, many younger sales people—especially in high-tech industries—are receiving single, large payments. Because people who are compensated this way, as opposed to receiving steady payments throughout the year, are more likely to save all or part of the windfall, they may be ideal prospects for significant gifts—especially if you help them with financial planning.

Good fields for prospecting include the technical selling arena and securities broker-dealers. An aggressive performer in the latter can earn $250,000 to $500,000 a year by the third year. About 50 percent of brokers earn between $31,400 and $103,040 per year. The median annual earnings level is $48,090. The highest-paid 10 percent take in more than $124,800; the lowest-paid 10 percent receive less than $22,660.

It's not difficult to find these sales pros. First make a list of those organizations listed in business directories with sales between $5 and $250 million annually. Pick up your phone, call, and simply ask for the name and telephone number of each organization's top sales professional. You can use this same approach to identify affluent sales managers.

● **Look for industries that add bonuses to compensation.** Even though the real estate market has been tight, compensation isn't for its executives. The average base salary for the CEO is $283,000 plus an addition $269,000 annual bonus. And, many managers share the wealth: bonuses average between $40,000 and $80,000.

Where will you find these affluent professional prospects? Entrepreneurs all, the great majority (71%) are in private practice. To find them, you're best strategy is to network at their meetings. A good way to meet the "movers and shakers" in the professions is to arrange to attend (or better yet to speak at) a conference or meeting of such professionals such as the American Bar Association, the Association of Certified Public Accountants, or the American Medical Association. Your local chamber of commerce probably has a full list of such organizations.

In many parts of the country, for example, you'll find professional women and minorities have formed their own networks: in the Pacific Northwest, for example, OWL—Oregon Women Lawyers—meets on a regular basis providing opportunities to meet and greet up and comers.

■ **Don't ignore the educators.** College professors have been some of the greatest beneficiaries of the bull market of the past 30 years. TIAA-CREF has turned many higher education employees into unwitting millionaires because of the appreciation of stock invested in the CREF Stock Account. Appreciation has made $1 invested in 1952 worth $173 today.

HOME-BASED BUSINESS OWNERS

Today's home-based business owners are just as likely to run multimillion-dollar high-tech companies as they are to run cottage crafts businesses. And, because home-based businesses typically have the lowest overheads, the profits can be significant!

● **Thirty-nine million people do at least some of their work from home.** Full-time home-based businesses totaled 12.1 million in 1992, an increase of 300,000 over 1991. Part-time home-based business owners hit 11.7 million, an increase of 1.2 million. Overall, the number of self-employed households grew 12 percent to 23.8 million. Just under half of those are owed by women.

● **Home-based professionals earn, on average, 28 percent more than the typical American worker—$34,5000 versus $24,908.** More home-based businesses are owned by women (58%) than men (42%), with 69 percent in the 36–55 age group. Management consulting (13%) and accounting/finance (10%) represent the greatest number of home firms, followed by computer technology, sales and desktop publishing, each with 8 percent. In terms of concentration of six-figure incomes, auctioneers are among the top 10 occupations in America.

● **A growing phenomena are new-style "mom and pop" businesses.** The Small Business Administration says that, between 1980 and 1986 (the last year for which statistics have been tabulated), the number of unincorporated business operated jointly—mainly by husbands and wives—increased by 62.7 percent. Some experts believe such businesses account for at least 1.5 million enterprises.

● **Cultivate the businesses "most likely to succeed."** According to *Entrepreneur* Magazine, these fall under the following categories:

- **Looking and feeling good** (exercise wear, cruise-only travel agencies, healthful deserts, and bicycle shops)

- **Just for kids** (educational books and toys, summer camps, child learning centers)

- **A healthy planet** (environmental "doctors," recycling consultants)

- **At your service** (event planning, gift baskets, desktop publishing, food delivery, computer consulting, specialty personnel, senior day care, mail order)

In launching her mail-order food preparation business catering to shut-ins and the elderly, Gretchen Cryer has joined a growing number of entrepreneurs tapping into the burgeoning mature market. The Extended Family delivers tasty, healthy prepared meals that can be popped in the oven.

Cryer is not the only savvy businessperson targeting American households age 55+ and many of the most successful are women. Fran Rodger started the top-of-the-line, $35 million Boston-based consulting firm, Work/Family Directions, to advise on eldercare issues; Vicki Thomas, a mature-marketing specialist in Westport, Connecticut, has been successfully producing videos for the over-50 crowd, ranging from *Dancin' Grannies* to *What, Me Pay for Nursing Home Costs?*; and Jerie Charnow has two private companies in Mineola, N.Y.: Long Term View, an insurance agency specializing in the needs of those in middle and later years, and Charnow Associates, which creates and manages personalized care plans for the elderly and their families.

THE BEST WAY TO CULTIVATE THE SELF-EMPLOYED IS TO OFFER EXPERTISE

Working for one's self is the American dream.

● **Look for those seeking to get started.** Many people interested in exploring starting their own businesses have significant assets. A not-for-profit dealing with health care issues, for example, might sponsor a seminar or panel discussion on the state of the industry.

● **Help them network.** The self-employed—especially those working from home—seek out opportunities to spread the word. Help them help themselves by hosting informal gatherings.

● **Write for their publications.** These are often local newsletters whose editors are willing—even eager—for useful copy.

● **Help them financially.** Show how charitable gift planning can help with retirement and succession issues.

Today, small business is big business. In Chapter 15 we'll discuss the non-glamorous, yet very profitable, side of low-tech business.

CHAPTER FIFTEEN

Pinpointing Affluence in Small Businesses

MEET TODAY'S MOST SUC-
CESSFUL SMALL-BUSINESS OWNERS. They're not flashy
with money, notes Dr. Thomas J. Stanley's *Marketing to the Affluent* and *The Millionaire Next Door: The Surprising Secrets of
America's Wealthy.*

■ **Older, solid citizens, they are often the owners of successful
low-tech businesses—running scrap metal, garbage, and ex-
terminating services.** Businesses that people who go to college
never think about doing. Stanley recounts the words of a very
successful salesman explaining why he focuses on such
prospects:

"My main target is the business owner. I look for buildings that are ideally in the low-rent commercial areas—you
know, the ones that somehow avoided being shut down by
OSHA.... This tells me that the owner does not throw his
money around, that he has money in his pocket, not in the
rugs, office rent, wallpaper, and office equipment. If he has
been in business for five years or longer, and in the 'right' type
of business, like tool and die, chances are very high that I have
located someone with lots of dollars to invest. He is probably
wealthy, not only because of his business revenue, but also because he is frugal as hell. Very often, when I talk to these types
of prospects, I find that they have never been discovered by
my competition. I especially like to find these types who are in

their 50s and early 60s and have been in business for 20 years or longer. They have a pile of money."

■ **Younger, more diversified individuals are buying established businesses.** Today's average franchisee is 40 years old and has a net worth of $329,704 before investing in a franchise. About 90 percent of all franchisees are college-educated, 20 percent are women, 11 percent are minorities, and more than one-third are "corporate refugees." More and more women are becoming franchisees—and not just in the industries you'd expect. According to Francorp Inc., 20 percent of franchisees in construction and home improvement were women in 1992, up from 12 percent in 1989.

In *McDonalds: Behind the Arches,* John F. Love estimates that one in four of the McDonald's franchisees are millionaires. What kind of investment do franchisees make in their businesses? Fees, working capital, and equipment costs vary from investment to investment but here's a sample:

Athlete's Foot	$175–250,000
Computerland	$162,300+
DryClean USA	$100–250,000
Mail Boxes Etc	$ 70–90,300
McDonald's	$600,000+
Mrs. Fields Cookies	$156–270,000
Pearle Vision Center	$300,000
7-Eleven	$ 93,465

"Franchising," says trend guru John Naisbitt, "is the most successful marketing concept ever created."

■ **Minority capitalism in on the rise.**

● **Asian-Americans represent the highest percentage of entrepreneurs of any ethnic or racial group in America, and are
tin the fastest-growing area of the U.S. economy today.** The
top six segments of entrepreneurs in the United States are:

Korean: 11.6%	Asian Indians: 10.4%
Chincse: 8.7%	Vietnamese: 8.3%
Japanese: 8%	Filipino: 4.4%

● **Minority women-owned businesses grew at triple the national average during the last decade,** according to a study
from the National Foundation of Women Business Owners
(NFWBO). African-American women own the largest percentage (39%) of U.S. companies owned by women of color (including Latinas, Asians, and Native Americans).

● **The number of successful black businesses is increasing
every year in fields as diverse as finance, software, and manufacturing.** According to *Black Entrepreneur* magazine, the 100
largest African-American-owned companies generated $14.1
billion in revenue in 1996. In 1973, the top 100 produced less
than $500,000.

● **Hispanics contribute significantly to the marketplace as
entrepreneurs and producers of goods and services, and as
employers.** According to M. Isabel Valdes in *Marketing to
American Latinos:*

"In 1992 there were 862,605 Hispanic-owned business in
the United States, up from 422,373 in 1987, with total sales
and receipts tripling to $76.8 billion from $25 billion. More recently, 1997 *Hispanic Business* magazine projections, based on
Census Bureau data, show the 'Golden Trio' states—California,
Texas, and Florida—with 456,000, 248,000, and 22,000 regis-
tered Hispanic business, respectively."

Marketing To Small Business Owners

■ **Read small business and entrepreneur publications.**

● **Read their trade publications.** Not only do they feature America's millionaires, many of the owners of these trades have also become multimillionaires through their vocation.

- *Pizza Today, Turkey World, Pork, Commercial Fisherman*

- *Exhaust News, Waste News*

- *Rock and Dirt, Pit and Quarry*

- *Bovine Veterinarian, Swine Practitioner, Equine Practice*

- *Tugboat Review*

● **Some of the better sources of small-business prospects lists are gathered by *Inc.* magazine, the "magazine for growing companies."** It reports on "The Inc. 100: America's fastest-growing small public companies" in its May issue; "The Inc. 500: America's fastest-growing private companies" in its October issue; and "The hottest entrepreneurs in America" in its December issue.

● ***Forbes* Magazine offers a yearly issue on "The 200 Best Small Companies in America."** *Forbes* "Up & Comers" may not be driving the economy, but neither did IBM or McDonald's 30 years ago. To qualify, a company must show substantial earnings over the past five years, carry a small debt load, and be recognized by Wall Street. *Forbes* also selects the "best of the best" for its "Small Company Honor Roll."

● **Other good list sources for small businesses include:**

- *The Macmillan Directory of Leading Private Companies*

- *Dun's Business Identification Services*

- *Directory of Women Business Owners* published by National Association of Women Business Owners

- *Business Owner's Reverse Directory*

- *Minority Business Vendor Directory*

- Secretary of State—list of pension plans

- Secretary of State—list of recent incorporations

- Newspaper reports on small businesses

- Telephone book lists of retailers

- *Who's Who in Trade Associations*

- Contacts Influential

- Pension and Profit Sharing Plans Directory

- *Blue Book of Pension Funds*—Dun's Marketing Service

■ **Attend their meetings.** The National Association of Women Business Owners, a Chicago-based association with more than 4,000 members, holds meetings around the country. The National Minority Supplier Development Council (NMSDC), is another good source: the New York City-based association represents 15,000 minority businesses.

■ **Find those who might be selling their businesses.** Dollars in transition provide major opportunities. A workshop on tax implications might be of interest to these prospects. You can easily create a prospect list by reading the Businesses for Sale classified section of newspapers and trade publications.

SMALL BUSINESS OWNERS ARE TOPS IN BIG CHARITABLE GIVING

More than three-quarters of small-business owners contribute both money and time to charity. It makes sense for small business owners to care: there is a vital link between small business and the health of the community. According to a survey by Ernst & Young Entrepreneurial Services in Dallas, 78 percent of small business owners said they made personal donations to environmental or social causes, and 76 percent said they made contributions to charity through their companies.

■ **Small business people make outstanding volunteers.** Betty Lee Hagrty, vice president of public affairs at Mutual Benefit Life, asserts:

- Because they often live and work in the same community, they understand the needs and have a vested interest in better services.

- They can readily mobilize forces and develop company-wide involvement.

- They are cost-conscious, innovative, and know how to get things done on a shoestring.

- They have special talents in working with people and understand the value of one-to-one communication.

- As team players, they know how to organize fellow volunteers into an effective group.

■ **Small business people make outstanding charitable prospects.** The affluent index indicates that they are three times as likely (an index of 313) as average Americans to have household incomes of $50,000 and above! And, don't forget:

- They are often able to dip into two pockets: their own and their company's.

- Their stock is often privately held and higher appreciated.

- They are often looking for innovative ways to fund retirement and pension plans.

- They are often receptive to vehicles that address succession planning.

However, it is the truly entrepreneurial who lead the way in affluence. Let's look at who they are and what they want in Chapter 16.

CHAPTER SIXTEEN

Pinpointing Affluent Entrepreneurs

THE LARGEST SINGLE SOURCE OF WEALTH CREATION IN THE WORLD IS ENTRE- PRENEURIAL ACTIVITY. Six out of 10 of the truly affluent own their own businesses. More than 300 of the people on the 1999 *Forbes 400* list of wealthiest Americans were first-gener- ation entrepreneurs who started with little or nothing and build a major enterprise creating enormous wealth.

We're in the midst of an "entrepreneurial explosion." Between 1978 and 1980, for the first time in America's history, self- employment in the U.S. grew at a faster rate than wage- and salary-paying jobs. Smaller and mid-sized businesses, rather than large corporations, are experiencing the most growth. The "under 100" list is where the action is.

> **Seventy-eight percent of influential Americans believe entrepreneurship will be the defining trend of the twenty-first century.**
> Lighting the fuse for this explosion is the Millennium Generation, the children born after 1980 who have grown up with their parents' horror stories of working for corporate America.

According to *Working Woman* magazine, "In the 1960s there was a total of perhaps 7 or 8 million companies in the country—200,000 new annually. In 1989 we had a total of 19 million companies, with roughly one million start-ups last year alone." In 2000 there are over 30 million enterprises.

CIVIC ENTREPRENEURS—A NEW GENERATION OF PHILANTHROPISTS

Driven by the Baby Boom and older Gen Xers, a new generation of entrepreneurs, entertainers, financiers, and executives is finally starting to give its money away. According the 2000 version of the *U.S. Trust Survey of Affluent Americans* (XVIII), "while 36 percent of the affluent technology respondents cited as very important that *Money allows you to support charities you feel are worthwhile,* almost every respondent (99%) made charitable contributions in 1999."

Wealthy technology executives gave 6 percent of their after-tax income to charity last year, donating an average of $20,000. According to the U.S. Trust Survey of Affluent Americans the affluent technology respondents most often supported organizations that aid the needy (69%), education (67%), and religious institutions (67%). Those surveyed were also committed to aiding children's causes (60%) and cultural (54%) and medical (52%) endeavors. Less popular with those surveyed, about one-third or fewer of the respondents made financial contributions to charities related to Public Affairs, Public Policy and Political Organizations (37%), the Environment (27%), Athletics (26%), and Animal Welfare (24%) in 1999.

As stated by *Time* magazine: "It's taken a while, but many multimillionaires of the technology boom are now giving something back. For many years, the multimillionaires of the booming technology industries didn't feel very secure in their newfound wealth and weren't at a point in their lives where they thought much about their legacies. Now that's changing. Silicon Valley CEOs, along with other newly rich Americans, are finally stepping up to the collection plate. And just as they've transformed American business, members of this new generation are changing the way philanthropy is done."

A growing number are treating charity like a business, demanding accountability and efficiency from a nonprofit sector never strongly associated with either trait. Many entrepreneurs believe is the responsibility of business leaders to right the social wrongs of the new economy according to 71 percent of the readers of *Fast Company* magazine, whose target population are the Generation X and Baby Boom entrepreneurs.

These modern philanthropists are spurring traditional charities in favor of projects and causes in which they can play an active role. Higher education, culture, and personal crusades lead the list. "It seems like this time, it's personal," observes Jack Shafer, deputy editor of Internet magazine *Slate.com* which tracks the USA's largest charitable givers. "They are very hands-on. They do lots of research before giving."

Many of those philanthropists who are emerging from the new fortunes define themselves as social or civic entrepreneurs. They want to solve defined problems in a specific way. They don't want to simply earmark money for "some vaguely benevolent purpose." They focus on performance. They try to make projects self-sustaining. If manufacturing products has been part of their wealth creation, they often make these products part of their giving. They believe strongly that equipping people with tools and investing in them to go out and create "wealth" is a vital part of their philanthropy. Their interpretation of the age-old equity and access challenge revolves around information and knowledge as the new currency and driving equalizer. While this may smack of naive optimism based on their own success, these wealth creators want their philanthropy to come out of the paradigm of a "hand up, not a hand out." Right or wrong, they don't want to hear about the have-nots and the negativity associated with this dependency syndrome. Their philanthropy is often targeted to broad economic and educational improvement first, with the belief that other forms of social and spiritual wealth will follow.

Impatient, restless, and activist, these rich are acting as "investor donors." Living donors are directing very large quantities of money, expresses Patricia Stoesifer, cochair of the Gates Foundation. "They're having a personal impact in deciding how to use the money. They bet big—don't shy away from risk; create benchmarks including expected earning streams; and focus on accountability."

What assumptions can we making about the new philanthropy? According to Tom Reis, Director, Venture Philanthropy at the W.K. Kellogg Foundation:

● The new wealth creators with early fortunes will move earlier into philanthropy than their predecessors, who generally took much longer to generate their fortunes and began giving seriously much later in life.

● Society's tough, intractable problems require new solutions, which will need to be more multi-sectoral in nature.

● Social entrepreneurship will demand a network of new systems and infrastructures.

● Systematic interventions will now be needed to help new donors avoid turn-off and fatigue. Philanthropy is a learned behavior, requiring both tenacity and patience. It needs to be taught.

● A potential for significant value exchange exists between and among existing and emerging funders and doers. The old donors bring wisdom, experience, and atrophy; the new are offering naiveté, enthusiasm, and capability. We need a respectful information exchange.

● Collective efforts are needed if we are to attain sustainable social change. We must create and work within new networks.

MARKETING TO SOCIAL AND CIVIC ENTREPENEURS

When cultivating today's entrepreneur for a charitable gift, beware!

● Unlike traditional donors, they have no time and are used to getting pitched all the time. They're used to selling themselves and they expect to be sold to.

● They don't respond well to ultimatums. Their giving is on their time line, not yours.

● On the other hand, you need to make your pitch quickly and succinctly. You only get one chance.

When marketing to today's entrepreneurs, recognize they have differing psychographics. According to a study conducted by Yankelovich Partners, there are five entrepreneurial "types":

● Idealists (24%) start their businesses to work on something special. They're highly creative, but frustrated by administrative details.

● Optimizers (21%) are confident and savvy. They enjoy the personal rewards of ownership.

● Substainers (15%) are more conservative—they work hard at keeping the enjoyable, balanced life they have.

● Hard Workers (20%) tend to sweat the details in order to build larger businesses.

● Jugglers (20%) do it all themselves. They're high-energy owners who feel pressures on time and cash flow.

How Can You Find the Hottest Entrepreneurs?

Entrepreneurs are often invisible to fundraisers as they usually plow back all of their financial resources into their privately held enterprise, sometimes operating out of an apartment or garage and maintaining a modest way of life.

■ **Look to the young.** *Entrepreneur* magazine remarks that whereas "twenty years ago, teenage entrepreneurs would mow lawns or deliver papers for extra money, today they start auto detailing businesses and computer companies making thousands of dollars a year before learning to drive."

● **Be sure to read entrepreneurial publications in addition to business publications regularly.** My personal favorite is *Fast Company* magazine which focuses on younger entrepreneurs in six hefty (300 plus page) issues a year. Many of the entrepreneurs quoted and profiled provide their direct e-mail addresses!

■ **Organizations abound for entrepreneurs: attend their meetings and conferences.** Each year, *Entrepreneur* Magazine hosts a national conference. The Association of Collegiate Entrepreneurs in New York City boasts 1,400 members nationwide and is starting high school chapters while the National Association of Private Enterprise, a Fort Worth, Texas-based association has 70,000. Most cities have a local association as well, with modestly-priced networking events, workshops, and seminars.

Although entrepreneurs tend not to differentiate between their work and play personalities, what people do for a living is only half of their lives; how they relax is another indicator of affluence. The next chapter examines this in detail.

CHAPTER SEVENTEEN

Pinpointing Affluence by Hobbies and Interests

E ACH WEEK, YOUR LOCAL PAPER'S SOCIETY PAGES—ALONG WITH THE WEDDING AND BIRTH ANNOUNCEMENTS—CHRONICLE THE LOCAL AFFLUENT SCENE. Regional magazines spotlight their comings and goings. And, of course, some—along with the truly wealthy—are highlighted in national magazines: *Town and Country, Glamour, Mirabella*—to name just a few. You've located affluents by age, gender, household, and workplace. Now you're ready to look at their common "psychographics"—attitudes, values, and lifestyle interests. Alternatively known as geodemographics, cluster or lifestyle marketing, psychographics jolts demographic marketing up a few notches.

Geodemographics is "a holistic approach to marketing," says Michael J. Weiss, author of *The Clustered World: How We Live, What We Buy, and What it all Means About Who We Are.* "It doesn't just consider demographic information like age, income, and marital status. It also looks at the effect of whether people live in a city, a small town, or a rural area. It looks at life stage—whether you're young and single, a couple with kids, or a retiree. And it also looks at other factors, specifically how you behave in the marketplace."

● **There are now cluster systems in 25 countries** with nearly every country having its neighborhoods of Old Money Flats and New Family Suburbs and Working Class Villages and Waterfront Retirement areas. The global cluster system MOSAIC, from Experian Information Solutions Inc., which has classified common lifestyles in 19 countries. The consuming patterns of each of these lifestyle types tend to be the same, whether you're in Australia, Italy, or England.

● **Among adults, there are six key global values segments, residing in 35 countries, but to varying degrees:**

- **Strivers**—the largest group—place emphasis on material and professional goals. Slightly more male than female, they are heavily represented in developing Asia, Russia, and developed Asia.

- **Devouts**—22 percent of adults—are more heavily women. Tradition and duty are very important. Most common in developing Asia and the Middle Eastern and African countries. Least common in developed Asia and Western Europe.

- **Altruists**—18 percent of adults, slightly more female and older with a median age of 44. Interested in social issues and the welfare of society. Found more in Latin America and Russia.

- **Intimates**—15 percent value close personal relationships and family above all else. One in four Europeans and Americans qualify, compared with just 7 percent of developing Asia.

- **Fun Seekers**—12 percent, the youngest group with male-female ratio of 54 to 46, are heavily found in developed Asia.

- **Creatives**—10%—hallmark trait is strong interest in education, knowledge, and technology. More common in Latin America and Western Europe. Along with Intimates, most balanced gender mix.

Do Affluents Share Common Psychographics?

It is logical to assume that people who have interests in common must share some common attitudes, values, and lifestyles. A good overall resource for finding what has been done for a particular sector is FIND-SVP. The company is a one-stop shopping center for market intelligence, industry analyses, marketing directories, and other valuable management reports.

AFFLUENTS HAVE THE FOLLOWING AREAS OF COMMONALITY

- Most upper-affluent Americans are solid, middle-aged citizens, with family values and often with grown children.

- The Work Ethic is alive and well in upper-affluent America. They see themselves as hardworking, self-made successes who thrive on giving of themselves; the more successful they are, the less they want to retire.

- The Upper-Affluent are optimistic. They believe their own economic situations will continue to improve or, at worst, hold steady.

- The goals and aspirations of the Upper-Affluent reflect solid values, not a desire for prestige.

SOURCE: *Success in America: The CIGNA Study of the Upper-Affluent*

While its fees are often too high for not-for-profits, you can use it as a resource to discover the company who initially paid to do the research. These companies will often share the research with not-for-profits gratis. FIND-SVP's *Information Catalog,* published six times a year, is **free**. You can be put on the mailing list by calling 1-800-FIND-SVP.

The real affluents are those with an affluent mind-style. According to a Louis Harris study of 500 households with a minimum of either $100,000 in income or a net worth of $500,000 excluding the value of the primary residence, affluents have common interests and goals. Those whose minds lead them to the values, lifestyles, and spending patterns of true affluence. You need to bypass those who fall into some demographic and other research groupings, but are not likely to display the psychographic characteristics that make them good prospects for significant giving to your organization.

However, there are differing psychographics among the affluent. The more traditional notions of wealth are found among the **Ultra-affluent**—those in households earning $200,000 or more per year (2.4 percent of all Americans). Their interest tends to be more materialistic than the other five affluent segments:

● **Trailblazers** (21%)—heaviest travelers; most likely to seek adventure and new experiences, most active investors; most computer savvy; most altruistic

● **Luxury Livers** (29%)—most image- and status-conscious; youngest and less often married; want to stand out from the crowd; focus on appearance and youth

● **Savvy Affluents** (23%)—most price-conscious shoppers; spurn ostentation; are savers rather than investors; focus on health, fitness, and self-improvement

● **Strained Affluents** (13%)—seek luxury that is out of reach; lowest net worth, but status- and image-conscious; conflicted between spending and saving

● **Contented Affluents** (14%)—oldest and most often retired; most likely to feel well-off; strongest interest in passing wealth to children; least computer savvy

ALL WORK AND NO PLAY WOULD MAKE JACK AND JILL PRETTY DULL

Affluents self-identify themselves through their areas of interest. If you're looking for a list of affluent individuals, remember that "birds of a feather flock together." Understanding the hobbies and interests of affluents can help you in two ways:

1) You can identify areas which might attract affluents to your organization and use an event, for example, to encourage new prospects to learn more about your non-profit.

2) You can identify leisure activities which attract affluents and use this in purchasing/creating prospect lists of up-scale individuals.

Affluent individuals share interests in common. Many affluent persons:

- own luxury cars, including antique and classic cars

- collect art

- are horse owners and/or breeders of Thoroughbreds

- own aircraft/jet/private planes

- have yachts (40' or more)

Note that aging has a powerful effect on leisure choices. Young people are much more interested in socializing, competing, and escaping from reality. Older people are motivated by pleasure and intellectual challenges.

HOW DO TODAY'S AFFLUENTS RELAX AND ENJOY THEIR LEISURE TIME?

■ **Many of the affluent are collectors.** In addition to buying lists from organizations associated with their interests, you can check the classified ads. Every day, affluent prospects place classified advertisements in newspapers and magazines detailing the sale of private aircraft, commercial real estate, yachts, and the like.

● **Their art collections aren't limited to antiques, paintings, and sculpture.** Fine crafts buyers are well-educated, well-traveled men and women aged 35 to 55. *Metropolitan Home* has been running feature stories about crafts since 1988 , and its photographs are often "propped" with hand-crafted objects. The typical reader is a 40-year-old married woman with a household income of $62,400. Almost one-third of the readers have homes worth $200,000 or more. One-fifth have second homes with an average value of $183,000.

AFFLUENT HOBBIES/INTERESTS

American Express Card Holders	IRA
Annuities	Mutual Funds
Boat Owners	PC Owners
Cable TV	Stock/Bonds
Cat Owner	Tennis
Contributor—Political	Vacation—Air Travel
Frequent Business Flyer	Working Couple

SOURCE: Survey Sampling, Inc.

● **The affluent don't just ride in Cadillacs and Lincolns.** Fifty percent of those with household incomes of $75,000 say a compact sport utility truck is their principal vehicle.

■ **"Americans are in love with the outdoors, and everything that has to do with the outdoors,"** says Derrick Crandall, president of the Washington, D.C.-based non-profit American Recreation Coalition (ARC). Today's seniors, laden with free time, unprecedented good health, and generally hefty retirement accounts are indulging in outdoor activities on pristine golf courses and rugged Elderhostel expeditions. Environmentally conscious Baby Boomers are flocking to exotic adventure travel destinations. Gen Xers and Ys—though surprisingly less physically active than other generations—have spurred the development of non-traditional outdoor activities and the creation of new recreational sites for snowboarding, inline skating, and telemark skiing.

● **Many of the 61 million grownups who play in the dirt are affluent.** Gardeners arc heavily concentrated among middle-aged, well-educated homeowners. The affluent and educated are more likely than the total public to claim gardening as a hobby or interest: an average of 43 percent of people in households making $75,000 or more per year and 37 percent of college graduates versus 31 percent of the total public. Among the politically and socially active Influential Americans, who tend to be affluent and educated, 50 percent do. Gardeners can be classified as Dabblers, Decorators, Cultivators, and Masters. The most affluent? Decorators (19 percent of gardeners, 11.5 million Americans). They have an average age of 49, are 59 percent female, with a median annual household income of $37,159.

● **Birdwatchers are above average in income.** Thirty-three percent of National Audubon Society readers have household incomes of $75,000 or more compared to 14 percent of the general American public.

● **Many of the 51 million fishermen have above-average annual incomes.** And, saltwater fishermen tend to be more affluent then their freshwater counterparts. Twenty-two percent of the former have household incomes of over $50,000 compared with just 11 percent of fly-fishermen.

● **Don't look for hunters**...lower-income people are more likely than those in high-income brackets to be frequent hunters. Less than 1 percent of people with 1990 annual incomes of $50,000 or more hunt frequently!

■ **Affluents are physically active.** The demographics of those who ski frequently reveal those with incomes above $75,000 are twice as likely to ski as the general population. Sixty-six percent of golfers have household incomes of $50,000 or more. Other sports affluents tend to participate in ranked by index against the U.S. average (index 100) include:

- tennis frequently   301

- racquetball   276

- boating/sailing   244

- bicycling frequently   222

- running/jogging   217

- motorcycles   212

- camping/hiking   186

The preferred television sport for affluent men is tennis. A third (33%) of male television tennis audiences have household incomes of $50,000 or more. Also scoring highly: NFL football (28%), college basketball (27%), golf (26%), and college football (25%). The largest male audience share for all sports is those with incomes of under $30,000, the second largest male audience share, for every sport category, is the affluent man.

■ **Media choices are an indication of affluence.** Generally speaking, the higher their income, the higher their readership. Seventy-one percent of those making $40,000 or more read the newspaper daily; 77 percent read Sunday compared to about half (56%) of those making less than $40,000 who read it daily; 59 percent on Sunday. Affluents are 39 percent more likely than average to watch CNN and 155 percent more likely to read the *Wall Street Journal*.

● **Book buyers,** 10 percent of the US adult population, and are dominated by women, professionals, and members of affluent households. Evenly distributed across all age groups, they have a slight bias toward the 18-to-34 age group. They are slightly more likely than the average adult to be childless, and slightly more likely to be employed.

● **Affluent CD buyers** (twice as likely to have incomes of $60,000 and greater) are heavily male (64%) and younger— aged 18 to 34 (57%). They are far more likely than average to be employed, and to hold a job in the professional or technical categories. They are less likely to have children.

The Affluent Index, published by Concert Music Broadcasting, notes that if we use an index of 100 to reflect average, an index of 175 reflects a 75 percent above-average incidence. Using this information, we can look at media choices for:

● **Those with household incomes of $100,000+** show preferences for Classical Music (383) on Radio, followed by Jazz (226) and All News (224). They choose Print over TV with *Forbes* (427), *Fortune* (344), and the *New Yorker* (338) leading.

● **Those with individual employment incomes of $75,000+** show preference for Classical Music (391) followed by All News (277), and New Age (258). They choose Print over TV with *Forbes* (625), *Fortune* (550), and the *New Yorker* (460) leading.

To find good media choices for affluent readership ask for a media kit. Take, for example, *Sunset* Magazine: 42 percent of its readers have $50,000+ annual household incomes, 35 percent have college degrees, 36 percent have taken a foreign vacation in the past three years, and 53 percent own homes worth over $100,000. *Golf Digest* boasts an average household income of $117,900. The median age of their readers is 49 years and 87 percent are college educated.

■ **The most affluent photo consumers view photography as self-expression, a creative ego-gratifying endeavor used to display talent and skill.** "Professionals," the wealthiest of the seven consumer lifestyle groups defined by Photo Marketing Association International, comprise 9 percent of consumers. They are largely men (70 percent) with an average age of 39.7 years, slightly younger than the 42.9 average. What further contrasts Professionals from the mainstream photo consumer is income, they average of $40,000 compared to $34,300, and their likelihood of working in a professional or managerial position: 45 percent versus 26 percent of the total.

■ **Affluent Americans regularly attend the performing arts, movies, and visit museums.** While 37 percent of all Americans visited a museum in 1998, a whopping 71 percent of people with graduate degrees made a trip that year, as did 66 percent of people with bachelor's degrees, according to the 1998 General Social Survey conducted by the University of Chicago's National Opinion Research. You'll also find a higher percentage of affluents attending live performances of opera, ballet, orchestral and chamber music, and theater than non-affluents.

TREATING THEMSELVES WELL

Affluent individuals enjoy their small luxuries. According to Judith Waldop, author of *The Seasons of Business:*

- People whose annual household income tops $100,000 are 97 percent more likely to indulge in fancy cooking.

- Sixty-nine percent of those with incomes about $50,000 think going out to the movies is great fun.

- Those with annual household incomes of $50,000 and over are the most likely to buy toys for themselves.

- The average purchaser of sugar-free candy is a married woman with a household income of over $60,000.

■ **Most of all, affluent Americans love travel.**

● **Focus on the seasoned traveler.** Demographically, it is a very attractive market for fund raisers. While 80 percent of all leisure travel dollars are spent by those aged 35-plus, a select group of just 8 percent of Americans—or about 14 million adults—drives the market.

This upscale group has an average annual household income of $46,000—50 percent above the U.S. norm. They're well-educated, with 60 percent having attended college, again far above the national norm. They're a mature group with an average age of around 50. And the overwhelming majority are married.

The "typical" Seasoned Traveler spends about $2,500 a year on leisure travel versus an average of only $400 in travel spending for other people aged 35 and over. Representing slightly more than one-third of all leisure travels in their age bracket, their travels account for nearly 60 percent of foreign vacation trips taken by Americans each year and for more than 40 percent of all domestic vacation trips in the U.S.

● **Timeshare travelers are another good affluent sub-markets.** Over half of timeshare travelers have incomes of $50,000 or more, compared with less than 40 percent of other leisure travelers. The median age of timeshare owners is about 47, and 23 percent are retired. Forty-five percent of timeshare owner are college graduates, compared with 20 percent of the general population. Many timeshare owners are Northerners who fly South for the winter. Forty-four percent have children living at home. According to a report conducted by Los Angeles-based Plog Research, "timeshare vacations are particularly family-oriented."

To attract upscale travelers, use special events. But understand that, for seasoned travelers, travel is a lifestyle. They see themselves as adventurous (61 percent versus 42 percent of average leisure travelers), experimental (58% vs. 35%), and experienced (53% vs. 27%) when it comes to travel.

● **Use print media to reach them.** More so than typical leisure travelers, seasoned travelers use printed sources of information about travel compared to television programs or videos. They enjoy reading travel publications, and they are more apt than the average traveler to pay attention to the ads in these publications.

● **Pick an attractive trip location.** Generally, seasoned travelers like to visit new places (62% vs. 47%), experience new things (60% vs. 45%), and go to places they've heard or read about (48% vs. 33%). Yet, they also enjoy returning to their favorite places (52% vs. 36%). They look for a good reputation and expect quality of service. They are looking for the best buy from well-known hotels, motels, and inns, airlines, and car rental agencies. Time is a key consideration. They want their vacation to be hassle-free. A strong group leader is a must. Specifically,

● **Canada, Mexico, and Orlando, Florida are the top choices among those over 50.** They are interested in long vacations, a good deal (this may suggest an American orientation in the next few years), and world cruises.

● **Single women are on the move:** Fifty percent of the solo-adventure-traveler market is composed of single women (with an average age of 47); it is estimated that women make up two out of every five business travelers in the U.S.

● **To reach high income single young males, be physical.** Try a special event that offers a type of adventure vacation— such as mountain climbing, sky diving, and cave exploring. This is especially popular in the West, according to the Travel Industry Association of America.

● **Be aware that ethnic and racial demographics impact on who does what.** While white, non-Hispanic Americans tend to be married couples traveling together and have older heads of households traveling (46-year-olds), a Travel Industry Association study found that compared with all U.S. travelers:

African-Americans:
Are more likely to travel for conventions and seminars.
Are much more likely to travel on group tours.

Asian-Americans:
Were more likely to spend more money when traveling.
Tended to be younger travelers (the majority were ages 18–34).

Latinos:
Tended to drive more.
Were much more likely to include children in travel parties.

PUTTING IT ALL TOGETHER

How could you use information about the common travel interests of affluent individuals to find a group of upscale prospects, create an event that would enable them to learn more about your organization, and raise funds? Let's use "ABC" Organization as an example. ABC Organization is considering hosting a travel event. It fits in well with its general mission of education and international understanding.

■ **Decide on an event that attracts the right group of upscale individuals.** Looking at some of the key indicators for affluence, ABC's Director of Development is interested in creating a travel package which will appeal to the more mature, adventurous individual. Having done her research on which particular type of travel event is most likely to attract this audience of affluent Americans, ABC chooses a leisurely sailing cruise to a relatively unexplored spot in Mexico. The organization locates a cruise company that specializes in these types of vacations with an outstanding reputation and negotiates to receive one free trip per 10 participants and a modest commission on each purchase.

■ **Focus on the right prospect lists.** Remember, we're looking for prospects with both the right demographics *and* psychographics. ABC contacts *Sailing Quarterly,* a new video magazine from a Denver-based company. Subscriptions cost $100 a year—a clue that they are attracting affluents—and sailing scores very highly on the affluent index of hobbies. She learns that the magazine makes the names of its subscribers available for rent. ABC also bought lists of newcomers to our city for those neighborhoods with a high incidence of "empty nesters." And, our travel company has agreed to mail to its own highly-qualified prospect list.

■ **Create a focused marketing plan.** How, in this world of crowded messages, will we attract the interest of those we are interested in? We decide to host a preview party to introduce our cruise. It will be a social event in itself. While our ultimate goal is to raise money by getting sign-ups for the cruise, equally important is to create enough interest to get the "right" people to attend the preview event. Even if they don't go on the cruise, they have moved closer to our organization and this gives us future opportunities.

● **The invitation stands out from the clutter.** Knowing our target list enjoys—in fact pays for the privilege of—receiving its information on video, we decide to package our event's invitation in video format.

Although we're looking a mid-life audience, we've been sensitive to issues of packaging: many in our audience suffer from minor arthritis. We've made sure the envelope we are mailing in can be opened easily. The contents—a letter and the video—provide a clear explanation of what is being offered with plenty of details. The photographs and models used reflect our target audience. Although the more active mid-life segment is our priority, we've also sent press releases and placed announcements in the local senior newspaper and contacted the "Over Fifty" clubs in the churches and temples.

● **Holding the event.** The event is scheduled for late afternoon. Our active prospects who work will appreciate not having to leave work mid-day and the daytime positioning will also be appreciated by the more mature audience who dislikes driving at night. We've checked our logistics carefully. Parking is nearby; there are no physical barriers to entry and exit.

We're offering both decaffeinated and regular coffee along with cookies. We've made sure there are plenty of places to sit with small tables to place refreshments upon.

Our facilitator is, herself, mature. She speaks slowly and clearly. Her handouts are printed in 12 point type. Illustrations are appropriate, showing healthy, vibrant mature individuals engaging in active but realistic travel activities.

Congratulations! You've done everything you can to assure success in attracting your target group of affluent individuals. Have a wonderful travel event and use the good feelings generated to begin the job of converting your attendees into donors.

PART IV

FUND RAISING STRATEGIES THAT MAKE SENSE

> By redirecting your focus from the small base of wealthy to the broader base of affluent prospects, your organization will increase its success in fund raising.

To get affluent individuals to give, our development strategies will need to change to accommodate affluence rather than wealth. A decision to focus on affluent individuals will change the way you do your fund raising.

Affluents won't automatically make the significant gifts they are capable of giving and that your organization craves. Affluents can make the four- to six-figure annual gifts that will enable your organization to reach its fund raising goal but, according to Independent Sector, affluent Americans actually give a lower percentage of their incomes than less affluent individuals:

● those with incomes between $60,000 and $74,999 contributed 1.9 percent of their incomes.

● those with incomes of $75,000 and $99,999 contributed 1.7 percent.

You'll have to rethink your development strategy and concentrate on building an organization that is responsive to the demands of a more sophisticated broad base of donors.

■ **Chapter 18** reviews the underlying implications for raising more money. First proposed in my book *Targeted Fund Raising* (Precept Press), I have refined them for your use.

■ **Chapter 19** explains why we need to focus on renewing and upgrading. A committed affluent donor *cannot and will not* makes gifts of assets but *can and will* make five- and five-figure annual gifts, year after year, bringing his/her total gift giving well into thousands, even hundreds of thousands, of dollars.

■ **Chapter 20** recommends focusing on planned giving: American life expectancies are steadily increasing. Would you be willing to give away a major portion of your assets when you are in your sixties, knowing you'll be living into your eighties, nineties, or beyond?

CHAPTER EIGHTEEN

Raising More Money: Overall Assumptions

WHILE PINPOINTING AFFLU-ENCE IN THE 21st CENTURY is not intended to teach the broad skills necessary for running a strong development program*, it does make some overall assumptions based on how I view fund raising.

These overall assumptions form the foundation for a development strategy that focuses on raising increased shares of major donor dollars. They are:

● **Your fund raising must be logical**

● **Your fund raising cannot be adversarial**

● **Your fund raising will not be democratic**

IS YOUR DEVELOPMENT SHOP WORKING LOGICALLY?

The key to raising more money is to pair your best donor and prospects with your best fund raising methodologies, and continue matching—donor by donor/prospect by prospect— those

---

*A fuller description of the points made in this chapter can be found in *Targeted Fund Raising: Defining and Refining your Development Strategy* (Precept Press).

with lesser abilities with the less successful methods of fund raising.

If you have made the commitment to pair the best donors and prospects with the best fund raising methodologies, you must structure a development program that:

- Works from the center, out

- Works from the top, down

- Focuses on outputs, rather than inputs

■ **Are you working from the "center, out"?** Take advice from America's first fund raiser, Ben Franklin. He advised an eager colleague "to apply to all those whom you know will give something; next to those whom you are uncertain whether they will give anything or not, and show them the list of those who have given; and, lastly, do not neglect those who you are sure will give nothing, for in some of them you may be mistaken."

How do you plan your strategy from the center out? By consciously starting with those closest to your organization, committing the greatest share of your time, energy, and resources to those most likely to support you:

- Members of the Board

- Staff

- Current donors, volunteers, and members

- Past Donors

- Retired and past board, staff, volunteers, and members

**How well do your board, staff, and volunteers
support your organization?**

If your "family" does not contribute at a meaningful level at the start of each fiscal year, what
type of a signal are you sending out into the
community?

For this reason, I strongly recommend that *every*
fiscal year begins with a planned "family" campaign before you seek support elsewhere.

Commit 70 percent of time, energy and resources to acquiring, renewing, and upgrading this group. The remaining
30 percent of your development efforts should be concentrated
on expanding your base, moving from the more logical
prospects to those less likely to give.

■ **Are you working from the "top, down"?** How do you decide
who gets the most personalized approach? Of course, you can't
treat all prospects equally. How do you decide pragmatically
who belongs at the top?

A "quick and dirty" way is to simply run two lists of your
organization's supporters. The first identifies all donors to the
last complete fiscal year (and/or current year if you are far
enough into this) in descending order—largest single gift-giver
first and proceeding down to the smallest gift-giver last. The
second lists the cumulative giving histories of all donors, going
as far back as your records are accurate. Again, names appear in
descending order.

Or, you can use a more scientific approach. Ken Burnett, in
Relationship Fundraising, suggests awarding points according
to recency, frequency, and monetary value. You can vary the
points and values to suit your organization, as long as they are
always consistent within the organization.

An example:

- **Recency**

  - Award eight points to a donor who last donated within the last six months.

  - Award four points to a donor who last donated 6–12 months ago.

  - Award two points to a donor who last donated 12–24 months ago.

  - Award one point to a donor who last donated more than two years ago.

- **Frequency**

  - Take the number of donations and multiply by four points.

- **Value**

  - Award one point for every $50 value to a maximum of 40 points.

■ **Are you focusing on outputs rather than inputs?** What percentage of gift "sales" actually close in your organization?

Good intentions don't count: you need to have a plan and a goal. Set a specific target date/amount with your volunteers and staff such as "each of us will aim for four acceptances at $1,000 or greater by (date)."

Keep the "span of control" tight: don't load your volunteers and staff with more prospects than they can move along. Three to five names is a logical number. As volunteers and staff report back to you with results—an appointment set, delays because of scheduling, a turn-down, a gift made—you can add additional prospects.

Be results-focused: It really doesn't matter how many names are in your prospect pool, what matters is how many of them convert to being donors at the gift level(s) you've identified as logical.

IS YOUR FUND RAISING IS BASED ON ADVOCACY RATHER THAN ADVERSARIAL RELATIONSHIPS?

Few people are saints. Most of us won't give up food, shelter, clothing, and health care in order to make a gift. The "pocket" we pick for charitable giving contains what's left: the same one we use for recreational and entertainment decisions.

The good news is that, over the years, the costs for necessities of life have dropped in absolute dollars. Those making over $50,000 have approximately 12 percent of this to spend from this disposable income pocket.

People choose to spend on your organization. You must:

- Identify those with interest

- Have access to them

- Work to build ongoing relationships

- Separate desire from fulfillment

■ **People must have interest.** Generous givers have a distinct "charitable" profile. According to Independent Sector's *Giving and Volunteering Survey,* there are distinct differences between generous contributions (3 percent or more of household incomes) and non-contributors. Generally speaking, the characteristics that distinguished generous givers are:

- Positive experiences when young: They were members of youth groups, volunteers, members of student governments, and/or had seen personally adults they admired helping others or were personally helped.

- Active religious involvement and religious or spiritual commitments.

- Positive attitudes about charitable organizations.

- Positive reasons for giving and volunteering.

- Positive attitudes about themselves and others.

■ **You must have access.** No matter how wealthy an individual is, s/he is not a prospect if you can't reach him/her! Possibly, s/he is a suspect and, in time, you might be able to find a starting point—a common area of interest to explore.

Providing access is a primary role for all members of the "family." On a regular basis, it's important to review both prospects and suspects to see if anyone in the organization can "open the door." Don't limit this function to the board—sometimes it is a program staff member or a volunteer who can provide the initial contact.

Access allows you to build on general interest and differentiates your organization from all the others working in the same field. Without access, you can rarely build a relationship.

■ **Work to build ongoing relationships.** We cannot force people to make gifts. Have you ever actually heard of a fund raiser using a knife or a gun to get a gift? Of course not! Yet many of us continue to think—and, in turn, to teach our volunteers— that we will have to "pull" contributions from unwilling individuals.

The difference between advocacy and adversarial fund raising is always shown by its results. When we build relationships, allowing for interest to grow and flourish into commitment, we can ask for—and get—meaningful gifts. When we beg, we receive the smallest amounts people think they can "get away with."

Advocacy fund raising takes more time than adversarial fund raising. Often, trust builds slowly. You may receive a modest, test gift from a new donor who waits to see how you handle it before making a greater commitment. Too often, the donor is disappointed: the organization appears to dismiss the prospect and doesn't keep in touch. The donor, in turn, decides s/he is not needed or appreciated.

■ **Don't confuse desire with fulfillment.** Most individuals want to be philanthropists. They just don't know how. Work with your prospects to identify what projects interest them. Show them what can be accomplished with varying support figures.

● **Help them to reach larger goals through pledging.** Get lower-level affluents to think big: invite your prospects to make their gifts by pledging a comfortable gift quarterly over a year or more. Remember a gift of $250 quarterly for a year is $1,000. For 10 years, it's $10,000.

● **Ask for upgrades.** Money loses value over time. Your $1,000+ donor needs to be encouraged to grow to $1,250. An annual upgrade of 10–20 percent is reasonable. Ask donors to consider upgrades as part of the annual renewal strategy.

● **Rethink your definitions of major giving and major donors.** A donor who gives—even modestly—year after year is likely to give your organization significant dollars. And, s/he is your best prospect for a bequest gift.

● **Make it easy for your donors to give again and again.** Be sure to offer a variety of methodologies for making gift giving easy—accept not only checks, but credit cards and electronic fund transfers.

MY OWN TRUE STORY

My family decided it wanted to be of help to relief efforts in Africa and the Middle East. We made four small gifts to organizations which sent us direct mail solicitations.

- Two organizations took more than a month to say thank you. We felt unappreciated and decided not to give again.

- One organization said thank you immediately but focused on getting an additional gift. We felt appreciated but pressured.

- One organization said thank you, provided additional information, and told us we were important. We felt appreciated and receptive to their next appeal.

In fact, over just three months, the last organization moved us from a one-time gift to a monthly, automatic payment pledge. Although the monthly amounts are still modest, our cumulative giving is not. *We gave nearly $2,000 over 10 years and are still giving.*

We consider ourselves philanthropists, not donors!

Do You Accept That Fund Raising Is Not Democratic?

Your development shop cannot do everything. The decision to raise more money is best accomplished through a more focused strategy concentrating on major donors. That, in turn, requires more commitment from staff and volunteers. It will take more training, more time, and more effort. *However, it does not take more money.* In fact, fund raising costs compared to income received (rate of return) will decrease.

You may not be able to continue a "buck shot" approach to fund raising, with equal staffing in all areas. Rather, you may choose to eliminate or scale back on less effective methodologies and put your energies into doing a better job with a smaller, more rationally chosen audience.

The overall assumptions discussed in this chapter are the building blocks of a strong development strategy. Understanding them and communicating them to staff and volunteer fundraisers is an important first step. Commit to them now as they form the strong foundation on which rests your ability to raise more money. Once your formal and informal gatekeepers have accepted them, you're ready to move on to the next chapters where we'll focus on specific strategies that make sense with affluent donors and prospects.

CHAPTER NINETEEN

Focusing on Renewal and Upgrading vs. Acquisition

A SHIFT IN EMPHASIS from *conquest marketing* with the focus on new customers to *relationship or aftermarketing* is the single most important concept for fundraising in a new century.

Repeat business is the secret to success. Sam Walton, founder of WalMart, America's most successful retail chain, understood the importance of customer loyalty. Walton asserted "That's where the real profit lies, not in trying to drag strangers into your store for a one-time purchase based on splashy sales or expensive advertising."

Having an ongoing relationship with your donors means working smarter, not harder. It follows the *80/20 rule of marketing* which suggests that 80 percent of a company's business probably comes from 20 percent of its customers and that, often, that 80 percent comes from repeat purchases by the 20 percent.

Indeed, common sense would indicate the wisdom in this. A truism is that a satisfied customer will send five people your way, while a disgruntled customer can be counted on to bad-mouth you to 20 prospects. Given this, it's safe to say that alienating donors or prospects is a risk you can't afford to take!

THE DEMOGRAPHIC EXPLANATION FOR A SHIFT FROM FOCUSING ON ACQUISITIONS TO A RENEWAL STRATEGY

Our population's growth is due to the length of life is increasing dramatically even as numbers of "new" adults are decreasing.

■ **The Census Bureau projects the U.S. population will grow from 272 million in 1999 to 286 million in 2005.*** Those consumers are generally going to be older, as the still-dominant Baby Boom continues to move into middle age. Today, 35.5 is the estimated median age of Americans. By 2005, the median age will be more than a year older, at 36.6. The 40- to 44-year-old group will become the largest, with 22.4 million; surpassing the 35–39-year-old population; 45- to 49-year-olds will become the next-largest group. In another age shift, 20- to 24-year-olds will also grow to outnumber 35- to 39-year-olds.

■ **The population pyramid is inverting:** In the 1970s and 1980s there were always more and more new prospects as the Baby Boomers reached adulthood. But from the mid-1990s and beyond, we've been dealing with the same prospects, over and over again.

---

*The recently released Census 2000 figures reveal a total population of over 281 million, suggesting that the estimate of 286 million in 2005 may be conservative.

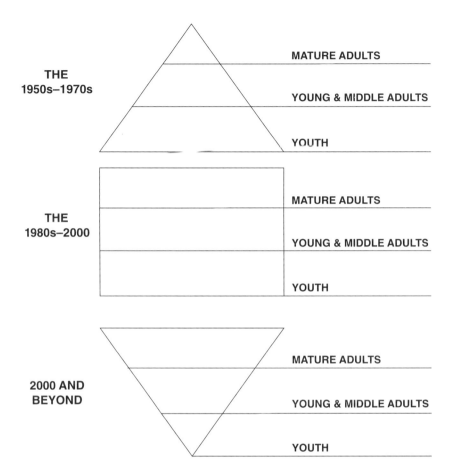

● **During the 1950s through the 1970s, we had a large number of children and teenagers,** a middling number of young through 40s adults, and a very small grouping of mature adults and the elderly, forming the traditional population pyramid.

● **In the 1980s through 2000, the pyramid's base of Baby Boomers moved into their adult years.** In 1986, the first of the Baby Boomers turned forty, clustering in the middle of the pyramid and "bulging" it into a rectangle.

● **Because people can only get older, as we move into the twenty-first century, our rectangle becomes top-heavy with**

older individuals. By 2030, the median age of our population will be past 40 with more than a third of the population over age 50. As today's massive boomer cohort of 81 million (76 million by birth and additional millions through immigration) passes from middle age to "the third age," the population pyramid inverts.

Why the American population is "bulging" in the middle

Between 1992 and the year 2000:

- Births—reflecting the tail end of the Baby Boomlet—declined slightly from 4 to 3.9 million annually through 2000.

- The Baby Boomlet—moving into the teen years—reversed the decline in this age category (Baby Busters) seen between 1980 and 1994.

- Baby Busters—The pool of 25–34-year-olds decreased by 5.5 million.

- Late Boomers—The pool of 35–44-year-olds increased by 5.4 million.

- Early Boomers—The age grouping of 45–54-year-olds-today's 35–44 year old Baby Boomers—showed the largest increase from 25.7 million to 37.1 million by the turn of the century.

- World War II Babies—The age grouping of 55 to 64 year olds grew from 21 to 24 million.

- Depression Year Babies—Those 65 and over rose from 32 to 35 million.

Population Projections of the United States, by Age, Sex, Race, and Hispanic Origin: 1992 to 2050

■ **The fastest growing age group is the oldest one.** Life expectancy in the USA in 1900 was 47 years. Today, it's 76.

● **The United States has more than 4.1 million people aged 85 and over.** That puts 1.5 percent of the population in the group aged 85 and over. By the time the Baby Boomers in the United States reach their early 80s (about 2030), the population in that age group will have swollen respectively, to 7.5 million. This will be just the beginning as the Baby Boomers in the United States enters the pipeline of the oldest old.

● **Today there are an estimated 66,000 centenarians. A Census Bureau study predicts their numbers will increase more than twelve-fold by 2050, to 834,000.** Among those who already have made it to 100, women outnumber men 5 to 1. Seventy-eight percent are white, 13 percent black, 6 percent Hispanic, and 3 percent Asian.

● **Life-spans of 120 years and longer may become common by the middle of the twenty-first century.** With a few more medical breakthroughs, some people alive today may live for centuries. Most people entering "old age" in the years ahead will be more healthy, more fit, and more energetic than any previous generation, thanks to biotechnology. Older people are not only the fastest-growing demographic group in developed countries, but will also become the future's wealthiest group. They will have had more years to accumulate wealth through investments, and they will have paid off their mortgages, thus lowering their housing costs and increasing their disposable incomes.

● **Boomers expect to live and work longer.** Within the next 35 years, "people are going to be turning 100 and feeling like they are at 55 today," according to Ronald Klatz, president of the American Academy of Anti-Aging Medicine in Chicago. "Retirement as we know it today will cease to exist," says Roger Herman, a business futurist.

Less than 40 years from now, when middle-aging Baby Boomers join the ranks of the elderly, the old will outnumber the young. There will be more competition for a smaller pool of young adult prospects. If you don't work hard now to retain your best donors, you may not be able to replace them with new ones.

How Can You Keep Your Donors?

Question: If your organization has a donor base of 10,000, what happens if your *renewal rate* is 60 percent?

Answer: You can only count on 6,000 donors in the next year. You must replace 4,000 donors just to stay stable.

If the renewal rate is increased to 70 percent, you'll retain another 1,000 donors.

If the renewal rate drops to 50 percent, you'll have lost half of your base of support.

● **Unfortunately, too many not-for-profits are treating their donors as if they are easily replaceable.** Understanding that successful relationship or aftermarketing requires a carefully thought-out and ongoing strategy, where should you begin?

PUTTING THE DONOR FIRST

- A donor is the most important person ever—in person, by telephone, by mail

- A donor is not dependent on us; we are dependent on him/her.

- A donor is not an interruption of our work; s/he is the purpose of it.

- We are not doing a favor by serving our donor; s/he is doing us a favor by giving us the opportunity to do so.

- No one ever won an argument with a donor.

- A donor is a person who brings us his/her wants. It is our job to handle them satisfactorily.

Adapted from L.L. Bean Company's Credo

■ **Commit your organization to donor service.** To increase your renewals and upgrading, you must be willing to do the following:

● Recognize that service to donors is a profit strategy.

● Commit the necessary resources to make donor service work.

● Understand that donor service requires a total systems approach.

■ **The strongest tool you have is your database.** But, if you are not coding information about those on it so as to capture relationships and interests along with transaction histories, you're

throwing away powerful clues to your prospects' likely donation triggers. According to Ken Burnett, author of *Relationship
Fundraising,* to keep proper records of your donors you need to
do six things:

1. Choose an adequate system with multiple fields of information.

2. Input data carefully.

3. Undertake continual, thorough cleaning.

4. Update your records continuously with all donor trans-
   actions.

5. Regularly add any new information gleaned from cor-
   respondence, mailing returns, research, the telephone,
   or other sources.

6. Use your data conscientiously and responsibly.

In addition to being able to store demographic information, you'll want to be able to segment your donors by gift histories: marked by recently of last gift, frequency of giving,
monetary value of gifts over life, and last gift amount.

You'll want to be able to segment them by how "close" to
your organization they are. Determine which of the following
categories best describe your *current donors:*

● **Advocate donors:** repeat donors who actively promote
your organization to others, often serving as volunteers and
board members.

● **Client donors:** repeat donors who demonstrate loyalty to
your organization by consistently "purchasing" a variety of
charitable packages (from memorial giving to attending special
events as well as a gift to a crisis appeal).

● **Repeat donors:** a donor who has made gifts in two con-
secutive fiscal years.

● **Trial donors:** making their first gift to your organization.

● **Returning donors:** making a second gift after a hiatus of a year or more.
   In addition, you have:

● **Lapsed donors:** non-responsive for two or more years.

● **Prospects:** non-donors with a rational reason for being on your data base.

● **Suspects:** non-donors you don't know why you're retaining on the data base.

■ **The creative use of your database is the key to building relationships.** Creating donor loyalty should be your priority. Once you've located an affluent donor, you don't want to lose him/her. Don't let your donors go without a fight. Use your data base information effectively. Every fund raiser needs to become a "computer wizard." According to Eugene Schwartz, respected direct mail author and consultant, "unless you know how to use your own computer without relying on someone else, you're helpless—and will ultimately be left behind."

BUILDING DONOR LOYALTY

There are two basic factors in creating donor loyalty—both requiring effective, two-way communication:

- Donor satisfaction with the way you respond to their gifts

- Donor satisfaction with your organization

■ **Create donor satisfaction with the way you respond to their gifts.** Terry Varva, in *Aftermarketing: How to Keep Customers For Life Through Relationship Marketing*, reminds us that "from the customer's perspective, a purchase is most likely viewed as initiating a relationship. The customer feels considerable desire or need for a continued interaction with the selling organization."

SUCCESSFUL AFTERMARKETING

Shows donors that your organization:

- appreciates their patronage

- wants to maximize their satisfaction

- cares about their concerns

- is interested in their suggestions and input

- wants their repeat gifts

Adapted from Terry Varva, *Aftermarketing*

● **Demonstrate to donors that your organization truly appreciates their support.** The largest share of customer (and donor) attrition is actually a cost of doing business poorly. Out of every 100 individuals who stop supporting you, only 4 move away or die:

- Fifteen have made a decision that another organization can serve them better.

- Fifteen are unhappy with your organization (and are telling others that).

- Sixty-six think you don't care about them.

● **Bond with your donors: Staying in touch is the single best means for creating donor loyalty.** Work diligently to increase trust and interaction by moving your donors from "awareness" to "identity"—establishing a sense of relationship and community. Your goal: to create a willingness to be an "advocate." These describe the different levels of trust and interaction in your relationship with your donors.

●   **Focus on high renewal percentages rather than maximum profit.** Effective customer-retention programs often result in a 25 to 100 percent boost in profits. The average U.S. company loses 10 to 30 percent of its customers each year—because of poor customer service. And, it takes five times as much work to find a new customer or donor as it does to renew an existing one.

●   **Thank donors properly.**

> "It leaves a lasting positive impression of you and your organization. If you don't acknowledge a gift, no matter how small, it may prevent you from obtaining a renewed contribution. Once again, it's a matter of customer satisfaction."
>
> Philanthropist, Stanley Marcus—Honorary Chairman of the Board, Neiman-Marcus

●   **Call even before the thank you letter goes out.** No, you can't do this for everyone, but certainly make it a rule for those giving gifts of $1,000 and more or $500 and more or $100 and more—whatever level makes sense for your organization.

●   **Send out your acknowledgment letters promptly.** Make it a priority in your organization to respond within 48 hours. Let your donors know you consider their gifts important.

●   **Send out your acknowledgment letters to all donors, regardless of the size of the gift.** Many donors—especially women—test organizations to see how they respond. Why should a small donor give a second, larger gift if s/he doesn't hear back from you?

● **Treat your donors as individuals.** Indicate in your acknowledgment letters you know if they are new donors, ongoing supporters, renewing after an absence, upgrading their gifts, etc.

● **Demonstrate your donors' importance by getting names right.** Check the spelling on unusual names, verify marital status, and the use of titles. You should make a conscious decision about using first name salutations versus employing a more formal mode of address.

October is Customer Appreciation Month.

This is an ideal opportunity to acknowledge the overriding importance of your donors, volunteers, and staff.

■ **Thank them often and well.**

● **Install a new donor welcome program.** Put some effort into identifying what your new donor will appreciate receiving: in addition to the thank you letter, you might include a "hotline" phone number for any questions, a short fact sheet that summarizes your organization, and a case example of what gifts accomplish.

● **Keep track of the milestones in their donor histories.** Use your computer system to identify five-, ten-, and fifteen-year givers as well as cumulative giving of $500, $1,000, or more. Make a fuss about these special donors. Send a special certificate of appreciation to those reaching milestones or at certain giving levels. Mention milestones regularly in your newsletter.

● **Send a personal note.** Sixty-eight percent of Americans indicate they would like to receive more handwritten letters.

There are eight special times to show appreciation:

- For the good, solid, steady, no-complaints, no-noise donor.

- For the donor who has done you the favor of complaining.

- For the new donor who has just made a second donation.

- For a donor who has thanked you.

- For a donor who's had a tough time.

- When going out of your way will prevent a donor from having a problem.

- For a good donor who has the potential for bringing you new donors or increasing his/her giving.

- To make employees and volunteers feel good about serving.

SOURCE: *Managing Knock Your Socks Off Service*, Chip Bell and Ron Zemike

● **Demonstrate their importance to everyone.** Announce their visits over the loudspeaker or by having a welcoming bulletin board at the front desk displaying their names.

● **Provide them with a contact person and a "private" telephone number for their use.**

● **Publish a newsletter or magazine just for donors.**

● **Give them a premium of appreciation.** For example, a t-shirt announcing to the world that they are "five-year" donors or decals to display on their cars showing they're a "VIP" to your charity.

■ **Increase donor satisfaction with your organization.** Demonstrate the qualities affluents value. According to *Town & Country* magazine, these include:

- Disdain for the mediocre.

- Regard for education.

- Elevated levels of taste.

- An emphasis on "good name"—honesty.

- Respect for character, integrity.

● **Add to this, pragmatism.** Affluents look for what works. They are less "big government" in their view, but want the homeless housed and the environment improved, and they want the federal government to do it. They are fairly liberal on many social issues—abortion, homosexuality, for example—but are fairly conservative on economic issues.

● **Market philanthropic giving as if it were a product.** According to Eric Miller, author of *The Lifestyle Odyssey* and former publisher of *Research Alert:* "Affluents demand quality and want to see a return—experiential or otherwise—on their investment. As any product marketer does, a philanthropic marketer should make explicit the benefits of buying his product, i.e. making a donation. Affluents are well-informed, educated people; they want to know that their donation is going to make a solid, concrete difference. Show how the organization will use their gift. Provide them with a breakdown of everything their donation will make possible. Pragmatism and quality are the attributes that affluents desire in their purchases; make sure they are aware that their giving will produce a definite result."

● **Involve your donors.** Ask them to tell you why they give. Put their comments in the newsletter for everyone to see. Send them a survey, asking for their comments and concerns, and use the answers you get to improve your organization. Clip out an article of interest and send it with a note. Invite them to be part of a focus group. Share the results with them.

● **Encourage them to volunteer.** Donors who volunteer give more. If they're not volunteers, find out why. Is timing a problem? The need for child care? Safety issues? Have you clearly articulated what volunteers do?

ALWAYS REMEMBER,
A DONOR IS NOT A TRUE DONOR UNTIL
S/HE MAKES A SECOND GIFT.

In the twenty-first century, our goal must be to keep donors connected because:

• Acquisition fund raising is going to be more competitive and less productive.

• A committed affluent donor can continue to give, year after year, bringing the total gift giving well into the thousands, even hundreds of thousands of dollars.

CHAPTER TWENTY

Focusing on Planned Giving Rather than Current Gifts

*A*MERICANS ARE ACQUIRING *ASSETS IN RECORD AMOUNTS.* The Federal Reserve reported that the typical American family's net worth rose to $71,600 in 1998, up from a net worth of $46,400.

WHO'S GOT THE ASSETS?

Percentage of all families whose net worth falls into each category in 1995 dollars

Net worth	1992	1995
Less than $10,000	27.0%	25.8%
$10,000–$24,999	10.4%	10.0%
$25,000–$49,999	11.4%	11.6%
$1000,000–$249,999	20.7%	21.3%
$250,000 and more	15.2%	14.4%
Median family		
Net worth	$52,800	$46,400

SOURCE: Federal Reserve 1997

The gains appeared to be concentrated on wealthy families and affluent self-employed people. From 1995 through 1998, families with annual incomes above $100,000 showed basically no change in their sizable median net worth, which stood at $510,800 in 1998, compared to $511,400 in 1995. However, this group's average net worth—a calculation that captures the huge gains made by the wealthiest Americans—rose 22.4 percent to $1.73 million, up from an average net worth of $1.41 million in 1995.

● **In 1996, an estimated 4.8 million American households had a net worth of at least $1 million, up 118 percent from 1992.** More than one in four affluent households owns securities valued at $100,000 or more. The average household portfolio is worth $184,400. As a group, the affluent in the U.S. hold $2.1 trillion in stocks, bonds, mutual funds, and other securities.

● **For all but the wealthiest of Americans, economic status has been mainly the result of employment.** But that picture is beginning to shift. Salaries and wages increased just 5.5 percent in 1996. By comparison, capital gains shot up 47.8 percent. Taxable pension grew 8 percent and taxable interest increased 7 percent.

● **The big story is the rise of stock options and performance-based bonuses.** Dot-coms have set off a domino effect across corporate America. Eager to hold on to their brightest employees, even companies like General Electric and Honeywell are issuing "performance units." These are non-tradable "shares" designed to reflect the growth in corporate divisions, departments, or even product development teams. Like shares of stock, they have set vesting periods and appreciate in value over time.

Changing Financial Concerns

It takes about 15 years for our perceptions to catch up with reality, Americans are just beginning to understand that the majority of us are living well into our 80s and 90s, rather than the "three score and ten" we were told we would need to plan for.

● **The numbers of persons over 50 will skyrocket.** The 76 million Americans born between 1946 and 1964 will push the number of 50- to 64-year-olds from 33 million today to a peak of 59 million in 2020 with the first of the "Baby Boomers" hitting traditional retirement age around 2011.

● **In 1960, only one American in 10 was aged 65 or older.** Today, that ratio is about one in eight, and it could reach one in six within 30 years. Americans aged 85 and older have increased from 940,000 in 1960 to 3.1 million today and will reach 5.4 million in 2020.

● **Of all the people who have lived to age 65 in the history of the world, more than half are alive now.** The general U.S. elderly population grow 89 percent compared with the total population growth of 39 percent. People age 85 and over have increased 232 percent since 1960. The latest census figures show that 57,000 Americans have reached 100—a growth of 77 percent from the 1980s. And, projections through 2050 suggest nearly *one million Americans* will live past the century mark within 50 years!

● **The number of Americans who celebrate 100 years is dramatically increasing.** There were less than 37,000 individuals who could claim that distinction prior to 1990. But, by 2050, more than 834,000 Americans will have passed the century mark!

Right now, two-thirds of Americans are satisfied with their financial situation. According to the *1999 Money/Lincoln Financial Americans and Their Money* survey, four out of five Americans expect their standard of living to rise. Twenty-eight percent of households with $50,000-plus incomes anticipate saving between $10,000 and $19,999 this year. Seventy-nine percent of Americans with household incomes over $50,000 say they are saving for retirement.

But, as more of us live longer, our concerns will grow around two areas:

- How will I fund my retirement?

- How will I cover end-of-life medical expenses?

A comfortable retirement is uppermost in the minds of wealthy Americans.

That's what the Spectrem Group financial services consulting firm found in a survey of nearly 1,900 affluent households. Maintaining their current standard of living followed closely on the list of concerns about protecting their estates from taxes.

By the end of 1996, for the first time, retirement and pension plans offset regular savings accounts as the place most Americans regard as best for their money. The number of Americans participating is up 8 points since 1995 to 38 percent. One in three $75,000+ households puts away $500 or more monthly, with 63 percent indicating they invest in retirement and pension plans.

By understanding what is happening in our society, your organization's planned giving program can serve as a resource to its constituents.

● **Generally, money worries are up.** More than three out of five Americans (63%) told *Money* magazine they are concerned about and dissatisfied with their current financial situation. A bare majority (53%) think their children will be able to live better than they have themselves.

Twenty-eight percent of those with household incomes of $50,000-plus believe they would need $5 million or more to feel rich. When the same question was asked in 1984, 28 percent of the respondents thought they needed only $100,000 or more to feel rich.

The findings of a national survey, sponsored by the Visa Gold Card and conducted by the Gallup Organization, suggest that a preoccupation with saving money is a priority of many. More than half (53%) of those contacted reported being more concerned with saving for their future. This was primarily evident among female respondents and those with a college education. When asked to explain why saving is a greater priority today than it was in the late 1980s, the largest portion of respondents (32%) stated it was because they were getting older and approaching retirement.

● **Public concerns about retirement are increasing.** Retirement isn't what it used to be. Economic and demographic changes are forcing pre-retirees and young retirees to reevaluate how they're going to fund "the golden years": "A few years ago planning to live to age 90 seemed to be stretching it a bit," says Philadelphia financial planner Lydia Sheckels. "Now I suggest that my clients watch the Today show every morning when Willard Scott is sending birthday greetings to the 100-year-olds."

Having enough money for retirement is the second biggest financial fear among Americans today, after rising medical costs. Just 54 percent expect to be financially comfortable in retirement. A Merrill Lynch survey of adults ages 45 to 64 has shown that 45 percent of the respondents say they are afraid they will outlive their money and a whopping 69 percent see a risk of being overwhelmed by health care costs. Affluent adults of all ages and both sexes worry about the longevity of their assets. Forty-seven percent of women and 33 percent of men in households with annual incomes greater than $50,000 are "very" or "somewhat" concerned that they will outlive their retirement savings, according to the International Association for Financial Planning in Atlanta, Georgia.

Providing for a comfortable retirement is the most commonly cited long-term financial goal in the planners' survey, and it is cited more often by higher-income households (35%) than by the general public (24%). And, droves of Boomers and Gen Xers are dreaming of an early retirement. But, what we mean by retiring before 60 has changed. Many expect to continue working at a low-stress job or increase their volunteer work.

Age	% Hopeful of Retiring Before Age 60	% Hopeful of Retiring 61–64
Pre-retirees (55 and older)	19%	19%
Older Boomers (47–54)	36%	10%
Younger Boomers (36–46)	31%	9%
Generation X (35 and younger)	46%	6%

SOURCE: 2000 Retirement Confidence Survey sponsored by the Employee Benefit Research Institute (EBRI), the American Savings Education Council and Greenwald & Associates.

As Boomers march reluctantly but relentlessly towards retirement, they face some challenging questions. By the year 2030, the Baby Boom generation, which currently accounts for a third of the U.S. population, will be our senior citizens.

- Who will foot the bill when the large numbers of retired Boomers line up to collect their share of the already dwindling Social Security pot?

- Who will continue to pay up during the 15 to 20 years the average Baby Boomer will be in retirement?

● **Nearly 90 percent of Boomers are concerned about retirement, according to a Gallup poll.** Because many Boomers have had children later in life, what might have been several middle years of accumulation of retirement resources is now a time when the 19-year-old child of 55-year-old parents is starting college. Many Boomers will not be able to save enough money on their own for a comfortable retirement.

Percent of Boomers who:

• Plan to work at least part-time during their
  retirement years   80%

• Are very, or fairly, optimistic about their
  retirement years   69%

• Have given a lot, or some, thought to their
  retirement years   72%

• Expect to move to a new geographic area
  when retired   21%

• Expect they will have to scale back on
  lifestyle when retired   35%

• Expect to devote more time in retirement to
  community service and volunteer activities   49%

• Do not want to depend on children during
  retirement   9%

• Think you should be able to depend on
  family financially   68%

• Think they can count on self-directed
  sources of income such as IRAs and 401(k)s   68%

• Think they can count on Social Security for
  retirement income   48%

• Believe their generation will live longer
  than their parents' generation   67%

• Believe their generation will be healthier
  than their parents' generation   56%

SOURCE: AARP study, *Baby Boomers Envision Their Retirement,* February 1999

● **Boomers are redefining retirement.** With the door to retirement no longer light years away from America's "youth" generation, Baby Boomers will take on their new roles with enthusiasm. Jeff Ostroff, author of *Successful Marketing to the 50+ Consumer,* believes that when retirement comes Boomers will address their retirement concerns aggressively: "They'll know, for example, that retirement could last 30 years or more and that a long-term illness could wipe out all their savings. Tomorrow's prime-lifers will be unlikely to rest comfortably at night knowing they can depend on Social Security or Medicare in their later years. Tax increases, benefit cuts or freezes, and a growing imbalance between the generation of workers to retirees may all fuel these doubts."

Gen Xers are taking a proactive approach to their futures. A study by *Money* magazine reveals that 41 percent of people under age 35 worry about whether they will have enough money for retirement. People in their 20s save as much or better than people in their 30s or 40s, often maxing out the 401(k), putting together portfolios, and keeping debt low.

BEQUEST AND PLANNED GIVING ARE
GREAT OPPORTUNITIES FOR FUND RAISERS

Giving away assets during life rather than at death is foolish. As Americans understand their own increasing longevity and the financial implications, "ultimate" gifts—sacrifice gifts of assets during one's lifetime—will be made reluctantly, at best.

> Would *you* be willing to make a major gift in your sixties or seventies, knowing you have another twenty, thirty, or more years of living?

By focusing on bequests and planned gifts, many organizations will actually bring in more money from a broader base of supporters than they can through a focus on current gifts! The reasons—in addition to a growth in wealth many times greater than previously anticipated—include:

1. Material resources available for charitable giving are large and growing larger than previously appreciated.
2. Both the reality and self-perception of financial security are more widespread than ever.
3. The economic and emotional incentives to devote financial resources to charitable purposes increasingly shape the moral sentiments of wealth holders.
4. There is a new values-based approach to financial planning that is increasing the commitment of wealth holders to charitable giving by guiding them through a planning methodology in which they discern for themselves:
   a) their material potential for charitable giving
   b) the people and causes for which they care
   c) the combination of financial, family, and philanthropic strategies best suited to implement their objectives

> *Americans could have given an additional $250 billion to charity last year—without decreasing their net worth—by using gift-planning techniques* according to The Newtithing Group, a San Francisco-based nonprofit organization that promotes philanthropy.

The potential is enormous: Only 48 percent of Americans have wills, according to a 1996 American Express survey. Even more startling given that the vast majority of Americans are charitable in nature, only six percent of Americans say they have bequests to charities in their wills. Even among the wealthiest, those who in 1990 left estates of over $600,000, 8 out of 10 estates made no charitable bequests at all.

● **Only 17.4 percent of Americans whose estates were large enough to file an estate-tax return in 1998 made charitable bequests,** according to the Internal Revenue Service. Wealthy people whose estates are large enough to be subject to estate taxes leave only a fraction of their assets to charity. According to estate-tax returns filed in 1998, 6.2 percent of total estate value was distributed in the form of charitable bequests, compared with 8.8 percent for 1997 and 6.3 percent for 1989.

● **A major need appears to be education.** The majority of Americans do not understand either the need for a will nor the role that planned charitable giving can play in reducing estate taxes and passing wealth along to surviving generations.

As development officers we are beginning to do a better job: according to *The Chronicle of Philanthropy,* two-thirds of all existing bequests have been established since 1990. In addition, Americans reported to the IRS that they held more than 82,000 charitable remainder trusts in 1997, with a total fair market value of $60.5 billion. Adding in unitrusts, charitable lead trusts, and pooled income funds, assets in the four main types of planned gifts totaled $72.6 billion.

As family structure changes, there is increased potential for charitable bequests outside the family. The probability of making bequests outside the traditional family increased from 19 percent to 29 percent between 1983 and 1991. Today,

● **Only one household in four consists of a married couple with dependent children.** Baby-Boomer lifestyles, including divorce, remarriage, voluntary childlessness, and lack of commitment, have decreased a need to leave the money in the family.

● **Psychographically, an increasing number of Americans are "distancers."** Currently, they are 11 percent of those using financial planning. Demographically speaking, Distancers are unique because they tend to be divorced or remarried. They are involved in groups that become meaningful to them. Distancers are more involved in community affairs and organizations.

Older distancers living in retirement communities are 35 percent more likely to make bequests outside the family. Distancers leave adequate bequests to children, but they also make bequests that reflect their involvement in political, religious, or cultural institutions.

Recognize that persons of all ages make charitable bequests. Appropriately market your bequest program to different ages. Don't limit planned giving strategies to the "traditional" older prospect—over age 64, married or widowed, and wealthy. Today, there are numerous pockets of opportunity for the savvy development officer to consider.

The Internal Revenue Service analyzes estates for charitable bequests. In one year (1995) it found that in wills containing charitable bequests:

- 22 percent were established by people over 70 years old.

- 20 percent were created by people between 60 and 69.

- 30 percent came from people between 45 and 59.

- 28 percent were set up by those under 45.

Women have different charitable interests than do men and their charitable bequests support this. The Internal Revenue Service's analysis of returns for deceased individuals revealed the following:

Charitable Bequests: Where Men and Women Give Their Estate Assets		
	Female	Male
Arts and humanities	4.1%	1.3%
Religious	12.4%	6.8%
Private foundations	23.2%	38.5%
Social welfare	1.0%	0.4%
Educational, medical, or scientific	31.9%	31.3%
Other	27.4%	31.3%

Understanding The Asset Pool

The heady real estate market of the 1970s and early 1980s has made many older Americans and early Baby Boomers "home rich." Home equity constitute the largest share of net worth: 43 percent.

● **The majority of homeowners over 62 own their houses debt-free.** From 1970 to 1988, the median price of an existing U.S. single-family home rose from $23,000 to $89,300—faster by more than a third than median household income. Today's median home price stands well over $92,000.

● **Most of those who live alone own their homes free and clear.** Of the 13.5 million women and 8.9 million men living alone, the majority of women own their homes (53 percent, or 7.1 million). Thirty-eight percent, or 3.4 million, men do as well. Seventy-seven percent (5 million) of lone women and 55 percent of men (1 million) who own their homes don't have mortgages on their properties.

● **Baby Boomers will be receiving large chunks—69 percent—of their inheritance through real estate.** But few Boomers will be planning to move into their parent's homes. The majority of these homes will be paid off completely: charities should work with Boomers *now* to discuss transferring these assets into trusts—especially in the high-priced housing markets of New York, San Francisco, Los Angeles, Aspen, and Honolulu.

Top Counties or County Equivalents
ranked by median value of owner-occupied dwelling units

Rank	County	PMSA/MSA	Median Value of owner-occupied dwelling units
1	New York Cty, NY	New York PSMA	$486,842
2	Pitkin Cty, CO		$451,968
3	Marin County, CA	San Francisco PSMA	$354,150
4	San Mateo Cty, CA	San Francisco PSMA	$343,938
5	San Francisco Cty, CA	San Francisco PSMA	$298,866
6	Santa Clara Cty, CA	San Jose PMSA	$289,430
7	Honolulu County, HI	Honolulu PMSA	$283,596
8	Westchester Cty, NY	New York PMSA	$283,462
9	Santa Cruz Cty, CA	Santa Cruz PMSA	$256,098
10	Orange Cty, CA	Anaheim-Santa Ana PMSA	$252,662
11	Santa Barbara Cty, CA	Santa Barbara-Santa Maria-Lompoc MSA	$249,944
12	Fairfield Cty, CT	Bridgeport-Stamford, Norwalk-Danbury PMSA	$249,829
13	Ventura Cty, CA	Oxnard-Ventura PMSA	$245,263
14	Arlington Cty, VA	Washington MSA	$230,980
15	Alexandria City, VA	Washington MSA	$228,602
16	Bergen Cty, NJ	Bergen-Passaic PMSA	$227,661
17	Alameda Cty, CA	Oakland PMSA	$227,186
18	Los Angeles Cty, CA	Los Angeles-Long Beach PMSA	$226,446
19	Contra Costa Cty, CA	Oakland PMSA	$219,407
20	Morris Cty, NJ	Newark PMSA	$217,334

SOURCE: 1990 U.S. Census

Low interest rates provide opportunities to access the $846 billion in certificates of deposit. Next to real estate, Americans love interest-earning assets accounts. Deposits at financial institutions make up 14 percent. Other interest-earning assets, such as money-market funds and municipal bonds, and IRA or KEOGH accounts, each constitute 4 percent of net worth. Stocks and mutual fund shares account for 7 percent.

Marc Carmichael, publisher of R. & R. Newkirk's Charitable Giving Tax Service, asserts that continuing low interest rates are creating a bonanza for those not-for-profits who market to affluent individuals holding CDs. Because rates are so low, life income vehicles such as gift annuities, are highly competitive. Carmichael suggests planning informational mailings in March and September because the highest number of CD rollovers take place in April and October.

The largest intergenerational transfer of wealth in the history of the United States—from thrifty parents of the World War II generation to their adult Boomer children—has begun. Wall Street's steady growth is turning modest inheritances into golden eggs.

● **The almost universally cited 55-year figure of $10 trillion for the forthcoming transfer of wealth has been revised upward to as much as $136 trillion.** In *Millionaires and the Millennium: New Estimates of the Forthcoming Wealth Transfer and the Prospects for a Golden Age of Philanthropy,* authors John J. Havens and Paul G. Schervish suggest that their low-range best estimate is that over the 55-year period from 1998 to 2052 the wealth transfer will be $41 trillion, and may well reach double or triple that amount. They predict a golden age of philanthropy is dawning, especially among wealth holders and the upper affluent.

● **More than half (51%) of Boomers expect an inheritance of $100,000 or more.** The median value estimated is $135,000.

- 69% expect real estate

- 68% expect cash

- 33% expect stocks and bonds

An ever-increasing share of live alones are aging women. In 1994, 23.6 million persons lived alone, 12 percent of all adults. Among those under age 45, more men than women live alone. In the 45–50–54 age group, the number of men and women who live alone is about equal. But after that, women who live alone outnumber men by a growing margin with advancing age.

There are 14 million single women older than 55 compared to only 4 million single men. Moreover, most women marry older men. In 2010—the most distant year for which the Census Bureau makes household projections—29 percent of all U.S. households will be headed by unmarried women. Nearly half of elderly women are widowed, compared with just 14 percent of elderly men.

"The land of the old will be a land of women."

For every 100 women 85 years or older, there are just 39 men in the same age group. Elderly women now outnumber elderly men by three to two. Baby Boomer women will outlive their husbands by at least fifteen years.

Women are inheriting the estates of males in their families.

Women tend to save more of their incomes than do men.

● **Almost half of the wealth of this country is already owned by women.** Women actually control 51.3 percent of the wealth in the United States.

● **Forty-three percent of individuals with assets of $500,000 or more were women.** Women comprise 1.3 of the 3.3 million Americans classified as top wealth holders (annual reported income of $500,000 or more) by the IRS in 1992.

● **Women 18 years and older control about half of the investment wealth in the United States.** Women own 43 percent of stock portfolios valued over $50,000, and 45 percent of investments in other markets. While men as a group may earn more money, women make more of the critical decisions about household purchasing and exercise control over many family financial resources.

● **Women in the U.S. account for 50 percent of stock market investing, and their investment styles differ from men's.** Among other differences, women investors tend to focus more on long-term security, stability, and lowered risk. They must be doing something right; one research study showed that although single men trade 45 percent more than single women, they earn less on their investments overall.

● **Women alone are an increasing source of homebuyers.** According to the National Association of Homebuyers, single-women home buyers in 1999 were:

- 18% of all buyers

- 22% of first-time buyers

- Median Age: 41

- Median income: $39,700

MARKETING PLANNED GIFTS IN THE 21ST CENTURY

Affluents need help with managing finances. Despite their claimed wealth and financial concerns, only 20 percent of affluent households have a written financial plan. Most prefer to deal with one provider for all their financial business according to the Spectrem Group. Eighty percent of the general public—and 69 percent of households with annual incomes greater than $50,000—have never used financial planning services.

In general, those seeking financial planning services tend to be male, but the higher-income clients are more likely to be female (53 percent of them). Annual average combined (both spouses) income of financial planning clients is $87,039 with a median combined earned income of $57,623.

MATURE AUDIENCES

Our strategy for marketing planned gifts to mature Americans works just fine. Basically continue to send out your brochures and letters. Highly trusting Civics see you as an authority and welcome your information.

- **Offer mature individuals seminars, workshops, and other educational programs in financial planning.** *Beyond Middle Age: Planning for the Rest of Your Life* is a two-hour multimedia seminar produced by the Office of Public Responsibility of American Express Company and facilitated by a representative of Shearson Lehman Brothers. The American Society on Aging offers it free of charge to its members in several national locations.

WOMEN

Even young women need to begin making plans for their retirement. Women in their 20s, 30s, and early 40s appear reluctant to think about planning for retirement. Yet, the overwhelming majority of women (82%) surveyed by Oppenheimer Management believe they will be solely responsible for their financial well-being at some point in their lives.

Nine out of 10 American women are expected to be in charge of their own finances at one time or another. Today, more women than ever marry later and get divorced, and wives outlive their husbands by about seven years. And with the country's dominant population group (the Baby Boomers) aging, millions more well-educated women are facing the likelihood of a widowhood with money.

■ **Women need and want to learn about finances.** Unfortunately, many women—even among the affluent—seem to be "financially paralyzed": unable to plan for their financial future, despite being anxious about the future. A declining proportion of the population describe themselves as "quite competent" at financial matters like figuring out how to save money, finance a home, buy insurance, or plan their family's financial future.

The good news is that increasing numbers of women are confident about their financial prowess. In 1994, nearly 60 percent of women agreed with the statement, "I sometimes feel stupid when asking questions about financial matters." By 2000, that figure had fallen to 44 percent.

However, because they perceive themselves as having less control than men do over financial aspects of their lives (61 percent of women do not have pension plans versus 54 percent of men), women are eager to attend financial planning seminars.

● **Many older women have minimal financial experience beyond handling the household budget.** The AARP's Women's Financial Information Program has assisted several thousand midlife and older women to assess their financial situations and options through workshops sponsored by a variety of community-based nonprofit groups at 140 sites throughout the United States. Many of the attendees are newly widowed, divorced, or separated.

While, as a group, women are "financially fairly savvy," many older women have not taken responsibility for handling their own financial resources.

According to a survey of its readership by *McCall's* magazine:

- 41 percent have never had a bank loan in their own names.

- 33 percent do not have their own checking accounts.

- 46 percent do not have savings and investment objectives.

- 44 percent have never personally made investments in stocks, bonds, mutual funds, or real estate.

- 59 percent have no income-replacement options in the event they become disabled.

- 42 percent don't know their entitlements under their own and/or their spouse's Social Security and pensions.

- 43 percent are without a financial plan to prepare for retirement.

While women are definitely taking a more active role in managing finances, Jan Warner—a Columbia, South Carolina lawyer who runs SoloSource Inc., a service that counsels divorced women on financial options—estimates that three-quarters of his female clients, most of whom are age 40 or older, come to him without the financial know-how needed to make it alone comfortably.

"Midlife and older women often find themselves in very precarious positions when suddenly faced with death or divorce," says Barbara Hughes, WFIP specialist. "They may have to make major financial decisions on investments, taxes, insurance, pensions, etc. in a very short period of time."

● **The best way to get a married couple's financial services business is to market to the woman,** according to American Express Financial Services. "It's the woman that gets the husband to sit down with the financial advisor," explains Jane Tuffe, marketing direction for the women's market at the Minneapolis, Minnesota-based company. "We try to get the couple by going through the woman."

● **Professional women need to pay more attention to their long-term financial futures.** A Gallup study commissioned by New York Life shows that although 82 percent of female executives initially called themselves "well-informed" about retirement planning, more than 72 percent of the 220 professional women polled turned out to be only "vaguely or not familiar" with fundamental investment concepts like compounding, inflation, and tax deferral compared to 53 percent of the men surveyed. Women were also wary of taking on even minimal investment risks, with half the women preferring low-risk (and low-return) investments exclusively.

A 1999 Deloitte & Touch survey, *She Said: A Study of Affluent Women and Personal Finances,* finds that affluent women with an average annual income of $155,000 expect a high level of personal service from financial service advisors. Half of the women in this study indicated that they are not taken as seriously as men in their dealings with financial providers.

Women have a strong sense of financial worth and enjoy managing their money. They:

- Want to keep financial affairs as simple as possible.

- Want to maintain control and independence in handling their finances

- Expect financial service advisors to provide education and guidance.

- Rely on people they know and trust to provide advice on investments.

- Expect personalized, proactive, and efficient service with money-management matters.

- Need help in developing specific plans to protect their income and savings in their retirement years.

BABY BOOMERS

Don't treat Baby Boomers like their parents. Boomer financial concerns are much broader than those of their parents.

● **The Boomer generation isn't necessarily looking to early retirement as a desirable goal.** Financial planners can help those seeking to plan for financial independence with a career-of-choice rather than early retirement.

● **Because Boomers married later and had children later, many—when they hit their fifties—will still be struggling with tuition payments.** Robert Hewitt, president of the International Association of Financial Planners, believes that, as the first broadly college-educated generation, Boomers will save more than their parents did for their children's tuition.

● **Boomers are the "sandwiched" generation.** In the next 10 to 15 years, as much as $41 trillion dollars will trickle down to

Boomers from their parents. But, for many Boomers, the question of inheriting from parents is *not* the issue. The issue is dealing with their parents' aging now.

● **The average boomer women will spend more years caring for aging parents and grandparents then for her children.** *More than 22 million U.S. households are involved in some kind of eldercare.* That translates to some 14.4 million full- and part-time employees who are also caregivers. Eldercare issues have exacted a price on the workplace—between $11 and $29 billion per year, according to the insurance company MetLife.

> **Portrait of a caregiver: typically female, age 46, employed, and spends 18 hours a week helping out her mother.**
>
> Pressured to juggle the responsibilities of an elderly parent and a career, she's on a path that could lead to absenteeism, lower productivity— even resignation. Observes Denise Spiewak, Senior Director at Kelly Assisted Living(R) Services, "Eldercare is to this new century what child care was to the '80s and '90s—a 'hot button' issue that can go a long way in retaining employees and keeping productivity high."

According to *Modern Maturity,* 20 percent of older adults live more than 100 miles from their children. And, people who went to college (24 percent of Baby Boomers and the overwhelming majority of affluent Americans), tend to live further from their parents than those who did not. Planned giving vehicles that help Boomers to deal with eldercare issues will find a niche among adult children.

● **Boomers change jobs more often.** Despite loss of future retirement savings and withdrawal taxes for those under age 59½, 68 percent of American workers opt to cash out of their 401(k) plans when changing jobs according to Hewitt Associates LLC. However, the larger the balance, the greater the likelihood workers won't opt for cash payment—among all age groups. Eighty percent of Baby Boomers over age 50 take cash payments for balances less than $3,500, but only 44 percent do so for balances between $20,000 and 24,000, similar to Generation Xers.

●   **Among parents of children aged three or younger, education is the biggest concern they have for their children's future,** according to a survey by Gerber Products Company of Fremont, Michigan. Twenty-six percent of parents are concerned about the quality and cost of providing an education for their children. Market planned giving as a way to address their concerns for providing for their children's college educations.

And concerns about financing a college education rise with income, finds the American College Testing Program of Iowa City, Iowa, in a survey sponsored by *Money* magazine. While 28 percent of all family decision-makers worry about college costs, this proportion rises to 45 percent among those with household incomes of $50,000 or more.

Understand that Boomers have trust issues. Just as Boomers are reaching their peak saving years, they've lost confidence in traditional money managers. Because of events in the late 1980s and early 1990s, many Boomers have little faith in banks and the banking system. Boomers are seeking out new sources of expertise.

●   For example, Gary and Rebecca Milburn of Kirkland, Washington, founded the Baby Boomers Association for A Better America. They publish a monthly newsletter emphasizing retirement planning. In concert with professional financial consultants, the association organizes seminars on a wide range of financial planning strategies. Gary Milburn formed the support group because the thought of his own retirement "scared the hell out of him."

●   Another group, the American Association of Boomers, headquartered in Washington, D.C., claims 6,000 members in

43 chapters, with the most active in Fort Worth, Texas, Colorado Springs, Colorado, Boca Raton, Florida, and San Francisco, California. It, too, offers financial planning seminars.

Baby Boomers' concern for the future coupled with a willingness to look for help in nontraditional sources is good news for not-for-profits—although there's been some slippage in our credibility, most Americans still give highest marks to our charities and not-for-profits when asked "whom do you trust."

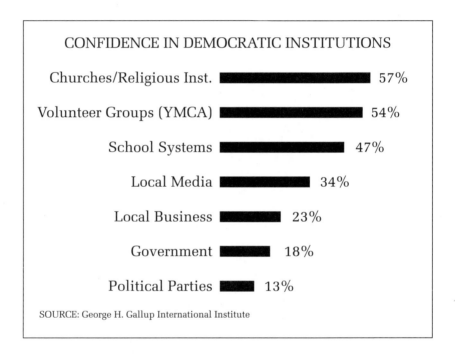

Interestingly, more so than their parents and grandparents, young affluents are loyal to financial advisors. Those under age 50 will hold strong loyalty to a good financial advisor, an indication of the importance they put on personal relationships.

ADVISOR LOYALTY		
	New Generation Affluents	Traditional Market Affluents
Enjoy investment decisions	53%	62%
Want one main advisor	72%	67%
Need advice for major decisions	45%	37%
Don't know how to find advice	32%	27%
Advisory firms overcharge	36%	34%

Because the Baby Boom is such a large group, you need to look for niches of opportunities. These include:

■ **SMUPPYS**—those Baby Boomers who are "Saving More Until Past the Parenting Years." Among married Smuppys, a two-career, two-income household is the norm with more than one third of them having incomes of $50,000 or more a year; 9 percent more than $75,000. The net worth of the oldest Smuppys averages $175,000.

Saving through non-profits may be an ideal way for them to combine their need to put money aside for the future education of their children or for their own retirement with their values. Smuppys tend to be community activists—not simply talkers, but doers. And this commitment is increasing with age. Sixty-four percent of these Americans had done some kind of volunteer work, compared with 54 percent for the same age group two years earlier.

■ **MALAs (Mid-life affluents living alone)**—an increasing number of Americans are never marrieds or single again through divorce or death. Because they lack the fallback position of a second income, singles are placed in greater jeopardy when it comes to job loss, serious illness or other emergencies. Singles also suffer from a bigger tax bite than do their married friends.

And, at death, singles are "singled out" just as they are in life by the IRS: there is no marital deduction. Not-for-profits can help by explaining the four tax-planning options: tax deferral, tax exemption, tax reduction, and tax shifting. Charitable remainder trusts, especially, are a good vehicle to market to this group.

■ **Small Business Owners**—Many entrepreneurs are so caught up in the day-to-day aspects of running their business that they neglect thinking ahead to retirement. That's a mistake: a strong retirement plan has significant current tax advantages and it helps attract and keep qualified, key employees while enabling business owners to safeguard the future for themselves, their families, their employees and their business.

In addition to workshops focusing on the financial aspects of retirement, not-for-profits can address planning for the social and psychological aspects—often devastating for entrepreneurs. Their concerns often include:

- Will I retire completely?

- How will I adjust to having more free time?

- How will my relationship with my spouse change?

- If I'm no longer the boss, how will I define myself?

Another area concerning entrepreneurs that not-for-profits can address is succession planning. Researchers at the Family Business Program of Oregon State University have found that only 30 percent of all family businesses are passed on to the next generation and only 13 percent stay in the family into a third generation.

■ **Market planned gifts to Boomer parents through their Boomlet children.** "Civic" in nature, like the mature generations, young children embrace financial responsibility. Offer to educate children on financial facts of life: provide parent-child workshops; set up contests using games such as The Game of

Life, Payday, The Allowance Game, Monopoly, and Monopoly Jr.

■ **Use planned gifts to reinforce mid-life and younger affluents' "sense of specialness."** Many younger adults have grown up in a world where sophisticated financial planning is a mark of status. *Money, Inc.* and *Entrepreneur*—these magazines owe their success to an audience that equates financial planning with the American Dream. The Upper-Affluent like to see themselves as in control of their financial affairs. Research suggests that Baby Boomers' attitudes towards money are very different from those of persons raised during the Great Depression years—less cautious, more willing to spend.

GENERATION X

Don't ignore young adults. More than any other generation, the Baby Bust—Generation X—places great importance on long-term financial planning. Nine out of 10 Xers told the American Bankers Association that accumulating money for retirement and developing a financial plan are top goals in their lives. But 40 percent believe banks are not committed to meeting their financial needs (compared to 24 percent of those 65 and older). Offer seminars and workshops that allow them to meet each other. Don't patronize them and you'll gain their appreciation.

How Northwestern Mutual Life Insurance got its #1 ranking: pinpointed segmentation.

A sample ad titled "Life Insurance for Living" introduces three prospect groups:

Bob (Mature Civic): After 24 years on the corporate ladder, Bob was able to say "enough" and start his own charter boat business. Because way back, he bought the right kind of life insurance.

Jim (Mid-life Boomer): Jim was swept out of his job by a merger. He's got two kids in college, and a mortgage on a house with a sweeping view...but he'll make it through. Because 20 years ago, he bought *Life Insurance For Living*, from us.

Kevin (Young Adult Gen Xer): Jobs don't come with a lifetime guarantee anymore. But Kevin's not worried, because he's covered his future.

AUDIENCES OF DIVERSITY

Proactively court audiences of diversity. Black Americans have less trust in investment advisers, less exposure to the stock market in their upbringing, and a cultural preference for real estate and insurance over stocks, according to a survey conducted by Yankelovich Partners comparing the investment habits of 500 African-American and 732 white, non-Hispanic households with incomes of $50,000 or more. And, just as surveys show audiences of color are asked less often to give, so are they less visible to financial planners.

MARKET BY PSYCHOGRAPHICS

Rather than segmenting by demographics, use psychographics in your planned giving marketing program. Affluent consumers can be broken into five segments with attitudes and motivations relevant to financial services and aging/retirement:

1) Self-reliant Savers (13%)—optimistic about both their situation and the U.S. economy.

2) Strapped Spenders (8%)—spend too much and save too little.

3) Worried Frugals (10%)—trust outside advisors but negative about their own financial futures.

4) Credit Consumers (16%)—have little interest in passing on an estate.

5) Savvy Investors (53%)—see a bright future for themselves and the U.S; sophisticated and confident, they actively seek out advisors.

By now it should be clear that repositioning your development program to focus on planned giving—along with renewal and upgrading—offers tremendous potential. Next, we'll review the methodologies you should use to support this approach.

PART V

BUILDING DONOR AND PROSPECT
INVOLVEMENT

The final chapters of *Pinpointing Affluence in the 21st Century* build on the implications of Part Four.

Given that we will work logically, we'll start with our best prospects. How can we best cultivate and solicit them? To encourage people to make larger gifts, staff and volunteers must be willing and able to carry out fund raising via face-to-face cultivation and solicitation. Yet, we often spend more time and resources on less effective fund raising methodologies.

■ In **Chapter 21** we'll discuss two keys to more effective face-to-face fund raising:
    Why do we hate to ask?
    How can we ask more effectively?

Given that we want to create advocates rather than adversaries, we need to promote involvement. Certainly the best way to create higher levels of involvement is through volunteerism.

■ **Chapter 22** explores the relationship between volunteerism and giving and provides a check-list of ways to show your volunteers they are valued. It also suggests how to find new volunteers.

Given that our resources are limited, we need to make all communications as effective as possible. While it would be nice if every communication we held with our best donors and prospects could be done in person, this is not reality. How do you use non–face-to-face methodologies to supplement your efforts?

■ **Chapter 23** provides numerous hints for more effective non–face-to-face communicating from the telephone to videos to direct mail to the internet.

CHAPTER TWENTY-ONE

Face-to-Face Cultivation and Solicitation

"THE REALLY DIFFICULT PART IN BIG GIFT FUNDRAISING IS NOT IN GETTING PEOPLE TO GIVE MONEY, IT IS IN GETTING PEOPLE TO ASK," according to Ken Burnett in *Relationship Fundraising.* Yet, **people are more than twice as likely to give when asked than when they are not.** Year after year, Independent Sector finds this to be true. In fact:

- Among the 74 percent of respondents to Independent Sector's *Giving and Volunteering Survey* who reported that they were asked to give in the past year, 85 percent contributed.

- While among the 25 percent of respondents who were not asked to give, 36 percent contributed.

The very best way of reaching donors and prospects is through face-to-face fund raising. However, an informal survey by Glenn Brady, development director of New Hope Village, suggests many fund raisers aren't doing this. His polling of 70 professionals showed that only two spent more than half their time in face-to-face contact with donors.

WHY DO WE HATE TO ASK?

There are many reasons but they can be summed up under three main areas:
  1. Fear of rejection by the prospect
  2. Lack of confidence in our organization's "selling" ability
  3. Concerns about offending

Let's look at each of these in turn:

1) FEAR OF REJECTION

Nobody wants to be turned down; we take it personally. And, we expect our prospects to say "no." This assumption is tied in to our treating of donors and prospects as adversaries. Secretly we feel that we are forcing "them" to give.

This is ridiculous. The very best fund raisers can't make people give; we can only facilitate the process. Even "guilt" only works if the prospect wants it to work!

A True Story

I had been asked by the Oregon Trail Chapter of the American Red Cross to advise them about increasing annual giving. They claimed they did not have a logical group of prospects to ask.

I was puzzled and asked: What about your blood donors?

Their answer: We do have 142,000 blood donors on file—but they wouldn't be interested in giving.

My reply: You ask people to give blood—the most precious gift of all—and you don't think they care enough to support you financially? Think about it.

P.S. We asked and they gave generously.

Instead of assuming rejection, anticipate that the prospect is eager to enter into a partnership with your organization. After all, s/he let you in the door and is now sitting with you in his/her home or office!

■ **A confident attitude is essential.** How important is that first impression? Bert Decker, a speech expert and trainer, says "The impressions made in the *first two* seconds are so vivid that it takes another *four minutes* to add 50 percent more impression—negative or positive—to that communication."

Those first two seconds are based primarily on visual impressions—our posture, movement, dress and appearance. Studies by Dr. Albert Mehrabian at the University of California, Los Angeles support this: His research shows that the verbal element accounts for 7 percent, the vocal for 38 percent and the visual for 55 percent.

Generally speaking, women are more sensitive to nonverbal cues—especially facial cues—and they transmit more accurate nonverbal cues to others.

■ **Defensive body language antagonizes a prospect. Assertive body language encourages the prospect.** But body language is something too many people ignore, according to Alan Grisman, a public speaking consultant in Pittsburgh. "A lot of people are unaware that their body language gives off messages."

You'll make a better impression if your body language is open and friendly: sit or stand facing the other person with your hands and arms relaxed.

Look directly at your prospect, putting a smile on your face and in your eyes. People with low self-esteem use more eye contact when receiving negative messages than when receiving positive ones, while those with high self-esteem do just the opposite in each case.

ENHANCING THE VISUAL FACTOR WILL STRENGTHEN YOUR MESSAGE

Eye communication comes first:

- Hold eye contact for five seconds.

- Don't avoid your prospect's eyes.

- Don't close your eyes when speaking.

Convey confidence through your posture:

- Stand tall.

- Don't rock on one hip.

- Direct your energy slightly forward.

Consider your dress and appearance:

- Be appropriate.

- Conservative is better for business.

- Dress and groom up, not down.

Your smile and gestures propel your message:

- Find your nervous gesture and stop making it!

- Practice smiling—do it with your whole face.

SOURCE: Bert Decker, *You've got to Be Believed to Be Heard,* St. Martin's Press, NYC.

■ **Learn to "read" body language, facial expressions, and common gestures.** According to Doe Lang, author of *Secrets of Charisma,* be alert for:

● **Body positions**

- If someone turns away or shrinks back from you, you may be invading his/her personal space.

- If s/he takes a deep breath or stands tall, s/he's wary of you.

- Be aware that people who live in high-contact cultures, including Mediterranean, Latin American, and Middle Eastern countries, typically stand about a foot apart when they interact, face each other directly, and engage in lots of eye contact and touching. At the other end of the continuum are northern European cultures where people stand farther apart and try to avoid accidental touching in social or business settings. Most Americans fall somewhere in between the "contact" and "non-contact" ethnic groups, generally standing two feet apart, or sitting four to five feet apart during social conversations. Hispanics tend to use less space than Anglos when interacting, while African-Americans stand farther apart.

● **Facial clues**

- Pursing the lips: disapproval or concentration

- Licking the lip: self-reproach

- Drawing brows together: anger, anxiety

- Sticking the chin out: belligerence

- Keeping eyes down: insecurity, evasiveness

- Staring with narrowed eyes: a threat, a sign of aggression

- Smiling: it's genuine if it reaches the eyes!

● **The meaning of common gestures**

- Tapping the foot: nervous, impatient, annoyed

- Leaning back: at ease

- Leaning forward: interested

- Tilting head to one side: sympathy, interest

- Looking at you sideways: mistrust

- Putting hands behind the back: uncomfortable or defensive, afraid of revealing self

- Hunching shoulders: a heavy burden, fear, discouragement

- Crossed arms: can be simply a comfortable position or could show s/he is unconvinced

Remember, when contradictory messages are sent through both verbal and nonverbal channels, most adults see the nonverbal message as more accurate.

2)   LACK OF CONFIDENCE IN OUR ORGANIZATION'S "SELLING ABILITY"

You must create a cycle of:

- AWARENESS

- INTEREST

- INVOLVEMENT

- COMMITMENT

● **Awareness: Don't assume your "unique selling position" is understood.** Too often, we don't do a very good job articulating what makes our organization different from others serving similar populations. We assume our prospects and donors know and understand what we do and how we do it. Can your donors articulate what makes your organization stand out from others in its sector?

What's the difference between these fine organizations, all of which serve youth?

- Boy Scouts of America

- Boys and Girls Clubs of America

- Campfire, Inc.

- Girl Scouts of the USA

- The YMCA

- The YWCA

Unfortunately, the best organizations don't necessarily win. In *The 22 Immutable Laws of Marketing,* Al Ries and Jack Trout warn that all that exists in the world of marketing are perceptions in the minds of prospects. The perception is the reality. If you are not communicating well, "number two" may preempt your leadership position.

● **Interest: Make your organization come alive!** We are often "tongue-tied" when it comes to giving specific examples of the fine work our organizations do. We expect others to know and understand what their support accomplishes. It's important to train both staff and volunteers to articulate what your organization is all about, using case examples, testimonials, and specific facts and figures.

Let me tell you exactly what your gift will accomplish...

- "$150 covers the shipping costs of 100 units of red cells to support national relief efforts such as the San Francisco earthquake and the Charleston, South Carolina recovery from Hurricane Hugo."

- "$1,000 would enable us to build classroom storage cabinets to house materials for Youth Education programs including Neat Kids/Safe Kids, Where I'm in Charge, Babysitting, and Basic Aid Training."

Examples from the American Red Cross, Oregon Trail Chapter

● **Involvement: Building commitment takes time.** Many times prospects will make trial gifts of modest amounts before committing to a significant contribution. Unfortunately, we are often impatient. Too often, we are concentrating so hard on our organization's bottom line and fund raising goals for the year that we try to move a prospect along more quickly than s/he is ready. *Remember, the typical major gift cultivation will take 34 months.*

On Patience:

"You can't sell a vision in 10 minutes.
Sometimes you have to marry the girl."

Philanthropist, Stanley Marcus
Honorary Chairman of the Board,
Neiman-Marcus.

Encourage your prospects and donors to explore multiple pockets of involvement: volunteerism, attendance at events, and advocacy of your organization are valuable gifts of time and effort that bind the giver to you.

● **Commitment: Loyalty must be nurtured.** Remember that *APPRECIATION* closes the donor cycle and opens it again to a possible higher level. You must get to people's hearts and minds before you can get them to give. Because of the importance of this step in setting the stage for an ongoing relationship, it was discussed in depth in Chapter 19: Focusing on Renewal and Upgrading vs. Acquisition. I urge you to review this chapter over and over again.

3)   CONCERNS ABOUT "OFFENDING."

● **Money is still the deepest, darkest secret of all.** Do your family members and closest friends know what **you** earn? We tend to be more open talking about sex than we are about money. Fund raisers and volunteers shy away from "offending." We worry that asking someone to give more than s/he is capable of doing is a terrible faux pas.

The truth is that most individuals are flattered rather than offended when we ask them to be a more major contributor than they have thought themselves capable of being! Learning an organization thinks you are better-off and more astute in acquiring assets than you are is **not** an insult. *We often project our own insecurities about money onto others.* We assume that because we couldn't—or wouldn't—give a particular gift amount, our prospects can't—or won't—as well.

● **To avoid offending, understand the difference between philanthropy and fulfillment.** While most individuals *want* to make a difference, they often are uncomfortable with *how* to make this happen. Research has shown that breaking the total amount down into yearly, quarterly, or monthly amounts often lessens the resistance to the higher gift level. Interestingly, very often, once prospects are offered to option of giving $10,000 as $250 quarterly for 10 years, they decide they'd prefer to give it all at once or in larger payments!

MAKING THE CALL

Your goal should be to make more calls to more people. Rather than waiting for the "big" prospect, you should visit with as many of your repeat donors as possible. You could also visit with any new donors. And, interested prospects capable of giving a larger than average annual gift (typically, a minimum of $250) to your organization.

How do you structure a first visit with a prospect? There are six distinct steps you want to pass through:

- Thanking your prospect for his/her time and past support

- Asking what s/he knows about the organization

- Adding to his/her knowledge

- Inviting him/her to be a partner

- Showing him/her how to make it happen

- Thanking the prospect

BE APPRECIATIVE

■ **Always start your call by saying thank you!**

● **If your prospect is a past donor, let him/her know you know.** Try to be specific—indicate you're aware of when and why the gift was made.

> "Sally, thank you for seeing me. Our organization is grateful for your ongoing support. Your gift this past Fall to the scholarship fund was most generous."

● **What if your prospect is not a donor?** Still thank him/her—for giving up valuable time.

> "Bob, thank you for taking time from a busy schedule. Our organization is most grateful for your willingness to see me."

● **Indicate you know your prospect's time is valuable.** Set out the time parameters and stick to them unless your prospect invites you to stay longer! This accomplishes two things: it encourages the prospect to pay full attention to you because the time commitment is limited and it forces you to move through the necessary steps in asking for the gift. Most introductory visits can be conducted in 20 minutes or less.

> "Bob and Sally, I know you're busy and I appreciate your willingness to see me. I'll take twenty minutes of your time and promise to be out promptly at 2:15 pm unless you ask me to stay longer."

MAKE YOUR PROSPECT AN ACTIVE PARTNER IN THE CULTIVATION AND SOLICITATION PROCESS.

■ **Involve the prospect—you need to make this a dialogue, rather than a monologue.**

● **Ask what s/he knows about the organization you represent.** There's a reason the prospect was willing to see you. Find out what it is. If this is a past donor you should find out why s/he gave what s/he did. If this is a new friend, why is s/he interested? Does a family member make use of your organization? Does the family have a particular concern that might relate to your mission?

● **Master the art of listening.** According to Letitia Baldrige, an internationally recognized etiquette expert and the author of *The Complete Guide to Executive Manners,* "the tendency not to pay full attention to the person speaking is one of the most common forms of rudeness in society today." Baldrige asserts that good listening is the basis for any real communication and is one of the highest compliments one individual can pay another. In order to find the basis for interest, you must hear what your prospect is saying. To improve your own listening ability,

Six barriers to effective listening:

1. *Our minds won't wait.* Our thoughts can race along from four to 10 times faster than most people speak. While we wait for the words to come, the mind tunes in and out. As a result, only a few words penetrate—we miss the point.

2. *We think we already know.* We assume we know what a person will say, so we listen with only "half an ear." Most of the time, our second guessing is wrong.

3. *We're looking, not listening.* We're too busy assessing the speaker's appearance or mannerisms.

4. *We're busy listeners.* Only part of our mind is on the speaker. We're giving part of our attention to another project.

5. *We miss the big ideas.* We end up listening to words rather than ideas. Whether because we're impatient, distracted, apathetic, or upset, we catch a phrase here and there but miss the main point.

6. *Our emotions make us deaf.* When someone offers opposing ideas to ours, we unconsciously feel it is risky to listen. We're busy planning our verbal counterattack and don't want to hear something that could make us question ourselves.

SOURCE: Leann Anderson, Anderson Business Resources

you'll need to practice. Listening well is not an easy skill to master.

● **Use Leann Anderson's seven tips to improve your listening:**

1. *Think like your prospects and donors.* Keep their viewpoints, needs, and concerns in mind. By listening carefully, you'll know what kinds of questions to ask. Especially if a prospect or donor is upset with your organization, s/he appreciates someone who will listen patiently.

2. *Limit your own talking.* You can't talk and listen at the same time—and nothing is so eloquent as a well-timed silence. Practice saying nothing for 15 seconds...when someone stops talking, the tendency is to rush in to fill the void.

3. *Concentrate and focus.* You can't do two things well at the same time. Devote yourself to the speaker. Look for visual cues and body language.

4. *Be an active listener.* Be all there—squirming, side-long glances, passive body language—telegraph to the other person that you're interested. Lean in towards the speaker, smile, maintain eye contact, take notes (if appropriate), and use reflective responses like "Yes," "I see," and "Uh-huh."

5. *Accept controversy; don't jump to conclusions.* Keep your own emotions under control. Sometimes words, issues, personalities, and behaviors can trigger us emotionally. Don't stop listening while you think up a snappy answer.

6. *Repeat and summarize.* Be sure you've heard what your prospects and donors are saying. Verify by restating the information or asking for clarification.

7. *Practice your listening skills, and help others practice theirs.* Don't save good listening for a major donor prospect—use it all the time.

● **Women and men do listen differently.** While both sexes make eye contact with people they like, women are more likely to maintain it. In general, as indicated by Dr. Lang, a woman tends to look at others when she is speaking to them (usually because she's looking for a reaction) while a man is more apt to look at others while he's listening to them.

BUILD ON WHAT YOU HEARD

■ **Add to a prospect's knowledge by linking your comments to what s/he has said.** Acknowledge a key point in their earlier response and provide a specific example of something happening in the organization that is relevant.

> "Sally, I'm not surprised to hear your interest was triggered by your family's frustration in getting information on your son's problem. I hear similar stories all the time from our friends. We're trying to do something about the lack of readily available crisis information by publicizing a hot-line number..."

This accomplishes two important things:

- It tells your prospect you heard what they said and listened actively.

- It gives you a chance to "dangle" a first or upgraded gift project idea.

Be Positive In Asking The Prospect To Make A Gift

■ **Invite him/her to be a partner by choosing a project of interest.**
This is the time to ask, not just for money, but for involvement.

> "Bob, I'd like to invite you to be a partner in fur-
> thering our organization's outreach efforts.
> Would you be interested in helping us to fund
> the hot-line project?"

● **Now—be quiet!** One of the reasons we don't listen well is
that we don't wait for people to speak! We find silence so uncomfortable that we rush in to fill the void.

- Try a simple exercise: Ask someone to keep time. Tell
  him/her when you think 15 seconds have passed.
  (Don't count!) Chances are you'll guess far short of a
  quarter of a minute.

Remember, we want to encourage a dialogue. Learn to pause
fully after speaking—for up to 7 seconds. Give the prospect a
chance to respond to your ask. S/he might agree this is an area
of interest or suggest another area you should explore.

Once You've Agreed on an Area of Interest, Help Your Prospect to Make a Meaningful Gift

■ **We all know it takes money to make a difference.** You can't
change the world for pennies anymore. Let your prospect know
the full cost of the project. Ask if s/he can consider funding
the entire amount, either as a current gift or through a pledge.
Again, listen!

Don't be afraid to invite a donor whose gifts have been
modest to consider making a significant financial commitment
if s/he has expressed excitement and interest in your project or

program. Most people are flattered, not insulted, to be considered major gift prospects.

"Sally, I'm excited that you are interested in the hot-line. We've gotten some preliminary cost figures and know it will take $25,000 to make this happen. I can provide you with the specific breakdown. Can you consider being the full sponsor for this important project, either by making a current gift or pledging $5,000 a year over five years?"

● **Again—be quiet! Let the prospect respond.** S/he is the best judge of what s/he can do. Of course, you can help—maybe the gift would be more do-able broken into quarterly installments or, even, monthly payments. Five hundred dollars a month doesn't seem as large as $5,000 a year but, in fact, it adds up to $1,000 more.

● **Accept that you may not wind up with the full amount you hoped to receive.** In spite of your conscientious research and attractive presentation, you may not get what you hoped to receive. Don't take this personally. There may be a personal situation of which you are unaware.

DO YOU KNOW WHAT YOUR PROSPECT'S OTHER CHARITABLE RESPONSIBILITIES ARE?

As the newly appointed Executive Director of Development for a large university, I decided to visit with the chair of our development board. The CEO of a large, publicly-held company, "John"'s salary of $300,000+ was a matter of public record. Yet, his yearly gift to our university was a modest $2,000.

I waited in his outer office while John said goodbye to his previous appointment. When he greeted me, he mentioned, "that was the fund raiser from ABC College. Did you know my oldest son graduated from there?" I hadn't.

John continued. "I have six children. My wife and I sent them all to private elementary and secondary schools. All six went to college, with five continuing on for graduate degrees. Three are now working for their Ph.D.s. In addition to the $75,000 in tuition I spend yearly, I proudly give 24 educational institutions yearly gifts of $2,000 each—double matched by my company. Sorry to ramble...was there a specific purpose for this visit?"

I told John I was there to thank him for ongoing support. It was truly meaningful.

If the prospect responds with a lower figure, encourage him/her to consider helping you find a co-sponsor: recruit your donor as a fund raising volunteer!

CLOSE AS YOU BEGAN, BY SAYING THANK YOU

■ **Don't overstay your welcome.** Handle any housekeeping items quickly and leave. Mark Twain* told the story about attending a meeting where a missionary had been invited to speak. Twain was deeply impressed:

"The preacher's voice was beautiful. He told us about the sufferings of the native, and he pleaded for help with such moving simplicity that I mentally doubled the 50 cents I had intended to put in the plate. He described the pitiful misery of those savages so vividly that the dollar I had in mind gradually rose to five. Then the preacher continued, and I felt that all the cash I carried on me would be insufficient, and I decided to write a large check."

But, Twain added, the preacher went on and on "about the dreadful state of those natives, and I abandoned the idea of the check. And he went on. And I got back to five dollars. He went on, and I got back to four, two, one—and still he went on. And when the plate came around...I took 10 cents out of it."

---

*related in *Accent on Humor: The Wit and Wisdom of Wealth and Philanthropy,* Cindy Chamberlin and Ronald A. Knott, Editors

CHAPTER TWENTY-TWO

Encouraging Volunteerism

MAURICE GURIN, writing in *Advancing Beyond the Techniques in Fund Raising,* deplored philanthropy's continuing depersonalization. He noted that, "long gone are the days when donors gave directly to the poor and needy; organizations have long since assumed that role. But until fairly recently, volunteers provided in-person solicitation of substantial prospects for support."

Volunteers serve as your organization's best advocates. They provide the community's "endorsement" for your not-for-profit, encouraging persons of affluence and influence to follow their lead.

> Word of mouth is the most powerful purchase driver, according to *Yankelovich Monitor,* which tracks consumer trends. Seventy percent of consumers consider their friends top sources for advice on new products and 82 percent turn to them for information before making purchasing decisions. The trend to buy what friends buy is stronger today than ever, jumping 12 points—from 21 percent to 33 percent—since 1994.

Gurin expressed his belief that "in soliciting large gifts, volunteers derive the kind of satisfaction that increases their own interest and commitment. Depriving them of that satisfaction could well have serious consequences for fund raising and for philanthropy in general."

Philanthropist Stanley Marcus, Honorary Chairman of the Board, Neiman-Marcus asserts that "Being a good citizen is a happier way to live."

"I consider volunteerism and board membership as being one of the important and very special phenomena of this country, and one of the factors that makes it great. As far as I am concerned, it is my way of paying back all that my community has done for me."

There is a direct relationship between volunteering and contributing. People who give their time have been shown to give more money as well. Consistently, respondents to Independent Sector's annual *Giving and Volunteering Survey* indicate that those who both volunteer and donate give nearly twice what those who do not volunteer contribute. The 1999 survey notes that contributing households with a volunteer gave over two and a half times more on average than contributing households where the respondent did not volunteer.

Fortunately, volunteering is in, according to *Worth* magazine: "...Whereas the charitable of the 80s wanted to be photographed making the scene at black-tie galas, the 90s ideal is to spend one's spare time helping out at a soup kitchen, tutoring ghetto teenagers, or bedsitting someone with AIDS. Check writing is now considered ersatz, a salve to the bourgeois conscience. Under the new code, involvement alone is deemed worthwhile, either for givers or the recipients of assistance." This trend has continued strongly into the twenty-first century.

WHO VOLUNTEERS?

One hundred million Americans volunteer according to Independent Sector's 1999 study, *Giving and Volunteering in the United States*. Fifty-six percent of Americans reported that they volunteered at some point in 1998—a 7 percent rise over 1995 and up from a quarter in 1977. This is the highest rate of volunteering in more than a decade. An estimated 109 million adults aged 18 and over volunteered in 1998 (the latest statistics available), up from 93 million in 1995. Eighty million adults volunteered in 1987. The volunteer workforce represented the equivalent of over 9 million full-time employees at a value of $255 billion.

- Volunteering is up not only with the general population, but especially with certain ethnic groups. Forty-seven percent of African-Americans and 46 percent of Hispanics volunteered.

- A higher percentage of women (62%) than of men (49%) volunteered. Men who volunteered gave slightly more time than women: 3.6 hours per week as opposed to 3.4 hours for women.

- Forty-three percent of seniors aged 75 and over reported volunteering—an increase of 8 percentage points since 1995. *A strong argument in recruiting older volunteers: volunteering adds longevity.* Giving time to charitable causes may play a key role in living longer, healthier, and happier lives. Researchers tracking 300 women found that those who had been members of a club or had volunteered with an organization were less likely to have suffered a major illness over a thirty-year period and tended to live longer!

Why do people volunteer? More than eight out of 10 people (86%) said they volunteered because they felt compassion for those in need. Nearly three-fourths of the respondents (72%) volunteered because they had an interest in the activity or work, and 70 percent volunteered to gain a new perspective on things.

■ Corporate America is placing a greater value on employee volunteer programs as a resource for achieving strategic business goals.

● Eighty-one percent of companies surveyed by the Points of Light Foundation in 1999 connect volunteering to their overall business strategies, compared to only 31 percent who did so in 1992.

● Respondents to the survey unanimously agreed that corporate volunteering helps create healthier communities and improves a company's public image; 97 percent say these programs improve employee teamwork.

● One-quarter of U.S. companies now offer either paid or unpaid sabbaticals, according to the Society for Human Resources Management in Alexandria, Virginia.

■ **Baby Boomers volunteer in large numbers.**

● **Boomers are most likely to fit our profile of "influentials,"** a consistent 10 to 12 percent of Americans who fill our society's need for role models and opinion leaders. The majority of Influentials (54%) are between the ages of 30 and 49, compared with just 41 percent of the adult population—Baby Boomers. Boomer Influentials are America's product leaders, social activists, advisers, and information seekers. And, they tend to be more likely than the general population to have high incomes: 28 percent of Influential households have incomes of $50,000 or more, compared with 15 percent of all households.

● **Boomer Singles volunteer**—for the networking. How can MALAs (Midlife Affluents Living Alone) meet someone now that the bar scene is passé? A Long Island, New York charity group, Singles for Charities, was started to encourage unmarried, divorced, widowed, or separated people to participate in charitable projects. It now has chapters in numerous cities.

How Can You Keep Your Volunteers?

Treat them as well as your treat your donors—if not better. John Kenneth Galbraith commented in his book, *The Scotch:* "Every community needs a great many communal services. To pay for them is expensive; and only a poor class of talent is available for money. By rewarding such men with honor and esteem, the very best men can be had for nothing."

> When our goal is to recruit "traditional" volunteers—white, middle-to-upper class, older individuals—the need is to focus on retention.

According to Joanne Drune, writing in the *NonProfit Times* on "Managing the New Volunteer," today's volunteer expects your not-for-profit to:

- Better respond to his/her needs and desires

- Offer new activities

- Better structure hours and days of service

- Offer volunteer activities that are time limited

- Provide training and education that include self-improvement and professional advancement

- Offer opportunities for couples and families to volunteer together

■ **Thank them properly, often, and well.**

● **Send out a written thank you,** signed by the CEO or appropriate highest-ranking individual in your organization when your volunteer begins his/her serve.

● **Hold a yearly volunteer appreciation event.** Give it an outstanding program—one people *would* pay to attend. But, *never* charge a fee to your volunteers. You might want to tie your recognition event into National Volunteer Week, celebrated in April each year.

● **Keep track of the milestones in their volunteer histories.** Use your computer system to identify five, ten, and fifteen year volunteers. Send them a special certificate.

● **Make a fuss** about these special individuals in your newsletters.

■ **Herald their importance to everyone.**

● **Announce their visits over the loudspeaker** or by placing a welcoming bulletin board at the front desk with their names.

● **Create a special t-shirt** just for them.

● **Tell the world they're "VIP"s** by providing them with decals for their cars.

■ **Provide them with "fringe benefits."** Milton Murray in *Accent on Recognition* suggests:

- Free library cards

- VIP parking passes

- Escort services to parking lots in the evening

- Reserved seating for institutional activities and events

- Passes to lectures, games, and other programs

- VIP emergency hospital admittance cards bearing vital medical information

- Free or discounted cafeteria meals

- Discounts on registration fees for classes or services rendered by your organization

WHAT ARE THE BARRIERS TO ATTRACTING AND RETAINING ETHNICALLY AND CULTURALLY DIVERSE VOLUNTEER LEADERSHIP?

The Chronicle of Philanthropy, in a special report entitled "The Challenge of Ethnic Diversity," notes that, while efforts are being made to serve and solicit a more diverse constituency, our not-for-profits have a long way to go.

> When the goal is to attract non-traditional volunteers—non-white or Hispanic as well as younger persons—not-for-profits must focus on being inclusive rather than exclusive.

Most organizations need to broaden minority representation on their boards and staff as well as learn how to recruit volunteers and cultivate financial support in minority communities they previously ignored. Cultural diversity is a fact of life in today's—and tomorrow's—society. Diversity can bring innovation, creativity, and better problem solving. A culturally sensitive, diverse volunteer pool enables organizations to better understand and serve their equally diverse clients and donors. Failure to understand cultural differences can lead to painful misunderstandings, poor performance, and unmet expectations on both sides.

Black, Asian, Pacific Islander, and Hispanic Americans often do not feel their participation is genuinely wanted and valued. Your not-for-profit may not be perceived as welcoming minority participation. *To encourage diversity among your volunteers, you must show you are inclusive rather than exclusive.*

■ **There are four key barriers to participation:**

1.   Formal qualifications for participation. Your organization may be exclusive or have either financial or occupational restrictions. Few minorities are persons of inherited wealth. This often means that they are not "networked" into the clubs, social events, and occupations you look to automatically when seeking high level volunteers.

Though increasing numbers of minorities are successful entrepreneurs, many are putting their profits back into their businesses. Making sizeable outright gifts to your organization may not be possible. But, while they may not be able to make the largest gifts on your board, they can bring "wisdom and work."

2.   An organizational inability to assess the "talent pool" of minorities. Traditionally, we've looked for board leadership in the corporate sector. Many minorities are not making it in corporate America. The problem is not simply one of racism. There are few role models, few means by which even ambitious minorities can rise. Talented Black, Hispanic, Asian, and Native Americans often choose to run their own businesses because they are intimidated by lack of access to the corporate "Club."

3.   A refusal to recruit aggressively. Many not-for-profit organizations have not been pro-active. Not-for-profits must make an explicit commitment to increase participation and make special efforts to recruit minorities. To find persons of color possessing the qualifications you desire in volunteers, you must seek out networking opportunities at professional meetings, social and church events.

● **Make direct contact within non-white communities.** Demonstrate your respect for the diversity within your local Black, Hispanic, Asian, and Native American communities by participating in or cosponsoring festivals and celebrations. Festivals, fairs, and other community events draw large crowds and provide an ideal opportunity to build awareness for your organization.

●   **Recruit one-on-one.** Regularly make use of alternative media and community-based organizations for identification of up and coming minorities. Chapter 12 offers a number of suggestions pertaining to organizations, directories, and media resources within the Black, Hispanic, Asian, and Native American communities. Review these for volunteer recruitment as well.

4.   Cultural insensitivity. Don't insult the individual by making race or ethnic background the sole criteria for your interest in recruiting a minority candidate: explain what qualities you think s/he will contribute to your organization because s/he is a successful businessperson or community leader. While contributing to the diversity of viewpoints on the board is always valid, it should never be the sole reason for recruitment.

Valuing diversity means recognizing and appreciating that individuals are different, that diversity is an advantage if it is valued and well managed, and that diversity is not to be simply tolerated but must be encouraged, supported, and nurtured. Often organizations fail to recognize:

- stereotypes and their associated assumptions

- actual cultural differences

- exclusivity of the "white male club" and its associated access to important information and relationships

- unwritten rules and double standards for success which are often unknown to women and minorities

- lack of communication about differences

Being sensitive to these four barriers to participation can help your organization to avoid the sin of "tokenism" where a person of color is recruited for his/her "hue" rather than "view." Too often, not-for-profits engage in "recycling" a small group of persons of color: a Black, Hispanic, Asian, or Native American individual is asked to represent the spectrum of diversity, over and over again, at a number of organizations.

Can not-for-profits succeed in attracting minority participation? Absolutely. Girl Scouts of the USA have been a real success story. Over just 10 years—in conjunction with an organizational pledge to increase diversity—there has been an increase of almost 20 percent in the number of volunteers, from 630,000 to 730,000. In part, the Girl Scouts' success resulted from their aggressive recruitment of minority women. The increase in minority volunteers parallels the dramatic change in the racial composition of the Girl Scouts over the decade. Whereas in the 1980s, the number of black Girl Scouts was negligible, today one out of four Girl Scouts is African-American.

Don't think of volunteerism as a "one way" street. Volunteers give as much as they get. Studies show those who volunteer live longer and have happier, more productive lives. Harvey Mackay, best-selling author and a successful entrepreneur, notes:

"My father told me at age 19 or 20 that 25 percent of your life should go back to the community. Little did I know at the time that volunteerism also enhances your skills. For example, volunteerism made me get up and give all those cancer and United Way speeches. Now I've become a fairly good public speaker. (Volunteerism sometimes requires me to) go out and ask for hundreds of millions of dollars—and get a lot of doors slammed in my face. But it's enhanced my selling skills. I've spent 40 years now with entrepreneurs, charities, or anyone who wanted help. The best thing (anyone) can do is get involved in something as a volunteer. Quite simply, you'll have a better chance to be successful and happy."

CHAPTER TWENTY-THREE

Asking Effectively through Direct Marketing Methodologies

YOU CAN'T ALWAYS MEET FACE-TO-FACE WITH YOUR BEST PROSPECTS. We've all got limits: there are many times when you can't deliver the message in person. More than half of all charitable giving in the USA comes from those earning less than $50,000 a year—wonderful people who probably don't have the potential for making significant annual gifts.

But, some do. Your best prospect research may not tell you who they are. You need these more modest donors to "self-identify" if they are major or planned gift prospects. That's when you need to rely on direct response vehicles.

The number-one fundraising challenge today and tomorrow is breaking through the clutter. How do you get prospects to respond to your materials and signal that they are interested? There are significantly more letters, phone calls, advertisements, special events, and (even) face-to-face visits asking Americans to give. Once-loyal donors have grown increasingly less willing to view themselves as "ours." Increasingly midlife and younger audiences will desire new products, be willing to throw products away before they are worn out, and actively seek that which is new and different.

This attitude will affect charitable choices as well as the purchases of goods. The "flavor of the month" dilemma is growing as mid-life and younger donors taste, try, and discard one charity in favor of another. And, it's not going to get better.

Your affluent prospects have grown up on Madison Avenue's increasingly sophisticated enticements.

- Thousands of new products—and millions of commercial messages—bombard them each year.

- The average person is on over 200 databases!

"Individualized" marketing has replaced mass-marketing and now, micro-marketing, according to Stan Rapp, co-author of *The Great Marketing Turnaround* and founder of the Rapp & Collins advertising agency. As computer power has grown more sophisticated—and more affordable—companies of all shapes and sizes have been able to gather increasingly sophisticated information about their customers' buying habits. Marketers are betting that even jaded consumers will pay attention if the promotions address their individual needs. Using information such as past buying habits, use of personalized coupons, and response to coded advertisements, marketers are approaching their prospects as a "segment of one."

Fund raising may have little choice but to follow. Newsletters, cards, brochures, videos, telephone, radio, television, and the Internet *all* have a role in ongoing communications. Your goal—regardless of which vehicle you use—should be to create as personalized an interaction as possible so that your prospect feels that you are focused on him or her.

Demographic targeting works for the arts.

Using testimonials from attendees as part of its membership invitation, the Atlanta Ballet segmented its direct marketing campaign, targeting subgroups of upscale Baby Boomers with families, empty nesters, and single Baby Busters.

The results? After just five weeks the mailing generated nearly twice the results of the previous year's effort after twenty weeks, $92,000 compared to $51,025 while costs remained the same.

● **Affluents are cautious about believing.** They trust their own ability to use gathered evidence (comparative ads and user surveys get information from more than one source) and make (or at least see) informed decisions based on the "facts."

Ranking for Ad Believability among Affluent Americans

1. User surveys	50%
2. Comparative ads	45%
3. Company representatives	35%
4. Hidden camera	20%
5. Celebrity endorsement	15%

SOURCE: *The Influential Americans: Who They Are, How To Reach Them*, The Roper Organization, Inc.

● **Affluents ask for more information and less hype in advertising.** They feel they can decide based on the facts. To sell them anything, convince them that it works, that it makes sense. Bear in mind that they are savvy enough with advertising to spot hype a mile away, and to be wary of claims.

"Skeptical" is perhaps the most apt word for their attitude—they've heard it all before; yet, they are not cynical. One of the luxuries of affluents is the belief that goodness is predominant, and that they can make things work out.

● **Enter the idea of "Permission Marketing."** According to Seth Godwin in his book of the same title, each of us is born with only a certain amount of time on this earth, and figuring out how to use it wisely is one of life's primary activities. 'Paying attention' to something—anything—is, in fact, a conscious act, requiring conscious effort. So one way to sell a consumer something in the future is simply to get his/her permission in advance. You'll do this by engaging the consumer in a dialogue, an interactive relationship with both you and the customer participating, instead of simply interrupting.

MARKETING HAS TO BE ABOUT CREATING VALUE IN THE MINDS OF CONSUMERS

The Re-emergence of Branding: Paradoxically, as choice and change increases, the need for order increases commensurably. That's where the re-emergence of branding fits in. According to Jack Meyers, author of *Reconnecting with Customers: Building Brands and Profits in The Relationship Age,* Consumers have an increased need to gain control over their environments. We seek out those relationships with which we feel most comfortable and with which we are most assured of being satisfied. And we narrow our choices to those relationships. A brand assures consistent delivery of differentiated and relevant promises.

● **A brand is a composite of how consumers feel about a product.** The personality they attribute to it. The reliability they count on from it. The confidence it earns from them. The affection they feel for it. And above all, their shared experience with the product. It's important because we can only keep track of a certain number of things in a category. Noted direct marketer Alan Rosenspan asserts that "Branding helps get you on the short list." Marketer Diana Bentley, writing *Hemisphere* magazine agrees: "In an increasingly complex and cluttered global marketplace, a brand is the manifestation of your organization's character and personality and, essentially, a guarantee of consistency, quality, and value."

● **A strong charity brand comes from strong beliefs and values.** Beliefs are at the heart of why charities exist and they are one of the most accessible parts of a charity's brand. That is why charities have among the strongest brands of any organization, commercial, public, or voluntary. Almost every purchase, no matter the product, is the result of an examination of self-worth: a car, a life-insurance policy, a new suit, perfume, shoes, a computer, a book. So it is with donations. In *The Art of Planned Giving: Understanding Donors and the Culture of Giving,* Douglas White suggests that "what is purchased is that faint, intangible heartstring between the soul of the supporter and a charity's programs or buildings or future."

Jay Chiat, partner in one of the largest advertising agencies, believes that enduring brands share one quality: comfort. It's a truism that everything recycles eventually. Marketing is returning to older, more basic issues. It's not about how new a product is—it's about how well that product resonates with people. Many larger not-for-profits such as The Salvation Army, the American Red Cross, and the YMCA have positioned themselves well. But, smaller, local charities can benefit from looking at who they are from this perspective as well.

● **Building brands used to be about creating messages that would endure for decades.** But, cautions futurist Johan Kramer, those days are over. Shorter product life cycles, a dynamic media landscape, and restless consumers mean that brands can become irrelevant within a few years, or even within a few months. Companies have to keep reinventing and revitalizing the messages behind their brands—not killing them but reincarnating them.

To keep your product new, you must constantly change the dialogue between the consumer and the brand says Sergio Zyman in *The End of Marketing As We Know It.* Every time you change the definition of yourself, you put your competitors, by comparison, in a totally different position. For your brand to be fresh, you have to refresh its meaning and definition over and over again. If not, consumers will take it for granted and your brand will fade with time and your volume decrease. However, you must first know the consumer's understanding and feel for the brand and its core foundational elements. If your organization stands, for example, for stability and continuity, you can't tell them about choice and change.

● **What words best describe your organization?** Does it have a clear personality? What if your organization's personae is perceived as solid and trustworthy by your heavily civic, mature donors but translates to staid and stuffy with the more inner-centered idealistic mid-life Boomers and out of touch with the reality young adult Generation X and the youngsters known as Gen Net? To create and deliver brand values you must choose, package and communicate beliefs effectively to both current and potential shareholders.

Joe Saxton, a British fund raiser has compiled several adjectives that might describe a charity's brand image. They include:

Passionate	Rigid	Compassionate	Large
Visionary	Bold	Outspoken	Dynamic
Tired	Focused	Inspiring	Leadership
Bureaucratic	Justice	Catalytic	Determined
Changing	Exciting	Cautious	Conservative
Fun	Rich	Established	Entrepreneurial
Staid	Persistent	Complacent	Other?

● **Start by building brand loyalty by identifying the common ground between donors and organization.** The Roper Organization's *The Influential Americans: Who They Are, How to Reach Them* offers some general rules-of-thumb to keep in tune with affluent lifestyles and mindstyles. All of these guidelines draw from (as well as support) the variety of data about affluents: they address the mindstyle of affluence, with respect to the affluents' somewhat sensitive reactions to high-pitched pleas and the special characteristics of the affluents (an increased appetite for information) that translate into an affluent predilection for articles (instead of ads that are long on hyperbole and short on information).

Roper's research recommends creating messages that:

- Emphasize discovery and exploration, not the known.

- Appeal to knowledge and judgment, not status.

- Challenge, not guarantee.

- Show action, not passivity.

- Provide news, not hype.

- Project decisiveness, not hesitancy.

- Reveal broad-minded sense of cooperation and independence, rather than competition.

WHICH DIRECT MARKETING METHODS MAKE MOST SENSE FOR REACHING AFFLUENTS?

■ **Affluents prefer the printed word over radio or television.** The problem is that the average American finds 22 pieces of mail in his/her mailbox each week, only one of which is personal, according to the latest U.S. Postal Services Household Diary Study. Households between the ages of 35 and 69 with higher incomes or education levels get even more junk mail than average.

Rules for Reaching Affluents

- Articles—as opposed to advertisements—are more effective for reaching Affluents. They trust the printed word more than do other consumers. Also, they spend more time reading.

- If you advertise, use specialty magazines and journals.

- Using radio and television? Pay attention to programming: public affairs and sports programs are good.

- Direct response campaigns—minus any hard sell—have strong appeal.

- Affluents spread the word among other affluents.

- Affluents often choose the quickest way to communicate: the telephone.

- They trust instant buying and aren't squeamish about giving their credit card numbers over the phone.

● **Don't automatically relegate your direct mail to the wastebasket.** The good news is that less people are throwing away bulk mail without reading it first. According to the Public Pulse, only 34 percent (down 4 points), report throwing away mail unopened. An even more optimistic view is provided by Jay Conrad Levinson, author of *Guerrilla Marketing Excellence,* who asserts that:

50 percent of bulk mail is read immediately
25 percent is scanned
10 percent is set aside for later reading
12 percent is tossed instantly

● **Use the right direct mail pieces.** While self-mailers are cheaper to produce, they practically never "out pull" an envelope with the promotional material enclosed. Third class mail gets a rather third-rate response from affluents, especially in the upper income segments. This, combined with the fact that affluents respond positively to personalized mailings, suggests it's worth the extra effort and cost for the higher response.

● **Start with the envelope.** If it isn't opened, nothing else counts. The best envelope for fund raising letters is a plain no. 10 or smaller in white, light yellow, buff, or light brown with a first class postage stamp, advises Jerry Huntsinger, the "dean" of direct mail fund raising. The address should be typed, with no window, no label, no teaser line, and no return address. Your changes of having it opened are almost 100 percent.

● **The letter sells.** In reality, what you get in most direct mail packages is a highly stylized one-page ad designed to look like a letter. Your letter must look good, so people will read it. In *Direct Marketing* magazine, Jeffrey Dobkin recommends:

> - Using Courier or another typewriter-style type to make your letter look like it was just typed on a typewriter.
>
> - Making the first line short and compelling. Its only objective is to keep the reader reading.
>
> - Indenting the first line of all paragraphs five spaces to start the eyeflow of the reader.
>
> - Limiting paragraph length to seven lines at most.
>
> - Staggering paragraph lengths so they don't all look the same, keeping the copy look fresh and visually interesting.
>
> - Using underlined, bold, and bulleted copy.

What about letter length? Mark McCormack, author of
What They Don't Teach You at Harvard Business School, suggests that when writing to influentials "Rank determines
length." McCormack believes the length of your letter should
be inversely proportionate to the importance of your reader,
noting that "if you're writing to the owner of a large company,
for example, the letter should be short. Two or three paragraphs
will do—one page at most. Lots of letters cross a CEO's desk
each day, and there's rarely time to digest them fully."

Not everyone agrees with McCormack. Jerry Huntsinger
believes strongly in the effectiveness of longer letters. I tend
to agree: it's not the length, it's the quality that counts. (Of
course, if you are targeting older affluents in your written appeals, the letters will need to be longer simply to accommodate a larger size type face: few people over age 40 can read
type under 12 points!)

● **The brochure tells, providing factual support for the letter.**
In *DM News,* Dean Rick reminds us that the brochure is meant
to be scanned or read in any order. It is less personal. It should
illustrate features, list benefits, provide proofs, make compar-
isons, and list details to lend credibility to what your letter
claims. You should test your package with and without a
brochure.

When using a brochure, it should:

- Make a visual impact.

- Make the brochure readable.

- Use headlines to tell a complete story.

- Start strong on the cover.

- Develop your big benefit immediately.

- Highlight the benefits and list the features.

- Restate the offer clearly.

- Feature a strong guarantee.

- Group your testimonials.

- Use the most effective format.

- Include all vital data.

● **Remember the "nine golden rules for readability."** According to Michael Collins in *Type and Layout: How Typography and Design Can Get Your Message Across:*

1. Elegant serif faces are comprehended by more readers than sans serif faces.

2. The use of high-chroma color, such as hot red or process red—especially in headline text—will increase comprehension.

3. People begin reading from the top left and move down to the bottom right.

4. Text color should be black.

5. Text in high-intensity colors is difficult to read.

6. The higher the percentage of colored background tint beyond 10 percent, the less comprehensible the text.

7. Black text on a white background is the most legible.

8. Any reverse-out text is much less legible than no reverse-out text.

9. Totally justified-setting text is much more legible than ragged-right or -left text.

● **Send a message with color.** Higher socioeconomic groups generally respond to complex and dark colors, lower-income groups to simple and highly saturated colors. According to Carlton Wagner of the Wagner Institute for Color Research, green attracts more sophisticated people than orange or yellow.

● **What are the hot graphic design trends?** Rose DeNeve, former managing editor of *Print,* notes that "Today design is an integral part of communication effort, as inseparable from it as words and thoughts are from content and meaning." Design should capture the attention of readers and pull them into the message.

- Use more graphics to explain information.

- Adopt more colorful art and use concise copy.

- Switch to a tabloid format for your newsletter.

● **Pay attention to timing:** avoid the appeal clutter: November is the number one month or fund raising mailings with 20.3 percent of total non-profit direct mail, followed by September (10.9%) and October (9.7%). According to Judith Waldrop in *The Seasons of Business,* "February is a low point for many Americans...the real winter winners are marketers who can reach consumers in their homes through the media, the mail, and home delivery."

● **Respect gender audience differences.** Men and women use language very differently. Research done by Stephen Pideon and Pauline Lockier, reported in the *Journal of Nonprofit and Voluntary Sector Marketing,* demonstrates that appeals written in gender-specific style have produced an 85 percent uplift in response.

MEN	WOMEN
Use commands and imperatives.	Tend to use suggestions.
Use interjections to change the subject.	Use conjunctions to change the subject.
Describe things in basic details.	Use many more adjectives in descriptions.
Use single adjectives to make a single point.	Use adjectives to elaborate.
Regard questions as requests for information.	Use interjections much less.
Use quantifiers such as "never," "all," "always," and "none."	Use questions to keep conversation going. Answer questions with questions.
	Make compound requests

● **Marketing to non-traditional audiences requires a sensitivity to cultural differences.** We've already explored the importance of accurate translation with non-English speaking audiences. But, don't stop there. For example, most Hispanics prefer cash payments in person: whereas more than two-thirds of all Americans hold credit cards, less than one-third of Hispanics have them. Many do not use checks: especially for working-class immigrants and families with strong ties to Mexico, there is distrust of banks and the postal service.

■ **Affluents enjoy making purchases via phone and mail.** More than three-quarters (77%) of Simmons' Exclusive Set (educated professionals between 35 and 49 with household incomes of $75,000+) order products or services by phone or mail compared to just 51 percent of lower-income households. Affluents also were more likely to purchase via catalogs, and made more purchases when they did so. The higher the formal education, the greater the use of mail-order services.

In *Fund Raising Management,* Roger Craver asserts that "the use of the telephone is particularly helpful for upgrading donors on your house file, for welcoming and bonding new donors to your organization, for alerting donors to special needs and emergencies, for thanking donors, and for basic research into the needs and interests of individual donors."

● **Although many people insist they hate telephone solicitations—up to 60 percent of consumers say they won't listen to an unsolicited sales pitch on the telephone, it works.** As Ken Burnett in *Relationship Fundraising* reminds us so eloquently: "How many people get out of the bathtub to answer a letter?"

- Typical outbound conversion rates from prospect to buyer are 6 percent to 8 percent versus 2 percent for direct mail, according to *Direct* magazine.

- Use of an 800 number increases the average incoming catalog order by about 20 to 25 percent. AT&T tested mailings in which the recipient could return a card or call an 800 number to order or request more information. Those who phoned ordered four times more than those who mailed in the card.

- An NPT/Barna Research study reveals that while women say they dislike telemarketing (and direct mail) appeals more than men do, they actually give more to those appeals.

● **The telephone offers several advantages over direct mail:**
it's immediate, it's personal, and it gives your better control
over your money. Comments Ann Herzog, a non-profit marketing consultant based in Arlington, Virginia. "With mail, all
costs are up front. Once a mail appeal goes out, all you can do
is wait; you have no control. During the Gulf War, many packages went unopened. That wouldn't have happened with the
phone. If an appeal isn't working, you can make adjustments
right away, instead of waiting four weeks for the responses to
trickle in."

Charlie Cadigan, formerly TransAmerica's Senior Vice
President and President of the Direct Marketing Association of
Washington, D.C. notes that "unlike direct mail, telephone marketing allows for immediate feedback. Within hours of calling,
an organization knows how members are responding, and what
issues they find most important and worthy of the organization's efforts."

● **Yet, many fund raisers—and their board members—often
hesitate to use the telephone, fearing it will be viewed as in-
vasive.** Much of this concern can be eliminated by preceding
the phone call with a pre-approach letter, explaining who will
be calling, why the call is being made, and when to expect it.*

It's equally important to understand the difference between
telemarketing (where success is measured by how many
contacts can be made in a defined period of time) and telecommunications (where success is measured by how many successful closings are accomplished).

---

*A full explanation of telecommunications—as opposed to telemarketing—is provided in my
book, *Changing Demographics: Fund Raising in the 1990s,* Chapter 12: Soliciting the Annual Gift.

A COMPARISON OF TELEMARKETING AND TELECOMMUNICATIONS

TELEMARKETING	TELECOMMUNICATIONS
High number of contacts per hour	Low number of contacts per hour
Short conversations	Long conversations
Less dialogue	More dialogue
Creativeness not too essential	Creativeness essential
Number of contacts more important than building long-term rapport	Goal is to leave prospect feeling good about the contact even if gift is not made
Much more rejection experienced by callers	Less rejection experienced by callers
Can be mentally exhausting and draining to callers	Mentally challenging with high caller satisfaction
Close supervision and control required	Callers work more on own

SOURCE: Scott Ashby Telemarketing Consulting

● **In addition to the typical outgoing use of telephone for fund raising, you should become familiar with 800 and 888, 900, and 700 numbers—all of which are *incoming* technologies.**

- 800 and 888 numbers (with the organization paying the cost of the incoming call) are essential for not-for-profits working over a large geographical area.

- 900 and 700 numbers have the cost of the call borne by the donor, by the organization, or some combination of both. The 900 number is a public number while the 700 is for a select group—"members only"—of donors of prospects.

● **It is getting harder to reach people by phone in certain parts of the United States.** The top unlisted MSA market is Las Vegas (64.6 percent unlisted in 1992); the next nine—all with over 55 percent unlisted—are California addresses: Fresno (63.1%), LA-Long Beach (61.7%), Oakland (61.2%), San Jose (60.2%), Sacramento (59.8%), Riverside-San Bernardino (57.7%), Anaheim-Santa Ana (57.1%), San Diego (56.5%), and Bakersfield (55.2%)

A TIP FOR CREATING AN AFFLUENT PHONE LIST

Reverse or criss-cross directories are backward telephone books, of sorts. Here you'll find listings arranged by street address followed by telephone number and name. This handy tool allows you to canvas specific neighborhoods. Remember human nature—most of us live with others like us, congregating by age, life-style, economic status, ethnic groupings.

SOURCE: *Power Calling: A Fresh Approach to Cold Calls & Prospecting,* Joan Guiducci

---

■ **Affluents and the small screen.** While affluents are less likely to watch television, when they do they lean towards documentary formats, news programs, and public television broadcasts. The infocommercial—typically a half-hour program in a documentary or news format—may be a strong marketing tool for your organization.

● **Affluents have more VCRs than the general public.** Eighty-five percent of affluent Americans own VCRs. Consider sending your story on tape to affluent audiences. Video increases information retention by 50 percent and accelerates buying decisions by 72 percent, according to a Wharton School study.

● You can maximize your organization's influence when using video, notes Dick Kindig, by:

1. *Use Reel Reality:* Let reality dictate perception. Make communication the servant of truth, not the other way around.
2. *Get Up Close and Personal:* Show the human face close up. If it is comfortable, sincere, and believable, then all the power of congruent non-verbal communication is available to reinforce the words of the speaker.
3. *Convey Complexity:* Supply the information needed for a meaningful decision.
4. *Clear the Air:* Pay your public the compliment of directly acknowledging their honest fears and objections.
5. *Command the High Ground:* Admit your bias frankly.
6. *Remember that Less is More:* Video doesn't work when you use it as an audio-visual re-enactment of passive prose.
7. *Show Trust to Your Audience:* Surprise them with honesty, self-effacing humor, confession, factual presentations.
8. *Communicate in Circles:* Build your arguments, don't go straight for the jugular.
9. *Fight in the Center of the Ring:* Don't corner your audience; allow them room to differ.
10. *Speak like One Who Listens:* Demonstrate that your point of view has been formulated with your audience in mind.

■ **Internet-based communication is here to stay.** Americans now send 2.2 billion e-mails a day, compared with just 293 million pieces of first class mail.

● **Who's online?** By 2002 a projected 45 million U.S. households will be online. While the average age of the annual 12 million recipients of direct mail solicitations is 66, the average age of the web donor population is just 42. That's not to say mature Americans aren't catching up: the percentage of Americans older than 55 who are online more than doubled last year to 9 percent.

Most importantly for fundraisers seeking affluent prospects:

- The average income levels of Internet users are almost double those of non-Internet users.

- Seventy percent of Web fans are college graduates with an average income of $66,000.

● **As Internet use continues to expand, the demographics of typical Internet users will increasingly mirror that of average Americans.** About 30 percent will be age 45 or older; 53 percent will be high school graduates or have less education and 61 percent will earn under $50,000.

- Men account for about three-quarters of total online traffic, while the number of women who use the Net has grown to about 30–40 percent.

- An estimated 16 million youths younger than 18 have Internet capability at home, and surveys show e-mail is their main online activity.

● **Philanthropy has begun to embrace the World Wide Web.** The Internet will revolutionize philanthropy. Jimmie R. Alford, a non-profit consultant and past chairman of the American Association of Fundraising Counsel, predicts that in 10 years half of all donations will be handled online. Traditional fund raising methods such as direct mail and phone requests will decline, while advertising messages will direct donors to the Website rather than publicize mission statements or solicit funding. The Web site will become the source for all charitable communication.

> You can give money to 640,000+ charities in the USA using www.allCharities.com.
> You can find out when and where to volunteer by typing your zip code into www.helping.org.
> You can look at Form 990s at www.guidestar.com.
> You can donate 15 percent of purchases when you buy at www.iGive.com.

● **The Internet will increase accountability between charity and donor by generating an immediate access point for all financial statements and current programs.** In addition, the relationship between charities and grant makers will also become more immediate and synergistic, creating a partnership between the two.

MARKETING THROUGH THE INTERNET

● **Currently, online giving is currently only a small part of total giving.** According to the newly named Association of Fund Raising Executives (formerly the National Society of Fund Raising Executives), in 1999 less than $200 million was contributed online: only 14 cents is given over the Internet for every $100 of total giving. However, the average gift is $55 which compares very favorably to the average for direct mail gifts.

● **Younger, more highly educated donors are demonstrating their willingness to give via the net.** WAMU, a public radio station in Washington, D.C. held a "cyber day" rather than an on-air fund raising drive. NSFRE reports that the effort generated over $225,000 and was so successful that the organizers repeated it two days later with no advance publicity and received another $77,000—a total of more than $300,000 in 72 hours.

● **There are an estimated 50 million "socially engaged Internet users" and "on-line activists."** According to Craver, Matthews, Smith & Company, they tend to be younger than the people charities reach through direct mail and represent a broader political spectrum. While the majority still have privacy concerns about giving via the Net, they believe that the Internet can provide education and feedback.

● **To reach donors via the Internet, remember that the Internet has unique attributes:**consumers pull information rather than have the message pushed at them as in traditional media. The Web isn't time-restricted, it is interactive, it is non-linear, it is multimedia, it is screen-based, it is dynamic, and it requires active retrieval.

● **An electronic newsletter or discussion list should be part of any Web marketing effort,** according to Richard Hoy of The Tenagra Corp., an Internet marketing agency. The Web is a passive medium; visitors have to type in your address to go to your Web site. Unless you remind people you're out there, you just have to hope they'll remember to come back.

To create a successful newsletter, Hoy suggests:

- Collect subscriber e-mail addresses on your home page rather than on a page buried deep in your site.

- The shorter your registration form, the more likely it is to be completed.

- When creating your newsletter, place hard returns after every 60 characters or so and keep it in plain text, or it may get garbled.

- Send the newsletter out frequently to keep readers interested.

● **A good website is a must.** You need to put time, effort, and money into creating one that catches attention. Michael Johnson's outstanding book, *Fundraising on the Net,* offers several examples of outstanding not-for-profit sites.

To lose your Web site's amateur status:

1. *Design for maximum readability.* Arts backgrounds and fonts can make a site difficult to read. Choose dark type on a solid white background.

2. *Make each page stand on its own.* You never know which page on your site a visitor will bookmark. Include contact and copyright information, as well as a navigation bar, on each page.

3. *Make navigation simple.* Sketch out how your information flows, and design a system visitors won't get lost in.

4. *Don't over-design.* Too many extras can slow load time and cause impatient visitors to move on.

5. *Include a response mechanism.* Involve your visitors by using contests or offers for special information, such as an e-mail newsletter.

6. *Keep the site fresh.* Update your content continually to give visitors a reason to come back.

SOURCE: Kim Gordon, *Enterprise* magazine

WE ARE TRULY FORTUNATE
in that most Americans do believe in the role of philanthropy
and want to support the efforts of the non-profit sector. That
commitment requires an equal commitment from us. Perhaps
the late Maurice Gurin, an outstanding fundraiser and the individual who first raised the "ethics flag" in fund raising, said
it best:

> "Americans respond to an appeal for support because
> they believe in the purpose of a philanthropic cause
> and trust the integrity of its representatives to con-
> scientiously advance its purpose. Public trust is es-
> sential for philanthropy; without it, there would be
> no claim nor climate for philanthropy. The require-
> ment of public trust explains why fund raisers' in-
> tegrity must be above question, why they are held to
> a higher standard than practitioners in other fields,
> and why they must familiarize themselves with ethi-
> cal concerns in fund raising."

**By now it should be obvious that the tools are readily avail-
able to allow us to find our best prospects and create the type
of enduring relationships to truly expand the base of philanthropy.** However, a fundamental concern—ethics—needs to be
part and parcel of your planning. Ethics refers to a standard of
conduct that indicates how one should behave based on moral

duties and on virtues arising from principles about right and wrong.

As mentioned in several places in this book, an eroding trust in not-for-profits is occurring. Donors and prospects do not take us on faith. Ethical behavior is a key concern of those who fund us. It's a key part of doing business today.

There are two overall areas which require our constant vigilance:

● Possible misuse of prospect research and data base management tools

● Increasing donor concerns about gift accountability and stewardship

When I wrote my first book to the fund raising community, *Changing Demographics: Fund Raising in the 1990s,* I concluded with a chapter on **Ethical Concerns for the Future**. In my other books I broadened my comments to include discussions on **Gift Stewardship and Accountability**. If anything, those concerns are even more pertinent and real today. I return to this all-important subject as a fitting conclusion to *Pinpointing Affluence in the 21st Century.*

SAMPLE FUND RAISING PRINCIPLES

1. We will value and appreciate our contributors and consider them stockholders with us.

2. We will consider the contributions we receive to be "special"—sent from loving people who have sacrificed to make their gifts possible. Our obligation, therefore, is to spend that money conservatively and wisely.

3. We will receipt all donations in order to assist contributors with tax-deduction record keeping for their gifts.

4. We will make needs and successes known to our friends. We will only use respected and honorable methods of fund raising.

5. We will honor all statements made in our fund raising appeals about the use of gifts and will honor the donor's intent, within the stated concepts of our Mission and Values.

6. We will not try to raise more money than we need.

7. We will allocate resources with preference for serving the most vulnerable.

8. We will not operate at a deficit. Although from time to time, it will be necessary to borrow funds for capital expenditures or to start new programs, we will seek to repay the loan as soon as possible.

9. When we make a purchase, we will pay the invoice within 30 days if possible. We do not intend to use the vendors' money.

10. We will not sell or rent our mailing list to those wishing to use the names and addresses of our supporters. Those individuals contacted us in good faith: we will maintain the tightest security on our list of friends and supporters.

With thanks to Catholic Community Services, Salem, Oregon.

Prospect Research and Data Base Management

Be alert to possible misuse of prospect research and data base management tools. Before forging blindly ahead in restructuring your development program and expanding your prospect research, pause to remind yourself that the use of demographic and psychographic tools brings with it responsibilities. Three key areas of potential abuse stand out:

- Who owns the information?

- Who owns the gift?

- Who owns the donor?

■ **Who owns the information?** Not-for-profits are becoming increasingly sophisticated in research prospects and donors. Whether handled internally or externally, the amount of information being compiled is staggering.

● **The American people regard privacy as a fundamental right and are not satisfied with the way some organizations currently collect and use information about individuals.** According to the Harris-Equifax Consumer Privacy Survey, an overwhelming 79 percent of Americans agree that "If we rewrote the Declaration of Independence today, we would probably add privacy to the list of life, liberty, and the pursuit of happiness as a fundamental right."

● **The American public expresses widespread concern with threats to personal privacy in America today.** Nearly four Americans in five (79%) expressed general concerns with 48 percent saying they were very concerned.

● **The majority of the American public (55%) feels the protection of information about consumers is getting worse, not better.**

● **Most people believe that consumers have lost all control over how personal information about them is circulated and**

used by companies. More than seven in 10 Americans (71%) feel that way.

● **Only 34 percent of those contacted believe individual public record information should be available to private investigators.**

● **Most people believe computers threaten personal privacy** with slightly more than three-quarters (76%) concerned about how personal information about them is circulated and used.

■ **Who owns the gift?** Our donors do not believe they are getting accurate information from the institutions that solicit them. Increasingly, charities find gifts of smaller and smaller amounts being restricted as donors take stewardship and accountability into their own hands. This creates a funding dilemma for organizations who rely on unrestricted monies for operating expenses and to "seed" the fund raising programs they conduct.

The demographics and psychographs of our emerging population groups suggest that, more than ever before, our donors and prospective donors will expect charities to *volunteer* detailed information on how their gifts will be used, and if any portion is earmarked for the costs of fund raising, explain how and why this is being done.

■ **Who owns the donor?** Look around any professional meeting of fund raisers...half are new to their jobs and the other half are looking!

Fund raisers mirror the population as a whole. Like the rest of our population, fund raisers are increasingly Boomers. And, job-wise, Boomers are more mobile than previous generations. Landon Jones, author of *Great Expectations,* attributes this, in part, to the fierce competition for top positions. "In effect, the entire generation will be like a large group of people being moved from a big room into a smaller room." Those Boomers who find advancement blocked at one organization often opt to move on.

The mobility of development officers brings up potential concerns. Will the donor transfer loyalty to a new organization? Will the development officer, in fact, encourage this practice? What must the fund raiser say when asked by the donor about the new agency s/he now represents? What if no gift has yet been received from the prospect, and s/he may, in fact, not be a good match for the first organization, but might possibly be sincerely interested in the development officer's new charity? These concerns are not new. However, the quickening tempo of job changes makes guidelines more important than ever, to avoid charges of unethical behavior.

GIFT ACCOUNTABILITY AND STEWARDSHIP CONCERNS

> Donors have two basic rights:
>
> 1) The right to expect that solicitations are made in the context of institutionally defined priorities.
>
> 2) The right to expect that gifts will be used as the donor intended.

Most donors vastly overestimate the share of their donation that goes to charity, according to a survey commissioned by the Connecticut Attorney General. The survey found that:

● Fifty-five percent said they would donate only if a charity kept administrative and fund-raising costs below 20 percent of all costs.

● Just 10 percent would donate to groups that spent more than half of all revenue on administration and fund raising.

Prior to commencing—or upgrading—your development program, the board and staff should agree on the principles that will govern its fund raising. These will need to be both general (principles and objectives) and specific (dealing with how you will handle areas of accountability and stewardship). The following stewardship and accountability guidelines are offered as a starting point for your organization's own comprehensive set of guidelines. The purpose of these guidelines is to provide a structure for board, staff, volunteers, and donors that answers commonly asked questions about your organization's policies for private contributions. They are based on sample guides first included in my books, *Targeted Fund Raising: Defining and Refining Your Development Strategy* (Precept Press) and *Transforming Fundraising* (Jossey Bass). Not all of this sample document may ultimately be relevant for your organization.

Sample Gift Stewardship and Accountability Guides for the "ABC" Organization

1. Who can accept gifts on behalf of the ABC Organization? Unrestricted gifts of cash in any amount may be accepted by the executive director; the directors of the various departments on behalf of their particular areas of responsibility; the Development Director, or members of the ABC Development Council on behalf of the organization.

Non-cash and restricted gifts of $1,000 or less may be accepted by the Executive Director; the directors of the various departments on behalf of their particular areas of responsibility; the Development Director, or members of the ABC Development Council on behalf of the organization.

All non-cash and restricted gifts of over $1,000 are reviewed for approval by the Finance Committee of the Board of the ABC Organization. The review will be scheduled within a 45-day period.

2. What types of gifts are accepted by ABC? Gifts are defined as follows:

- *Unrestricted:* Gifts of any amount without donor qualifications as to use.

- *Designated:* Gifts of over $100 directed to a general area of interest such as a department or program.

- *Restricted:* Gifts of over $1,000 with donor restrictions as to program/service usage within a designated area.

The ABC Organization accepts gifts of cash, securities, irrevocable planned gift arrangements utilizing bequests, life insurance, trusts and annuities, and in-kind and real property contributions, with the following guidelines:

● Stock gifts are attributed the median price on the day received.

● Gifts of real property valued at $5,000 and over should be evaluated by an independent appraiser. The ABC Organization does not assign a value for tax purposes to non-cash contributions, although it will assign an *internal* level for donor recognition.

● Pledges paid within a five year period are assigned full, current value. Until paid in full, they are considered to be "accounts receivable" and assigned 70 percent of value.

● Deferred gifts (including but not limited to annuities, unitrusts, pooled income vehicles, and irrevocable bequests) are assigned a value, and are adjusted for current value using actuarial tables for the age of the donor.

● Bequests that are revocable are assigned a value of $1,000. If the actual amount is known it is recorded for an *internal* level of donor recognition only.

3.   What forms of donor recognition does ABC give? All gifts to the ABC Organization are sincerely appreciated and promptly acknowledged with a letter.

Unless a donor requests anonymity, all contributors for the immediate past fiscal year are listed in the organization's annual report or an honor roll of donors.

Donors who contribute at and above $100 become participants in ABC's Donor Circles, with these levels of membership:

Members $100–$999 in annual gifts
Contributors $1,000–$9,999 in annual gifts
Benefactors $10,000 and above in cumulative gifts
Key Club   Bequests and other planned gifts

A personalized certificate of appreciation is provided to members of the PATRON'S CIRCLE upon request.

Donors who indicate in writing they have included the ABC Organization or a particular department in their wills or other planned giving vehicle become members of the Key Club. No amount need be specified.

4.   How does ABC recover fund raising costs from contributions? The ABC Organization raises funds on behalf of the organization and its entities through an intensified development strategy using personal solicitations, corporate and foundation proposals, direct mail, telecommunications, and special events.

All direct costs for fund raising are recovered from these efforts before funds are distributed.

● Twenty percent of each undesignated gift is assigned to the Office of Development to cover the costs of fund raising.

● For designated or restricted gifts, direct costs of fund raising are recovered by the following formula:

- 10 percent levy for gifts of up to $100,000

- 5 percent levy for gifts of over $100,000

This levy can be "paid" in any of the following ways:

- With donor agreement, taken from the gift

- With donor agreement, supplementing the gift

- With board agreement, taken from another source of revenue including unrestricted and designated funds or existing endowment monies

After fund raising costs are recovered, the ABC Organization allocates the remaining unrestricted dollars among its entities and departments. Recommendations for are made quarterly by the Administrators' Council.

5.   What levels of funding are required for a named endowment? A sum of $10,000 or greater establishes a named endowment fund. The first grant is made during July following completion of the first full fiscal year after the fund's establishment. The grant is limited to 5 percent of the interest income, with the remaining interest going back into the endowment to build principal.

6.   What levels of funding are required for trusts and annuities? The sum of $50,000 establishes a charitable remainder trust or annuity. Generally, trusts and annuities are made available to individuals aged 55 or older. Up to two beneficiaries may be named to receive payments. The trust or annuity must be funded with a vehicle which can be readily liquidated prior to payments commencing.

7.   What are the requirements for bequest gifts? Bequest gifts of any amount are welcome. Because it is difficult to anticipate the needs of the future, donors are requested to leave their bequest gifts to ABC Organization unrestricted or designated rather than restricted.

8.   What kinds of in-kind donations are accepted? Limited amount of office equipment, durable goods, and specific materials in good condition are accepted, subject to the approval of the Finance Committee, as described earlier. In-kind gifts are assigned no value by the ABC Organization. It is the responsibility of the donor to obtain a valuation for tax purposes.

9.   What is ABC Organization's policy for sponsorship, cause-related marketing, premiums, and incentives? ABC Organization recognizes that its name carries weight in the community. Before agreeing to lend ABC's implied endorsement to a for-profit entity through sponsorship or cause-related marketing, the Sponsorship Committee will meet, review the request, and advise the board. A decision will be rendered within 45 days of the request.

Fund raising appeals that in exchange for a contribution offer premiums or incentives (the value of which is not insubstantial, but which is significant in relation to the amount of the donation) will advise the donor of the fair market value of the premium or incentive and that the value is not deductible for tax purposes.

10. What are ABC's investment policies? As an ethical, responsible member of our community, the ABC Organization will not invest in stock and bond vehicles that either directly or indirectly refute its mission. These include stocks and bonds in tobacco, drug and alcohol products, and companies with a history of discriminating by race and ethnicity, age, gender, or sexual orientation. ABC does not do business with countries that ignore the civil rights of their citizens.

11. What is ABC Organization's stance on the use of paid versus commission-based fund raising consultants? ABC subscribes to the principles of both the American Association of Fund Raising Counsel and the National Society of Fund Raising Executives. It does not hire fund raisers on a percentage basis.

12. What is ABC Organization's stance on privacy of donor information issues? ABC recognizes that donors are at the heart of the organization's viability and that it has strong responsibilities to protect their privacy. For example,

- All donors are contacted prior to the printing of the annual honor roll in the September issue of our newsletter and advised that names are being listed. Donors are given the option of remaining anonymous.

- Donors are welcome to request and receive a complete copy of any written materials being held in their file.

- Only authorized staff and board members may view a donor file.

- Donor files remain on site.

Index